# THE ABCs OF PUBLIC EDUCATION

MASCOT BOOKS

www.mascotbooks.com

*The ABCs of Public Education*



I have tried to recreate events, locales, and conversations from my memories of them. In order to maintain their anonymity in some instances I have changed the names of individuals and places. I may have changed some identifying characteristics and details such as physical properties, occupations, and places of residence.

**For more information, please contact:**
Mascot Books
620 Herndon Parkway #320
Herndon, VA 20170
info@mascotbooks.com

Library of Congress Control Number: 2020916642

CPSIA Code: PRFRE0221A
ISBN-13: 978-1-64543-415-3

Printed in Canada

*I dedicate this book to all of the victims of abuse and bullying within school departments that lack the voice of justice. May they find peace and righteousness in the battle against the cruelty of this terrible problem that all Americans face. I also dedicate this book to my loving and supportive wife, Joyce, and our children, who were by my side through my fight to hold the bullies accountable and have them face the consequences of their actions. I continue to pray for the healing of those who were attacked and those who were the attackers.*

# The ABCs of Public Education

*Abuse, Bullying, and Corruption: A Story of Institutionalized Mobbing in Education*

DR. JOHN J. PEPI SR.

# TABLE OF CONTENTS

# AUTHOR'S NOTE

This story is based on the facts of a true story. Names and places were changed to protect the innocent. This story is told as a lived experience of the author that documents and presents firsthand knowledge of the facts. The names and places are irrelevant because the author's purpose is to show that this phenomenon can happen to anyone from anywhere, whether here in the US, or another country.

# PREFACE

After the torment I experienced over the years, I decided to write a book to help others who are victims of abuse and bullying. My intentions were not to look at my story and to feel sorry for myself, but to give hope to those who believe they are alone in suffering from workplace abuse. My desire to right this wrong was so strong that I decided in 2013 to go for my doctorate degree in educational leadership. Part of my degree requirements was completing a dissertation. The choice was easy, and I decided to conduct a study on workplace bullying in education. I realized through reading hundreds and hundreds of documents on this subject that there is a severe problem in our school systems across the country. I do understand that the problem is not just in education—such occurrences are pervasive in nursing and in private companies—but in this book, I will focus on education and how bullying not only affects the educator going through the abuse, but also the students as well as the whole educational community.

I became an advocate for the voiceless and will continue to advocate until justice is served. Advocacy goes beyond posting on social media, passing laws, or creating dialogue among others who have been affected. These are all good avenues for engagement, but calling out the bullies themselves will not only hold them accountable for their actions but also expose them for what they really are: BULLIES. If the bully is not exposed, they will continue to torment and abuse others. Telling my story is well overdue because after being bullied—coupled with union failure, politician failure, and a lengthy as well as expensive lawsuit—I received NO justice. My reputation was destroyed, and I could not receive any other position outside the city. If anyone googles my name, my lawsuit appears. I sued for defamation, and I may have lost my case, but not my passion of exposing the truth. The real problem was that other school districts, family members, and friends don't know my side of the story. This etched a black mark next to my name that was placed there by these narcissistic personalities.

My image, character, integrity, and reputation were all destroyed by these bullies, and they feel that they won by getting rid of me. Their destructive behavior forced me into retirement much too early, and they even proceeded to take my health insurance away by claiming I resigned. What they didn't take away was my pride, and therefore, I needed to tell my side of the story. I have the documents and other evidence that supports the truth. I will expose these bullies, and I am hoping that you have the courage to expose your bully. This book is for you to understand how devastating bullying is. Thank you for giving me the opportunity to share my story with you, and may God bless you through your challenges.

Dr. John J. Pepi Sr.
Founder and President
Pepi & Associates, LLC

# INTRODUCTION

I was in the courtroom with my family and friends behind me and my wife by my side. *Why*, I wondered, *am I here?* It hurt so much to see my character and reputation that I worked for all my life get destroyed by a bunch of self-loathing narcissists. My career and my name were destroyed, and for what? *Why are they doing this to me?* I thought, *This is not right.* At the lowest point of my life, I made a decision. I decided to write a book on my experiences so that people would know what actually went down—not just what the media portrayed, nor what the politicians and school department portrayed. I want to share the truth. The truth on abuse. The truth on bullying and the truth on corruption that I have lived through firsthand.

To give the reader the full understanding of what my family and I went through, I need to bring you back to where my career started. The Catholic school where I taught may seem irrelevant, but as you read about this situation that I went through, the pieces will fit together. You will see how my lifelong bully from childhood influenced my career and created a strain on my relationships with my siblings. The abuse would trickle from the Catholic schools to the public schools. This will give you a clear picture of how bullying becomes destructive, and how I stood up to these bullies even though it cost me my career.

The bullying I experienced at work, the false rumors spread about me—in which my colleagues accused me of dishonesty, stealing, and other falsified stories—ruined my reputation. The bully didn't care about my family. This could be your supervisor telling these falsehoods to the human resource department, your coworkers, or even the union who is supposed to represent you. Then, when you think it can't get any worse, the bullying escalates to what is called "mobbing," and, you, as the target, are getting it from all angles. I equate this behavior to the scene in the movie Jurassic Park, in which the raptors surround the target and get ready to attack. This mobbing can easily become institutionalized bullying. This has become a major problem in government, public school systems, hospitals, court systems, police departments, and other private or public corporations. It has negatively impacted many people within our society.

This is what I had to face. It is sad because I am a giver, and all my life I've want to give back, especially to underprivileged children who do not have much. My heart always roots for the underdog, and I look to find ways to help the underdog overcome their misfortunes. This trend seems to be the norm and certain bullies in leadership roles are a part of the problem. They use antics of blame, lying, deception, and manipulation to control and suppress the target. Bullies are self-absorbed, and they punish others with their vampire personalities that will try to suck the life out of you.

This book will help you understand that there are bullies out there, and people will not understand the pain you encounter from them. It is my goal, through what I have experienced, to expose that there is a problem that needs to be addressed. It seems that today, the problem is bigger than ever. There is hope for you, and I want to encourage you to continue to battle your bully, either legally or through exposure.

My expectation from this book is to give you optimism. After you read this book, I want to hear from you, so I can help you face this phenomenon head-on. Learn from my situation so you can avoid the same humiliation. Remember, it is not you. Even though the bullies should be the ones humiliated—a sentiment I understand especially after the torment my family and I went through—the healing must begin so that the pain does not destroy you. My wife and my four children went through a horrible ordeal in which they saw their husband

and their father's name dragged through the mud and watched our finances collapse. Some of these terrible memories still keep me up at night, but after I wipe away my tears, I am ready to share the reality of this phenomenon. I do understand that I will continue to make the bullies of my life unhappy because they fear one thing, THE TRUTH. So let's get started.

# 1

# START OF A CAREER

In 1981, I had just graduated from Urbanville College with a bachelor of science degree in psychology. Looking at my options, I truly didn't know what to do. At the suggestion of my sister, I decided to become a teacher.

However, with the passage of the unpopular bill Proposition Two 1/2, it was an inauspicious time to become a teacher. The bill limited property tax assessments, which limited spending in school departments across the state, reduced school district budgets, and marked a low point for the field of education. Teaching positions were eliminated, and the result was a large hiring freeze in the public school sector. I had just graduated from college, I had chosen to pursue work in a field I was excited about, but I didn't have a job. Not knowing what my future would hold, I decided to apply for jobs in other states. I was interested in three teaching positions: one in San Antonio, Texas; one in Long Beach, California; and one in New York City. I was ultimately offered the job in Long Beach, California.

The offer was exciting, but the problem was, I had two elderly parents. I was the last of five children. My mother was sixty-eight and my dad was seventy-one, and I did not feel comfortable leaving them. My parents were big influences in my life and my heroes. Neither my mother nor my father had an education past the eighth grade. They used their lack of education as a reason to make sure that their children were educated, and they were both excited that I chose to become a teacher.

I was faced with the dilemma of whether I should leave my parents and head to sunny California or stay in Urbanville struggling and looking for work. While I was contemplating that decision, I received a phone call from a priest who I knew was looking for a teacher at a Catholic school thirty minutes from home. I placed my decision to move to California on hold and went for the interview.

I was hired, which took a load off my mind because I was going to stay in the Urbanville area. God works in mysterious ways, because after that decision I met my wife. You know that feeling you get when it seems that everything is coming together? You start a new job and you meet the girl you will spend the rest your life with? This was a no brainer. I think my parents were happy, to tell you the truth, even though they never expressed it to me. I would not have minded leaving behind the cold January and February months, but being young, I could handle the winter. To cap off my streak of good fortune, I bought myself a new car, a brand-spanking-new Pontiac Phoenix, purchased right off the showroom floor for $7,500. For a kid out of college, that wasn't a bad deal.

I don't want to bore you with the days at the two local Catholic schools that started my career because I had a wonderful experience. I was able to coach basketball, officiate football, umpire baseball, and work at a sports camp during the summer. It's amazing to think that I started my teaching career making $8,800, but what was even more amazing was when I was offered to go to Urbanville Central Catholic and make $13,300. That's when my wife and I decided to marry in 1984, because I felt I was in the money.

I do hope you know that I'm being facetious, because if you are a teacher you know that your pay is just above the poverty line. But it wasn't the money; it was helping children grow to be young adults that was my motivation. I make this point because my heart has always been with the children. I knew what it was like not to have any money, and it was at that point I knew I would dedicate my life to the good of the children.

The nuns that I worked with at Urbanville Central were fantastic, and I loved my job. I was a hustler because I wanted a new house, like every other young married couple. I had an opportunity to start a cleaning business on the side because I had high goals, and I jumped on it immediately. One of my customers was Urbanville Central Catholic. I put in long hours, but my goal was to buy a house, especially with my first child on the way. In August 1987, we moved into our new house, we received a house-warming gift (our dog Scooter), and our first child was born. Like every American, we did what we had to do to make a living, but by the time our second son was born in 1989, our situation started to change.

As we were getting adjusted to the new house, the dog, and two young children, I told my wife that I would do anything I could to keep the pressure off our home life. I put in long hours with the cleaning business, officiating, and teaching. The biggest addition, I was hired as the new head basketball coach at Reservoir Regional High School. Still, in the back of my head I knew I wanted to go for my master's, and I had a burning desire to become an administrator. Teaching was great because many of my students would come back to say hi. I would see them at supermarkets, barbershops, in and out of the city. The nice thing is they never said anything negative about me and they were thrilled to see me. In other words, I tried my best to be a positive role model and a pillar in the Urbanville community.

A professor once told me that as long as you keep the kids in mind, you'll never go wrong as a teacher. So that's what I always look for, and I enjoyed getting up in the morning to show up at school. This would all change in 1991 when my first brush with workplace bullying occurred, but at that time I didn't understand the term or what was happening to me. The principal at my school, a nun, decided to retire, which opened up a slot to look for her replacement. Many applicants would come in for interviews and tour the school. They finally came up with the person who would be the new principal. Anna Marie was in her mid-forties and had three children. One was in high school, and two of them attended Urbanville Central Catholic.

There was a lot of significance in this part of my story that would later haunt me in my bullying experience in the Urbanville Public Schools. In 1991, I was also the athletic director at Urbanville Central Catholic, but my first confrontation with the new principal came almost immediately. Anna Marie cut my salary in half without notifying me. My first conflict with her was not really a conflict, but money was tight, and I asked her if there was a mistake. She claimed it was no mistake and she was looking to cut some corners, starting with my athletic director salary. Around the same time, the principal announced her new assistant principal, which happened to be a friend of mine, Missy. I was thinking, *Maybe things will be okay*. After a couple of days, Anna Marie approached me and said that my two boys could attend preschool for free at Urbanville Central Catholic to make up for the reduction in my athletic director salary. I thought that was a nice gesture.

The free tuition was a big help, and I figured everything was good because we didn't have to pay for preschool, but what I didn't realize was that this was the beginning of Anna Marie's manipulation, deceitfulness, lying, and evil tormenting.

At the end of the school year in 1992, she started a huge fundraising activity in which the school would put on a variety show, and the proceeds from the ticket sales would benefit the school. I was not one for doing variety shows (taking time away from education was not popular with me), but I did anything I could to help during the performance by doing stagehand work. During the middle of the show, I was backstage with Anna Marie. I was asked to pick up a riser that the students would stand on. She came up behind me and grabbed my ass, which made me jump. I didn't think anything of it, so I let it go.

The next day I was called to the principal's office. Anna Marie said she wanted to talk to me about the show, but strangely, she wanted me to sit next to her with the door closed. I told her I'd speak to her standing and she proceeded to get angry and said, "Go back to your wife." I felt really uncomfortable and puzzled. Why would she say something like that? In fact, I was embarrassed. What was she implying? I never told my wife or any of my colleagues. That ate me alive, and I thought about transferring to another Catholic school. I went to the diocese headquarters to ask for a transfer, and there was an opening at Holy Faith High School. The principal at the high school loved me and wanted to hire me. She even had me sign the contract to go to the school to teach history. That wouldn't last long.

Through the summer of 1992, I was waiting for the confirmation from the principal of Holy Faith High School, but I was never contacted. Instead I was contacted by the superintendent of the Catholic school system, Stan. He told me to report back to my old school. Confused, I showed up at Urbanville Central Catholic only to be greeted by Anna Marie, who started to excel in the art of bullying when she knew I wanted to leave. She said, "You think you are going to get away from me?" My heart was in my mouth, and I felt stress permeating throughout the building. This was going to be a long year! I needed prayers because I knew this was not good.

At first, I didn't know how bad this was going be. The 1992–93 school year kicked off inauspiciously when I was given all the duties in the school yard. Anna Marie instituted a new rule: every time a student suffered a scraped knee or a minor cut, I had to document it in the school-incident report log at the office (I did not know she would use this against me). I knew she was up to something, especially when she cancelled my cleaning service account for the school. I had to sell my cleaning equipment because the school had been my main account and it became a nuisance to keep the business going with only the smaller accounts. The biggest problem was I lost $3,000 a month in income, and I had a mortgage to keep up with. My wife and I not only worried about my teaching job, but also losing the cleaning account.

Despite losing my cleaning business, I went looking to replenish the lost income. A friend of mine called me up and asked if one of his friends could call me about a business idea. It happened to be someone that I knew through athletics. He introduced my wife and me to a multilevel marketing business. I hadn't heard of this business before, nor did I know that people felt negatively toward this sort of venture, but I trusted the people that introduced us. Even though we did not make much money in the business, the conventions we attended and the positive books I read were an asset to me, and what I read and the connections I made helped me through these bullying situations. The friendships I developed during this time still remain in my life today.

My closest friends that came out of this business were Ron and Claire. They continued to believe in my wife and I even thought we had a hard time in believing in ourselves. Claire was a positive influence on my wife, and Ron was with me, and they saved our sanity. I became bitter and angry given all the problems with Anna Marie and how she tormented me, and I believe this negatively affected the business. I had also lost my basketball job at Reservoir Regional High School. I built the program from having two years of zero wins before I took over the program, to qualifying for the districts. At least the athletic director told me the truth that the person who took my job was friends with a school committee member. That doesn't mean it didn't hurt. I learned the adage early in my life, "It's not what you know, but who you know, that counts." With all these issues weighing on my shoulders, there were two major factors that kept me going.

As Les Brown, a motivational speaker in the 1990s, said on one of his tapes, "If someone knocks you down, fall on your back. Because if you can look up, you can get up, dust yourself off, and move on." His inspiration, along with John Maxwell, Zig Ziglar, Tony Roberts, and Norman Vincent Peale, helped me through my most challenging times, including today. One thing I learned was that "leaders are readers," and that's what I became, a reader.

The second factor was my friendship with Ron, who took a real interest in my well-being as well as that of my family. In one session I had with Ron, he drew a cross on a piece of paper. Curious, I waited to see what he was going to say. He knew of the troubles the principal was putting me through at Urbanville Central Catholic School, and he said to me, "Don't let what is happening to you interfere with your faith." It was great advice, but unfortunately, I was so angry that I ended up leaving the church.

The start of the 1992–93 school year had three main challenges that heightened the bullying at school. At this point, who could I trust? The assistant principal, Missy, who I thought was my friend? No, she began harassing me on my plan book every day, stating that it was not good enough. When I asked where I should make the corrections, she responded that it was up to me to figure it out. How about my colleagues, you know, my fellow teachers? Besides, I was the one who left teaching history because they did not have a physical education teacher, and I was the only one licensed to teach PE. They would not have a prep period if I did not cover their classes; but wait, they avoided me like I had some kind of disease, which made it clear that I was in a no-win situation.

My aging parents had to witness what my young family had to go through with the Catholic school. My wife was now pregnant with our third child, and the uncertainty of me losing my job compounded the stress. My dad was a very devout Catholic and could not understand why the school was doing this to me. I wish I had an answer for him, but I didn't. It was at this point that my passion helping children was tested and my career being employed by the Catholic schools would reach its end.

Visiting my parents and holding in what I was going through was not easy, but teaching, holding down a household with two young children, including one on the way, was even harder. In September, we received a new student. She was in the eighth grade and had learning disabilities. Anna Marie placed her in the one history class I was still teaching. She told me, and not in a nice way, to "do something with her." I knew that this student's disability was severe but not impossible. I had meetings with her mother and told her that the Catholic school system was not well-equipped to handle learning disabilities. The mother told me that there was no way her daughter could go back to her neighborhood school because she was being bullied. I comforted her through her tears and said that I would help her daughter.

By the end of October, Anna Marie abruptly came into my class and told me she had had it with this girl and her mother. Anna Marie removed the girl from the class and placed her in the school's library. She told her that she would stay there the rest of the school year. This made me upset. The principal was not only targeting me, but now this thirteen-year-old girl. Remember, I was bullied as a child, so I am very quick to defend any young person being bullied. I decided to give up my prep periods and my lunch every day to tutor this girl, even though I received push-back from Anna Marie. I spent the whole school year instilling in her that you can do anything you put your mind to.

It wasn't until eight years later I found out what happened to this student during this time when she invited me to her college graduation. Her mother explained to me that her battles with the principal were daunting because she would not let her daughter socialize with other students or attend class. After having this heavy discussion with the mother, who had tears flowing down her face, I heard my name called. It was the student that I encouraged eight years ago. She introduced me to her family saying, "If it wasn't for Mr. Pepi, I would not be standing here with a degree." Since then, she has gone on to receive a master's degree and is holding down a great job. There is one example of the fruits of my labor, and how I deeply believe in not giving up on a child. I was very adamant helping children because when I was in the fourth grade, I was told in front of the class by a teacher that I would not amount to anything. All my life, I was working to prove this teacher wrong. To me, it was personal.

The other situation that occurred during the 1992–93 school year is still hard for me to handle without choking up. It was October 7, 1992, when I visited my parents. My mom made one of her pizzas that was out of this world. My dad asked about school, and I said it was excellent, as I always did, even though it was far from it. I just didn't want to worry them. My mom was seventy-nine and my dad was eighty-two at the time. They didn't need to hear this. My dad also asked me about the multilevel business which, again, I told him was going well. As the night came to an end, and the most powerful words that my dad said to me that night also happened to be his last words to me: "I am proud of you" and "I love you." You have to understand that "I love you" was not easy for him to say. We both had an understanding that we loved each other, but never actually said it. That would be the last time I would have quality time with my dad.

It was 4 a.m. on October 8, 1992, when I received a frantic phone call from my mother that my dad was unresponsive on the kitchen floor. I called 9-1-1 for her, and by the time I got to the house, my dad was already in the ambulance. Unfortunately, my mom did not sign a do-not-resuscitate form. My dad was clinically dead, but the EMTs revived him. When he was admitted to the hospital, he was in a coma. It became very difficult for my mom, my siblings, and myself to handle. My dad was a fighter, and for the eighty-two years he lived, it was his determination in life that gave me the motivation to push forward in my circumstances. As I sat in the hospital with my family, my thoughts were focused on the good times we'd shared. He had season tickets for the men's basketball games at the local college. We also attended all the home games for the local college's football team, and we went to Red Sox and Patriots games. He and my mom were my biggest cheerleaders in whatever I did. He attended all of my basketball games when I was the assistant coach at a private boy's high school and the head coach at Reservoir.

During this time, I began to feel that he wouldn't have wanted to be in this condition. Even though the doctors told us he had some brain function and that his heart was strong, I knew that at eighty-two, he would not be the same. Between the stress of the harassment I was going through with my principal and my father's condition, I was psychologically drained. My siblings, after hours in the ICU, decided that we should all go to work because nothing would change. The doctor told us he would call if there was a change in his condition. I told my siblings that I would drive Mom home. As we pulled into the driveway, a depressed and hopeless feeling came over me. Mom would have to stay home alone, and I had to go to work. I thought, *I wish I could take her home with me.* Given what was in store at work for me the next day, I should have taken my mother to my house and taken the day off.

The next morning, I arrived at school too soon, and I was mentally and physically exhausted. I was not in the mood to see children, or worse yet, the principal. I know it was Friday, and the older students (eighth grade) would always play their favorite game called Mat Ball. As I always did, I explained the rules, discussed the dangers of the game, and divided the class into teams. We were not even fifteen minutes into the game when a student rounded second and landed on the third-base mat. Unfortunately, he landed on another student's leg. All of a sudden, I heard the leg brake and the boy started screaming in pain. I cleared the gym floor, sat every student down, and had one of them go to the office to find an administrator. In other words, I went through protocol.

When Anna Marie came into the gym her first words to me were, "What did you do?"

"Never mind what I did," I said. "Let's worry about the child that is hurt." I knew all along that this was going to be a problem for two reasons: one, the principal had it out for me, and two, this injured child was the son of the art teacher. The art teacher happened to be a friend of the principal.

I wanted to call the ambulance because the child was in excruciating pain, and I wanted the principal to get ahold of the parents. I dismissed the class to the next period and I waited for the art teacher to come down to the gym. Once she arrived, I suggested for us to call the ambulance, but she wanted to call her husband who worked across the city. Forty-five minutes later, he showed up. Again, I mentioned the ambulance, but they refused. The principal, the art teacher, and the art teacher's husband dragged the child on a mat across the gym floor to the back seat of a two-door sedan while the child was screaming. At that point I told all three of them I would not assist them and that I wanted to keep out of the situation to protect myself. This was only the start of a firestorm.

There were many things that happened that day, especially spending the whole night at the hospital with my dad. To come into school and have the principal not even ask how my dad was doing was very hurtful, but having a child get hurt in my class and having them put the blame on me was worse. A week went by with no change in my father's status, but the pot was stirred at my school. I received a letter from the art teacher stating that because of me, her son's major-league baseball career was in jeopardy. (*Really?* I thought.) You couldn't even make this up. The likelihood of making the major league is less than 1 percent. That was not the worst part of the letter. She also informed me I was going to be sued for neglect. I did not expect support from the principal, and I knew I was going to be on my own on this one. Again, I was being tested, and with the Almighty God's guidance, I needed to be strong.

A couple of months later, the principal had a gentleman sit in on my classroom. I didn't know who he was. I taught my class like I always did. I took attendance, explained the rules of whatever game we were playing that day, and talked about the dangers of the game. After the class was dismissed, the gentleman approached me and introduced himself as an attorney representing the parents of the hurt boy. He told me they didn't have a case because I ran a "tight ship." That didn't stop the principal and the art teacher from turning up the heat against me. It got worse. They not only attacked me, but the boy who landed on the art teacher's son. Anna Marie called the Catholic high school that he was going to attend in the fall to tell them that the boy was a troublemaker. I found this out and since I was an alumnus of the school, I was able to get him in. Again, I spoke the truth, but once Anna Marie found this out, the bullying intensified.

My father's condition worsened. He was out of the coma, but he was on a feeding tube and didn't recognize us. The good-hearted people at the ambulance service volunteered to drive him home for Christmas for the last time, and he sat in a wheelchair. I didn't even know if he knew he was there. I could've used his strong guidance given my situation because I knew that he was a man who stood on principle. His strong faith in God and his relationship with Jesus gave me the comfort that he was going to be okay. The holidays came and went with my father being sent back to the rehabilitation center at the Urbanville County Hospital. Even though my wife was nine-months pregnant, I would still go up to the hospital to visit my dad, which brought tears to my eyes every time I saw him in that condition. I prayed that the good Lord would take him home and end his suffering.

On February 6, 1993, my wife and I were preparing to go out when her contractions started. By the time we got to the hospital, her water broke. By 11:30 that evening, our third son was born. I wanted my dad to see my son so my wife and I, at the beginning of March, brought him to the Urbanville County Hospital. My dad smiled, which consoled me that he saw my third born child.

My dad was not improving, and a week later he was placed in a nursing home. I knew deep down this was the best thing for him because none of us had the time and commitment to care for him, and we knew he would be safe there. After two weeks of him being in the nursing home, my mom indicated she didn't want to go home alone. Since I lived the closest to the facility, I offered my house, which she finally accepted. I promised that I would bring her back to the nursing home immediately the next morning.

The next morning, the phone rang at 5 a.m. I answered the phone, and my heart sank when I realized why the person had called. It was the nursing home to inform me that my dad had passed. After I hung up the phone, my mom sat up in bed and said to me, "He's gone." I confirmed with a lump in my throat. She started to tear up, and I went over to comfort her. My mom and dad had a wonderful life together. I was happy that my mom was with me and she didn't receive the sad news alone, but I regret that my dad died alone. That bothered me.

The line at the wake was long and deep with friends and family members lined up outside and around the corner from the Urbanville Funeral Home. Friends told me how it took hours for them to get to the casket, which made me feel proud of our family's integrity and character. I did take notice that no one from the diocese came to the wake except for some straggling teachers. I shouldn't have expected much. The next day there was a beautiful funeral, and because of my bereavement days, I had a few extra days away from school. After four days off, I had to go back to the hell hole. I knew my father would want me to carry on, but the end of the school year was in my mind. I was one step closer to the end of my teaching days in the Catholic school system.

April came and went, and to my surprise, I was still employed by the Catholic school system. I would get to see the 1993–94 school year. But there was new problem that had come up at the end of the 1992–93 school year, which again showed me that the principal purposefully set me up to fail and how manipulative she was. It was a simple fundraiser that gave them the final excuse to let me go unexpectedly.

Every year since I had started teaching at Urbanville Central Catholic School, I ran a basketball-shooting fundraiser sponsored by the Boston Celtics. I started this event so that my students could fully understand the benefits of donating to a charity. The end of the 1992–93 school year was no different. I usually scheduled the fundraiser for March, but because of my father's death, I pushed it off until May. After collecting donations—made by checks only—I would take the checks and the forms and send them to the fundraising department in a sealed envelope. The gentleman who ran the fundraiser was on vacation at the time, and I told him that school was going to be out early that year for summer vacation. He told me that he was going to call the school when he came back from vacation and that I could deliver the materials to the fundraising office. I made sure my school would make the appropriate arrangements, which I put it in writing to let the school office know when the fundraising organizer called that they would call me.

I called the school in June, July, and again at the beginning of

August to see if the organizer ever got in touch with the school, and the school said the organizer had not. At the end of August, just before school started, I received a letter from the diocese superintendent that I was to have a meeting ASAP. Confused, I called the office of the superintendent to schedule a meeting date. When I attended the meeting, Anna Marie was there with the superintendent, Stan, and they both accused me of stealing the fundraising money and money from a sports vendor. Despite letting them know that the checks were in the fundraising company's name and I had no balance with the sports vendor, these facts were not enough. The superintendent told me if I did not come up with the money, I would be terminated. Confused and upset, I went home to gather my evidence.

After gathering a letter from the fundraiser organizer confirming that I had done nothing wrong, plus sending all of the copies of checks, Stan responded by saying that I only did this because of the fear of being terminated. I had a letter from the sports vendor as well, but even with the proof, Stan suspended me for three days without pay. At this point I did not feel that fighting them would amount to much because they claimed that they did not follow labor laws because of their nonprofit status. I was worried about my job because they also did not put into the unemployment insurance, which meant that I would have no pay if I was terminated. To me, it was time to start looking for other employment. This was something I hadn't done since 1981, and it was very difficult for me to wrap my head around this.

The 1993–94 school year was a year from hell. I was thinking of trying to protect my wife and children of the torment that this principal was about to inflict upon me. It was all on me, and fortunately I believe I was young enough to handle it. It was at this point I began to second-guess my ability to teach, who my friends were, and who my enemies were. The first move I made was to remove my two oldest children from preschool to protect them. My wife wanted to know what was going on, and I decided to tell her what Anna Marie did to me. The both of us stayed up nights worrying about our mortgage and bills and the possibility of me without a job.

After informing the school that my two sons would not be attending, the preschool teacher pulled me into the office and began to beráte me. The first thing out of her mouth was "Do you know that I can report to the state that you are abusing your children?" I flipped! *You may pick on me,* I thought, *but my children are off limits.*

"Are you threatening me?" I asked. I stood up and pointed my finger at her and said in a loud voice, "Don't you dare!" I abruptly left and did not speak to her the rest of the school year. I did not know who to trust and who to turn to.

When I got home, I called my oldest sister because she was like a second mother to me. I trusted her and her husband. I received great advice from her, but she suggested that I call my cousin, Antonio, who was the executive secretary of the Urbanville Public School's teachers union. Against my better judgement, I called him with a knot in my stomach and a ball in my throat. I had many negative experiences with my number-one bully, and I knew Antonio was going to use this against me in the future.

It all started when I was five years old. My family shared a house with my uncle and aunt on the second floor and my parents on the first. My cousin Antonio was about fifteen years older than I was because I was a late baby. All of my siblings were married and out of the house by the time I was eight, but I still had to face my childhood bully, Antonio.

As I played outside, just the sound of my cousin's voice made me shiver. He would come up to me and shove me against the house. I was frightened by his presence. One day, I was so frightened, I ran inside and hid under the bed. My dad saw what was happening and told Antonio that if he did it again, he would report him (technically I think he told him that he would kick his ass). Even with that, I still had this sick feeling every time I heard his name. This was one of my childhood experiences of bullying, and now I had to call my bully about the Catholic schools? He didn't help, but later he used this situation to inflict more damage on my career once I entered the public schools.

How could I trust him, especially when he promised that he would get me a job in the Urbanville Public Schools as early as 1991? He would come back to tell me that my application was on the wrong desk or maybe his dog ate it. If I received a job in the Urbanville Public Schools in 1991, I would not have been in this situation. It would be 1997 that I would get my first job in the Urbanville Public Schools, but it was an outsider who helped me and not family (this is how teachers received jobs in Urbanville because of politics, but there are no problems in public education. Yeah, right!). I guess that is where they come up with "you can pick your friends, but you can't pick your relatives."

After we buried my dad, the harassment stopped. I did not understand why. Maybe it was the calm before the storm, or maybe things were getting better. Like I said before, I was naive back then. Obviously, it was the calm before the storm.

On March 17, 1994, I was called to the library by Anna Marie at 8:30 a.m. I was just going outside for duty, but the detour she created sounded important. As I walked into the library, Stan the superintendent was sitting at the table with Anna Marie. I knew what was coming, the big hammer—or was that my heart beating against the walls of my chest?

"Have a seat," Anna Marie said in a stern voice. As my knees knocked when I sat, I directly looked at the superintendent, but not once did he lift his head. After a seemingly long, awkward silence, Stan lifted his head and handed me a letter. As I read the letter, I tried not to tear up. I didn't want them to see that I was weak. Thoughts ran through my head about my parents, my wife, my bills, mortgage, and my children. The letter read: *"THE DIOCESE WILL NOT RENEW YOUR CONTRACT FOR THE UPCOMING 1994–95 SCHOOL YEAR."* Then I thought, *What am I going to say to my wife?*

As I headed to the door to leave the library, I turned to the two of them and asked, "Why?"

Their response was typical of a bully: "I don't have to give a reason." And with that, I left.

I couldn't even finish my day because every time I would see a staff member or child, I felt tears welling up. My life at the Catholic schools was just that: my life. I was loyal and always lent a hand, but when the new principal came to our school, the bottom fell out.

As the day ended, I could not go back to the school because I wanted to stay in bed. I had more than 100 sick days that I was not going to have the chance to use. I felt sick, emotionally and mentally, so I stayed out the rest of the year. This was only the beginning. Two weeks later my wife got laid off as a surgical tech when her hospital merged with another. Now we had to face a mortgage, bills, food, clothing, and the loss of two jobs. How were we going to care for our children?

I guess what I didn't understand then what I see today, that this was an example of workplace bullying. The other problem I realized later is that people look at me and see being a nice guy as a sign of weakness. I don't know if I am just naïve or if I am too loyal and trustworthy that I placed myself in this situation. The other problem I could not get over was the fact that this was the Catholic Church. The Bishop didn't have the common decency to meet with me. These were Christians. What does this mean? I don't know anymore. I do know this: I blamed God and questioned my faith. This was wrong, but at this time, I was confused and hurt. I had a young family, bills to pay, and pride all in one package. My future was uncertain, and I did something that you should never do, which is feel sorry for yourself.

# 2

# THE AFTERMATH

Finding a job under stress is not a good way to go through life. I had to work in different fields, such as selling insurance, pest-control sales, and driver's education, so that I could make any money I could. I didn't know if I was ever going to teach again. I did find out some things about myself. I am a terrible salesman because I could not sell anyone on the "what if?" What if you get sick? What if you get bugs? Not my fit. I did enjoy teaching driver's education, but I also had problems in that area as well. Behind the wheel I hit a house, I drove on the median, and I developed gray hair from terrible drivers. I did have great experiences meeting some great students from the public school systems throughout central Massachusetts, but the reality of losing my house loomed in the back of my head.

As I rode around with my students, I would think about my wife at home trying to keep the house in order. I am sure she had a sinking feeling, but I always assured her that everything would be okay, although I knew better.

I also had terrible hours because my driving students had to be picked up after school, which meant my work day finished around 8 or 9 p.m. This made it difficult to see my son's Little League games or any other function my children were involved in. Two years of not working meant added stress just to put food on the table.

In the city, there was a great organization that aided low- or no-income families in need with clothing, turkeys for Thanksgiving and Christmas, as well as other food items. We had given money and clothing to this organization in the past but never knew that we would be going to need food for ourselves. At this point, my wife was laid off from the hospital and we had just had our fourth child, our only daughter. The struggle was intensifying because the only income that was coming in was my wife's unemployment, my football games in the fall, summer camp, and teaching driver's education. This was just enough to keep the heat and electricity on, but not enough for food.

I then decided to take my wife to the welfare office in downtown Urbanville. I said to myself, "Why not? This is what it's for, right?" I mean, food stamps assistance (or EBT, as it's called today) is there when you are struggling, right? Wrong! The counselor called us into his office and proceeded to tell us that after reviewing our application, we were denied. But, he continued, if I were to move out of the house, then they would give my family assistance. What? What a hard lesson.

Our mortgage was way behind and foreclosure was getting closer, but our main focus was food. We decided to go to Catholic charities. I figured, the Catholic Church did this to us. I have been a devout Catholic all my life. They would help me, right? I am still in shock today that a Catholic organization that practices Christianity said no. Even the Bishop, after I sent a letter to see if we could sit down man to man, refused by stating that he believed Anna Marie and Stan and "did not feel the need to sit down." Not even to hear my side of the story. Unbelievable! Maybe that is why the priest sex scandal blew up in their faces—because they were not honest, open, or compassionate toward the victims. Nevertheless, it was December 1995, and as my anger grew toward the Catholic Church, I decided to leave the church. I made a big mistake blaming God for my struggles, and I didn't realize until later that Jesus was with me all along.

Since there was a lack of resources to receive food, my wife and I went to pick up a donated box of food. I was prideful, but I realized I had to put my pride in my back pocket. This was the worst experience of my life. I am not knocking people who needed the food because thank God they have this service, but for me to receive handouts and beg for food humbled me. I was supposed to be the one who helped others, but the roles had become reversed. I vowed and prayed that once I was on my feet, I would help those in need, and the Happy House of Urbanville would be the organization that I would do this for. They do a great job, and the organization is still helping others and is a gem in the city.

As I left the front door of the Happy House and approached our car, I saw my wife sobbing in the passenger's seat, and my heart sank. I didn't know what to do or what to say. I placed the box in the back seat and began to cry with her. The trauma was unbearable, but the worst was yet to come. Our home with all of our pride and future ambitions were about to come crashing down on us. I tried to hold back the mortgage company and hold on as long as possible. At thirty-five, I felt that I could hold them back and be strong for my family, but truthfully, I had no idea of our future. The Catholic school system had taken the air right out of our sails.

Depressed and not knowing what was going to happen next was as equally psychologically damaging as being bullied at school. Losing my dad (who was my best friend and whom I missed terribly) and watching my mother starting to show signs of old age as she approached eighty-one added to my depression. As I started to question my ability to teach, working at the driving school kept me sharp around children, but the pay was not that good. This kept me in the game.

My wife and the children kept me focused on moving forward but my mind was in the past. Struggling just to put food on the table, I was able to take care packages from my mother anytime I was able to. She also insisted on watching our third son, who had just turned two. It was at that point that things got worse. My mom stopped speaking from an illness and had to write everything down, the mortgage company was ready to foreclose our house, and I started to work for a pest-control company to try to get a full-time income.

It was 1995 when my mom was diagnosed with ALS, or Lou Gehrig's disease, which is the worst thing I have seen in my life. I watched my mom die a slow and painful death. My sisters and brother did a lot of the care for my mom as she became advanced in her illness. I had no choice but go to work to try to save my home. The stress built up, and I wanted to be a good father to watch my son play Little League baseball and Pop Warner football. We now had four children between the ages of one and eight, and I knew I had to be strong for them. But my heart was slowly bleeding, and I didn't know how long I could go on. My wife and I are proud people and did not want others to know of our struggles. Going to family functions or going to a ball game, we carried on like everything was normal. We waited to come home to break down in the privacy of our own house. We supported each other, and we knew we had to figure this out on our own.

As 1995 came to an end, my mother's deteriorating health placed her in a wheelchair. Watching her waste away to nothing made me sick. I prayed that God would take her because I couldn't stand watching her suffer. My mom was a prisoner in her own body. She knew what was going on but couldn't do anything about it. My siblings and I admitted her into a very clean and nice nursing home. There was nothing else we could do. One thing we all agreed was to be by her side when the day came that she passed away because we regretted that our father died in the middle of the night with nobody present. That was not going to happen to Mom.

Beginning January 1996, we took turns staying with her. Her feeble body just lay there, and at this point she was heavily medicated to relieve the pain. My three sisters and my brother would talk about our time with our parents. My experiences with my parents were different than my siblings' upbringing because I was a change-of-life baby, and my closest sibling was fourteen years older than me.

My siblings and I showed up to see Mom one Saturday. By late morning, my sister Jude wanted a cup of coffee. My oldest sister, Jane said she would go with her to the coffee shop. The three youngest children were left to stay with Mom. My brother, my sister, and me. As we continued to talk, we could hear in the background the heavy breathing of our mother as it seemed she was struggling for every breath. We all suddenly stopped mid-conversation. There was dead silence. We turned to our mother and realized that she had taken her last breath. She was now with our father in the presence of our Lord. Emotions came over all of us, but in a way, we were relieved that her suffering was over. We prayed over her when the other two sisters returned. They were devastated not being there, but like they said, "At least she didn't die alone." We said our goodbyes and left to make the proper burial arrangements.

I had good memories with my parents, and the time I spent with them will stay with me until the day I die. The wake and the funeral for my mom was packed, just like my dad's was, with relatives and friends. The day was filled with relief in knowing that my mom's suffering had ended. There were a few things that I knew would be missing in my life, such as her cooking and her unconditional love. My father was my rock, and my mother was the steady hand. Even though neither had an education beyond the eighth grade, they were very smart with finances and in organizing the home. We did not have much growing up, but I never knew that. Instead, we were rich in morals and values. We loved God, our country, and were proud to be Italian-Americans.

During the mercy dinner that was held after the funeral, my sisters wanted to go to my parents' house to start working on cleaning and starting the process of dividing our cherished belongings. I was not ready for that, but I understood why they wanted to get started. All of my siblings worked, and one of my sisters lived out of town. It was after they left the house that I drove over to see the house that I grew up in. I needed time to think, grieve, and reminisce in the peaceful surroundings of a place I called home.

It was very strange to be in the house knowing that my mom and dad were gone. In my heart I knew they were with Jesus, but there was a feeling of emptiness that came over me. I could feel their presence and

I thought back on the good times I had at the house. The Christmas Eve dinners, which were more like an open house. Sitting in the backyard talking about my work, sports, or any other subject that came to mind. Then it hit me: in one month, I would be losing my house. Emotions came over me, and I sat in my parent's living room with tears in my eyes. I felt that I was a failure.

Questions filled my mind as I sat there in grief. Was I a loser? Did I deserve this? The only one who truly understood where I was coming from was my wife. I knew that our vows said "for better or worse," but this was ridiculous. As dark set in the winter evening, I went home to my family. I know that I was their rock and had to be the leader of the household. That was one lesson I learned from my father: "Don't let anyone take your integrity and character away from you because those are the most valuable assets you own." I didn't understand when I was younger what my dad was saying, but as I grew into adulthood, he still told me that. My mom told me to "observe, observe, observe," and between the two lessons, that's what I did to fight the bullies. My senses developed through the years, and I could smell a rat a mile away.

For three nights, I went back and forth to my parents' house to think. I was worried about being thrown out into the street with my family, and I worried that the landlord of any apartment I found would not take in my dog, Scooter. He was a Bearded Collie, not a small dog, which would limit me on the apartments to choose from. But on the third night, as I was sitting on my mother's couch, it dawned on me that I was part owner of this house. It gave me new hope, and I knew that the best thing to do was to meet with my siblings.

I didn't realize that my sisters were talking about renting out the apartment when I approached them. My older sister said that my mother was leaving each of us with $5,000, and I was stunned because I knew they had very little. My first thought was to catch up with the mortgage and continue to live in the house I had. My older sister said this plan was crazy because I would not be able to afford the house, and it would place me behind the eight ball when the money ran out. I agreed, and my sisters and brother told me that I could pay them rent, but I told them that would be a stretch. We all know family disagreements are always fun, but this was serious; I needed a roof over my head. We had had bad family squabbles—I don't want to go there in this book—but what I will say is that I know some family members took my cousin Antonio's side of the story. I felt hurt, but today I understand that bullies are manipulators, and that was Antonio.

We eventually agreed that I would pay all of the bills on the first floor just like my parents did until I got on my feet and bought a house elsewhere. The problem? The other half of the house was owned by Antonio and his sister. This was an open invitation for him to continue to bully me. Antonio did everything in his power to make my family's life miserable. It was at this point I knew the bullying would come to a head, because I was older and had a family to defend. The problem now was that my bully had access to the same house I did.

It wasn't too long before I started failing as a salesman with the pest-control company, and my manager told me I wasn't producing enough business. With him on my case, it became obvious that I needed to get back into education. The question was how?

Working at the driving school was excellent, but the best thing was the connections I made with the director and the superintendent of schools in Urbanville. One day after my lessons, the director called me into his office. I thought, *Oh boy, what did I do?* He commended me on a great effort and asked me if I wanted to teach in Urbanville. I jumped at the opportunity, and before I knew it, I was at an interview with the superintendent himself, Dr. Richards.

The interview went well, and I thought getting hired in Urbanville would be a no-brainer. After leaving his office, I went home and waited for the school department to call me. I waited, waited, and waited. After two days, I decided to call the superintendent's office. The secretary got on the phone after talking it over with her boss. "The superintendent wants to meet with you," she told me. Now what?

As I entered the central office building, my heart was pounding. I thought it was strange—what possibly could go wrong? I entered the office and told the secretary that I was there for an appointment. She told me to have a seat and that the superintendent would be with me in about ten minutes. Ten minutes ended up being twenty, but to me it seemed like a week. I was finally called in.

My knees were weak, and it seemed like I just ran the Boston Marathon. He had me sit down and laid out something I never expected.

"What happened in the Catholic schools?" he asked.

At this point, I thought I was done for. The bullies won, I lost. I then went back to my father's advice to protect my integrity and character, as well as what the Bible teaches us: tell the truth. I laid out for him what happened at Urbanville Central Catholic, and he specified to me that Stan, the superintendent of the Catholic schools, had said, "He might be good for your system, but he is not good for ours." I left his office confused and believing I didn't get the job.

I walked into my house with my tail between my legs thinking I would never teach again. My wife saw the dejected look on my face, and we sat in the kitchen wondering what was next. As we talked about some of the options I had left, my phone rang. As I answered the unknown call, a voice I didn't recognize was on the other end. He stated that he was Bill, director of human resources for the public school system. Then I heard the magic words that we thought would never come: "The superintendent would like to hire you for the 97–98 school year." I accepted the offer, got off the phone, and hugged my wife in celebration. At this point, we thought it was the beginning of something special.

# 3

# THE OLD HOMESTEAD

Being a third-generation Italian-American makes me proud of my grandparents who passed through Ellis Island looking for a new beginning in a country called America. They didn't speak English, but they were fluent in a universal language called work. They knew that coming to America would give them the opportunity to create a brighter future not only for themselves, but also, and more importantly, for generations that followed. Both sets of my grandparents were born in Italy and migrated to the new world. They both had totally different stories, but they both worked hard so that they could own homes.

Times were tough, and they saw many injustices in their lifetime, including poor working conditions, child labor, and poor wages, just to name a few. They knew that working hard was the way out, and they never once looked for any help. They were proud people.

After my parents married, they moved to my mother's family home on Wilson Street in Urbanville, which was off Shrewsbury Street. As I stated before, my siblings were much older than I was, and many of the stories that were told on Wilson Street were just that, stories. When I was born in 1959, I only lived in the Wilson Street house until I was two. In 1961, my father's dad passed away, and my father wanted to move up to the Plantation Street home, which had been in the Pepi name since

1919. My dad's sister was living on the second floor with her family, and we planned to move in to the first floor with my brother and two of my sisters. My oldest sister was already married at that point.

By the time I was eight, all of my siblings were out of the house and married. I was basically an only child, which had its advantages. There were plenty of fond memories on Urban Hill and the feeling of comfort living in this house that I called home. My dad had a great garden that he took over from my grandfather, except it was much smaller than when my grandfather originally planted it. The house sat on an acre of land, and even though the surroundings changed since 1919, it was still a quiet neighborhood.

The only problem living here was the fear of my bully, my cousin Antonio, who would intimidate me and could make me cringe just from the sound of his voice. I want to give you an example of his bullying behavior. I was taking a break from one of my friends after an argument (you know, kid stuff—I had a great group of friends that I grew up with, but once in a while, we would have our tiffs). One day, sitting outside with my mother, my cousin showed up and asked why I wasn't out playing with my friends. He pushed my buttons that day, and later, once he found out our situation, he told me to call him. He then tried to orchestrate a fistfight between my friend and I at Holmes Field while he watched. I think he was getting a kick out it. Anyway, we didn't fight, and my friend and I went to his house to get away from my crazy cousin. I joked to my friend, "Hey, at least he is not related to you."

As long as I avoided my cousin, things were great. I was happy when he got married and moved out so I could have some peace. Living there for twenty-three years was special, and having a great relationship with my parents throughout is something I'll cherish forever. That is why after I ran into the problem with my mortgage, it was a good move to move into my parents' house. Little did I know how many problems I would soon be facing because of the move.

Moving and starting a new job all felt surreal, which I took as a sign of a new beginning. Getting used to our new life was tough at first, but it wasn't as emotional as I first thought. Maybe because we were moving into the Pepi household, which had been in my family for generations. I felt that it was only going to be temporary and would give us an opportunity to get back on our feet both with our credit and finances. In the meantime, I thought I would enjoy my new job and the huge yard that our children loved to play in.

My wife and I didn't have our children change schools or Little League teams for the first year. We tried to make the transition as normal as possible for our children, and we would travel across the city to take our two oldest children to school. We moved them the next year to become a part of the Urban Hill community. It didn't take that long in our new home until trouble started, but we were ready to protect ourselves.

Antonio was at it again. Even though he and his wife had a beautiful home in a suburb of Urbanville which was located west of the city, he had his eyes on Plantation Street. It is almost like a sick obsession for him, and for the life of me I could never understand it. He had two of his boys living upstairs from us, who harassed us every chance they had and often caused huge battles between our families. The drama compounded by my working in the Urbanville Public Schools because of Antonio's role as the executive secretary of the Educational Association of Urbanville (EAU), which represented the teachers in the district.

Antonio would try to get me to pay him directly for half of the taxes and the water bill because he would go up to city hall on behalf of his sons to pay. Right from the start I told him that we were capable of paying our own bills. This infuriated him, I think because I effectively took his control away. Isn't that just like a bully? They want control over you, but if you take their power away, the bully is neutralized. The bully loves power and would do anything to maintain that power. At this point, Antonio decided that bullying us more would make us so sick and tired of the abuse that we would move out. Well, guess what? I stood up to my bully, dug in my heels, and became unshakeable. Realizing that it didn't work, he decided to use his children to bully us out.

There were a couple of instances that helped me to understand that it was all a ploy to get my family out of the house. It was very evident on what Antonio's end game was. One Thursday night, his sons decided to have a party. Obviously, my children went to bed at nine, which is normal for small children. The night started with loud music and loud talking. It was a Thursday, and not only did my children have to go to school the next day, but I had to go to work at my new job in the morning. After warnings from the police and myself, the party only seemed to get louder. Calling the police only seemed to exacerbate the problem even more. They ended the night at 4 a.m. with drunk girls on the side lawn, passed out. This obviously was harassment.

The second instance was in the winter. As my wife was getting out of the car one day, she slipped on ice and fell in front of one of Antonio's sons. Instead of stopping to help her, he walked by and laughed. What a gentleman! This same son was the one I saw coming home from school, sitting on top of the side roof of our two-family house drinking beer. The cat they owned went out on the roof with him, and he decided to throw the cat off the roof. I believe that anyone who hurts a helpless animal is capable of doing anything. Let's put it this way, since these are my bully cousin's sons, the apple doesn't fall far from the tree. But Antonio's ruthless attitude toward my family and myself worried me that he was capable of something sinister, so I had to prepare for everything.

Whatever he tried, we stood up to him and stayed strong. When you face a bully, they do not like when you stand up to them. My wife, the children, and I always took the high road. We knew we had to stand our ground so that we wouldn't end up on the streets. It got so bad that he turned my siblings against me and blamed me for the fabricated problems at the house. You have to understand, the biggest ploy for a bully is to fabricate lies and stories to try to destroy his victims. This was his intention.

The plan of a narcissist is to divide and conquer, effectively pulling you away from your allies. It became more noticeable when I received the public school teaching position as a physical education instructor.

When I arrived at the union office to join, I was met by Antonio, who greeted me with a stern steer.

"Tell your wife to keep her mouth shut, and you need to follow the rules here in this school system," he said. Not one to argue and make a scene, I did not respond, but I knew that this was going to be tough with him as the head of the union and me as a teacher in the same school system. I hoped and prayed that I wouldn't ever need him to represent me because I knew it was not going to be pretty.

After many meetings with my family and Antonio, it was agreed that my wife and I would buy the house. He told his sister and my siblings that I put him through so much stress that he couldn't take it anymore. Yeah, right!

I thought it was a good thing to get him off my back by buying all of them out, but I didn't even know if I would get approved for a mortgage. I already foreclosed on a house, and I only just started working in the school system. I had to try because I needed to get rid of the negativity that we were living in. If it didn't work out, I would just tell the family, "Oh well." Maybe they would accept that and leave us alone. Only time would tell.

I didn't have to go far. The first mortgage company accepted our application for $140,000. What I didn't know was the housing and mortgage market at the time. I never heard of a sub-prime mortgage until many years later. I didn't realize that the mortgage companies were bullies as well, and the brokers gave everyone who was breathing a mortgage no matter what financial situation they were in.

Because we could pay the mortgage with earnings from my job, rent from the second floor, officiating football, coaching, and working at sports camp in the summer, I thought everything was going to work out. What I didn't know was the bully was at it again. His plan ultimately was to sell me the house and then find a way to have me lose it so that he could swoop in to save the day. He didn't realize that I was not going to let him do that.

I was working at summer sports camp one day when my wife

showed up. Our children went to the same camp, so I thought maybe they forgot their lunch, but then I saw she was crying. With a muddled look on my face, I asked her, "What's the matter?" What she told me made my blood boil, and I became enraged. She told me that Antonio had come to the house with one of his friends and told my wife that he was going upstairs to take the heating units and refrigerator out of the second-floor apartment. My wife said to him that the refrigerator was fine, but the heating units are the only means of heating the upstairs.

I agreed with my wife. "How did he respond?" I asked.

She started crying harder and said that he had made sexually explicit comments to her and proceeded to use other profanity. I lost it, but I knew that if I went after him physically, he would have me arrested. I had to be smart. The best solution I could think of was a restraining order.

I asked my boss at the sports camp for permission to leave, which he granted. We headed down to the courthouse, a place where I didn't believe I belonged, but the fear of what my cousin was capable of doing to us outweighed the trip. As we walked in the old courthouse, it was packed. Of course, it was 11 a.m., and the building was filled with all of the people who were arrested and awaiting justice. It just so happened that one of my former students from the Catholic schools was a police officer stationed at the courthouse. He saw me and came right over. He was very excited to see me (this is important, because my reputation was always excellent). After some small talk, and after I introduced him to my wife, he asked me what I was doing there. I gave him the short version of the story.

It was the most interesting trip to the courthouse I ever made because not only was one of my students was a police officer there, but another student from the same class was the clerk for the judge I needed to see for the restraining order. God works in mysterious ways, and I knew I was blessed. Things worked out fine, and the judge slapped a restraining order on Antonio. I thought it was over and I would be signing papers the next week. But guess again.

After my wife dropped me off at work, I assured her everything would be okay. As soon as I walked downstairs to watch the pool area back at the sports camp, one of my sisters came up the stairs, yelling at me.

"How dare you place a restraining order on our cousin!" she said. She told me she wanted money for the house.

"Get off this property now," I said. "I am done with family!"

From there, it got worse. Every day a family member called wanting their money. However, two of my sisters told me that they would forfeit their portion so that I could afford the mortgage. Thinking back, I was disappointed in my siblings except for the oldest, who worked to help me afford the house. My other siblings all seemed to back our bullying cousin over me. Anyway, the biggest problem was yet to come.

I received a phone call from the lawyer representing the bank, who told me that the deed to the house was frozen. He told me they were going to back out of the deal if it was not resolved immediately. Confused, I called my oldest sister, and she said it was true—Antonio had frozen the deed. The pressure built up even more. According to the siblings, who all wanted money, it was my fault. I understood that they wanted the money, but why blame me? I thought, *What did I do?* I just wanted to protect my family from a narcissist. They did not see it that way.

The stress was building. I had to look over my shoulder to see who was going to show up at my door. I thought, *I can't handle this anymore.* I decided only an attorney could help us. I went to the father of one of the girls I taught in driver's ed, who was an attorney. He was very helpful. One day, for an hour while my wife and I waited in his waiting room, we could hear our lawyer raise his voice to my cousin's lawyer. Right away I knew it was the best $700 I spent. After the hour was over, our attorney came over to us and asked if we can take the restraining order off him. "If we could do that," he said, "you can close on the house by 2 p.m." I told him we would make it work.

We went back to the courthouse and found my former student in the clerk's office. I explained the situation and she placed us in front of the same judge.

"I don't like taking restraining orders off people because it becomes dangerous," the judge told us. I agreed with him, but after I explained the reason, he said, "Okay, but if he continues to torment your family, come right back in and I will slap it on him again." I thanked him and left. We signed for the house at 2 p.m. that day.

The final request that we granted Antonio was to have he and his sister see the second-floor apartment where they grew up for the last time. My wife and I waited inside the house with the blinds down and the doors open so we didn't have to confront them. All I heard from him was profanity. What really bothered me was that his sister brought one of her daughters, with whom I taught at school, to the house. After they visited and took the refrigerator, my cousin stood in front of the house and in a loud voice, "Another Pepi owning this house, unbelievable. God Bless F— America." Then they left. All of a sudden, a peace fell over the house. It was awesome.

One thing that really bothered me, even still today, was the fact that Antonio sought to throw it in our faces that he grew up in the house, but so did I. My siblings grew up on Wilson Street, and none of them spent much time on Plantation Street. Another Pepi owns the house? So what? I was the third generation to own the house since 1919. In my opinion, it was not the sentimental value of the house, but the monetary value of the house that drove my cousin crazy. Another thing I learned was that my cousin must have had this sick obsession with the house because years later, and even to this day, he would drive by to look at the house. It was his mission for us to lose the house so that he could come in to save the day. As the book continues, you will see what his hidden agenda was.

The funny thing about this situation was that since he had been trying so hard to harass me, he forgot that a second appraisal had to be conducted. This was caused by the delay of the frozen deed. The appraisal came in at $185,000 instead of $140,000. I never told them, because of the aggravation they put me through. I was not volunteering that to anyone. We saved $45,000. Yes, God Bless America.

# 4

# THE SYSTEM

After losing my house, being abused by the Catholic Church, and suffering the stress of my uncertain professional future, it felt great to finally be hired by a public school system. I felt great, but I wasn't proud of the way I received the position. It seemed like "It is not *what* you know, but *who* you know." Still, I would have taken any break that came my way.

The new job came with some downfalls. Being thirty-seven, I felt like an old man compared to the other teachers in my department. I was given a mentor who was almost ten years younger than me. Despite the age difference, it was still a good fit, and we are close friends even to this day. I knew my schedule was going to be tough because I had to take my lumps as a rookie, and I was willing to do what needed to be done in order to continue my career.

The other downside was dealing with Antonio, the union head, especially given what he already put me through. He would throw obscure rules in my face when I didn't even know which rules to follow. That not only made me nervous, it also made me wonder what rules he was talking about. The union's rules? The school department's rules? Whose? I didn't know the answer, and eventually I would find out that there were two sets of rules, one for the state and one for Urbanville.

That was obvious. I just wanted to go to work every day and stay clear of the union as much as possible. If I didn't need the union, I was one happy man.

Other than that, there were many positives that outweighed the negative. I was back to teaching, and as a bonus, I was teaching inner-city children, who I loved dealing with. I also met two close friends, one who would eventually become my son's football coach, Tim, and I rekindled my high school friendship with Robert. These two friends stuck by me through thick and thin, given what was about to happen.

I was placed as a system-wide physical education teacher. One of the schools where I taught was a tough elementary school, and another school had students who were caught with weapons violations, which would take up my Mondays, Tuesdays, and Wednesdays. The two other schools were, let's say, easier to manage. On Friday, my supervisor didn't know where to place me, so he told me to go to one of the high schools and team up with my friend Robert. In all, I was assigned to teach in five schools on five different days, but who cares, I was happy.

It was also very helpful that the government had a surplus of money during this time, which meant all physical education teachers could purchase $300 worth of physical education equipment per year for the first three years that I was in post. This was how I was able to gather equipment so I could travel to all of my schools. My car became my office. The biggest benefit of this job was the people I got to meet and the older physical education teachers who knew how to have fun, which seems to be lost in education today. The physical educators' meetings once a month were enjoyable to go to because it felt like a reunion, but I also figured out very early on who not to trust within the staff.

The schools I taught in were tough, and I was trying to feel my way through that first year. I promised myself two things: I wouldn't take any days off for three years so that I could receive professional status (the first three years are like a probation period), and I would stay under the radar with central office. I just wanted to do my job, make sure the children were getting the best education as possible from me, and then go home. I tried to stay away from the constant soap opera in the teachers' room and the always-ongoing crisis with the administration, who seemed to create problems instead of solving them. The problem was that I was not at the top of the pay scale the first three years because the deal I made with the superintendent. I had to look for other work to offset the lack of pay.

Fortunately for me, I officiated football games, which helped us get by. When the city received a Century 21 grant that funded afterschool programs, I jumped on the opportunity to make extra money. I would receive an extra $35 an hour which offset the low teacher salary. Since I was a traveling physical education teacher, I decided to teach the afterschool program in two of the schools. Both of these schools were in tough areas of the city, and many of the other teachers thought I was crazy to stay after school for two hours to teach. I loved it. We went on field trips and did many programs with the children, which let the students see me differently and they were able to get to know me. I believe, even today, that the key to education is developing trust between students and teachers.

Someone once told me, "Children do not care what you know until they know that you care." Boy, is that so true. Even today, I see these children at stores and at sporting events, and they come up to me to thank me for helping them with their homework or for taking them on a field trip. What is heartbreaking is knowing that some of these children don't even have a father figure in their lives. I was that figure. I respected that.

My oldest son was heavily into sports and played football, basketball, and baseball throughout middle school. He would always bring to my attention the years that I had coached varsity basketball, and he would ask if I would do it again. It gave me some thought of getting back into it. When I lost my last job in coaching seven years earlier, it was because of politics, and I questioned if it was worth it. For my son, I thought it was a good move. Once I got the family's blessing, I started to apply.

I was able to find two jobs that were open at the time, at Milltown

High School and at Knox Regional High School. My first interview was with Milltown. The principal happened to be a member of the Urbanville School Committee. He liked me and referred me and another candidate to the superintendent. Both interviews with the principal and the superintendent went well, but I did not receive the job. I was beaten out by a former college coach who was more qualified for the job. Even still, it felt good getting back into the arena. The principal of Milltown ended up becoming the deputy superintendent of the Urbanville Public Schools. I bumped into him at my children's parent's night, and he told me that he had liked me and my qualifications, which made me feel good.

My next interview was with Knox, which was a little different than the other interview because it was in front of fifteen people. Some were parents and others where staff members at the school. I didn't expect a second interview, but soon enough I found myself in front of the principal, the athletic director, and the superintendent. Within two days I accepted the position, and when I told my son, he was excited. I was excited myself, but something was missing. I could not pinpoint what it was at first. Yes, I officiated football games, I was the only two-term president of the football board, I umpired baseball, I worked long hours in the afterschool programs, and I coached basketball. I had good teams, and I had great rapport with children, teachers, and the administration. But still, what was it?

I finally figured it out: it was that I wanted to make a bigger difference in the lives of children. After starting my first season, I took my first basketball check and bought an aboveground pool so that my family could swim during the summer while I went back to school to go for my master's degree in educational leadership. After careful research, I decided to attend Metro-City College, which had classes at convenient times so that I could go to school around my busy schedule. Every weekend, as well as for weeks on end during the summer, I went to school while I continued to teach, officiate football, and coach basketball for three years. To this day, I don't know how I did it, but I guess if there is a will, there is a way. And, of course, having a loving and supportive family makes the biggest difference.

This was a big challenge for me, especially since I had poor self-esteem. I would think back to my fourth-grade teacher saying I would not amount to anything. One of my sisters had received her master's degree, but nobody else in my family pursued an advanced degree. So my mindset was not where it should have been. It was my wife who encouraged me to do it, and I certainly didn't want to disappoint my children. I wanted them to know the importance of an education, and that in itself was a very valuable asset.

Working as a physical education teacher was very rewarding, and the time I spent in the elementary schools gave me encouragement to move on. The staff at the schools I taught in found out that I was going for my master's in educational leadership, and some would mention that they would love to work in a school where I was principal. That was a real boost in the arm. That kept me focused to continue pushing forward to get my degree.

I would not have accomplished this degree without my family behind me, and I have to give a lot of credit to the former superintendent of schools from one of the small towns outside of Urbanville. As my instructor, she tutored me in writing and helped me with the major project that I needed to complete at the end of the master's program. I worked hard on it, and I knew it needed to be done for me to obtain my degree. It was interesting that the struggle that I always had with my writing started to fade as I grew confident in my work. It was interesting that I started off in this writing class with forty-two students and by the time I finished, only eight graduated with me. I felt this was a great accomplishment.

After my project was accepted, my fellow classmates and I went out to celebrate in Metro-City at an Italian restaurant. We had wine and relaxed and told stories about what this meant to us in our professional career. As I sat there, I became emotional, knowing that I had been told I would not amount to anything by a teacher. This satisfied me because he was wrong. I told that story that night, and I felt proud of my accomplishment. The facilitator gave us all a gift, *The New Meaning of Educational Change* by Michael Fullon, which I read in a week. It was encouraging to know the importance in education to become a change agent to promote quality opportunities for students. I wanted to be that agent to my students, but my dream became my nightmare, and I became disillusioned.

I graduated from Metro-City College in 2003, and I was adamant to walk that stage. I wanted to do this for my four children to show the importance of an education. I also showed my wife that her sacrifices had paid off, and of course, I proved to myself that I can accomplish my goals and dreams as long as I focused on the end game.

The graduation was held at the Big Town Arena, and I was impressed by the professional ceremony that the college had. Sitting there with my family in the audience behind me, I couldn't help but be filled up with pride. I felt tears of joy, accomplishment, and the satisfaction of having placed my naysayers in my rearview mirror. I did it, and nobody could take that away from me. Now was the time to move from teacher to administration. What I didn't know was not everyone celebrated my success. The next string of events changed my life and the life of my family.

# 5

# THE JOB

Part of the license process for becoming an administrator included a practicum, which meant I would have a mentor who would oversee my administrative duties as I completed my required hours. In 2001, I saw that there was an opening at one of the toughest middle schools in the city. The children were great, but the students ran the school and not the administrators. My supervisor, Marsha, thought I was out of my mind to go there, not because of the children, but because there was a controversial physical education teacher there as well, plus the principal didn't dole out any discipline. Marsha thought I was just going there to teach physical education, but once she found out that I was looking for hours to do my practicum, she understood. She still thought I was nuts.

Once Marsha confided in me that she didn't have the time to go for her administrator's license. I was taken aback by that. *What does that mean?* I thought, *She is my supervisor with no license from the state?* It didn't register with me until years later, but thinking back, who would admit that? I knew she was politically connected (her father-in-law was the mayor of Urbanville, and her husband's siblings all had prominent positions within the school department and courthouse), but really? I let it go at the time because I needed to concentrate on my goals.

Anyway, in August 2001, I met my new coworkers and new supervisor, Bill. Even though I heard negative things about the school, I felt like I was at home. I not only loved the children, but also the staff and the administration. They loved having me on board, especially Bill. He and I hit it off well, and we both had the same beliefs about education. I knew that this was going to work, at least until I was set to graduate in 2003. After that, I figured, I would decide where to go from there.

Bill let me do plenty of work in administration, and it didn't take long for me to complete my hours for my practicum. I would even volunteer to stay late when there was an early student dismissal for a snow storm. I would make sure that every child got on a bus home. Since the school was on a hill, the buses would have a hard time making it to the school in the snow, but I felt it was great because I was piling up my hours. Parents, teachers, and students all believed I was an administrator because of how I handled myself. I had earned their respect, and they listened when I gave the students guidance. They learned right away that I was a disciplinarian, and that seemed to resonate with them.

The next year, due to a grant awarded to the city, our school system planned to turn the larger schools into several smaller schools. They were going through the process of implementing the program in my school. That summer I was asked to go to a conference on the new plan, to be held at Mt. Hilltop Resort. Not only did I accept the invitation, all expenses paid, but I really loved the idea. It made a lot of sense to take large, urban schools and make smaller academies that were both manageable and logical. Spending a week in the mountains with the clean summer air was wonderful. The conference was very informative, and I was excited that the school district was going to institute the plan for the good of the students.

After that summer, I was more excited to become a part of an innovative plan that I knew would work in my middle school. Just the fact that I was going to benefit from this and that I was asked to be a part of the change made me feel the school had plans for me. The 2002–03 school year was going to be the first year this plan was implemented, and I was going to be there for the opening. The other positive was that I would be signed off on my practicum in April 2003, which meant I would graduate with a master's in educational leadership. Exciting!

I was surprised to find out who my representative from Metro-City College was. He was the former human resource director from the City of Urbanville, and he was the representative who would sign off on my practicum. He and my mentor, Bill, raved about my work ethic and how I handled the students and teachers. The former human resource director asked if I was related to another Pepi. I was shocked when he mentioned her first name, and I told him she was my oldest sister, Jane. He happily told me how wonderful she was and that they had gone to school together. He then proceeded to ask me why I didn't see him for a position earlier. I told him my cousin was supposed to help me get a position, but every time I asked about the application, it was either placed on the wrong desk or it was lost. He asked me who this cousin was, and I told him it was Antonio.

"Everyone has skeletons in their closest," he told me. I knew that Antonio had done it to me again. A typical bully.

I sat down at the end of the 2002–03 school year, about a week after my graduation from Metro-City College, with the principal of my school as well as Bill. They proceeded to tell me that Bill was going to retire at the end of the 2004–05 school year and that they would love me to take over his position. I was pumped! I knew then my education was working for me already. I never expected what was about to happen to me at the beginning of the 2004–05 school year, which changed the situation entirely.

The 2003–04 school year started off excellent. I continued to do administrative work to assist Bill. I worked around my prep periods and after school to continue to ingratiate myself in the community. My relationships with parents, students, administrators, and teachers was strong, the administration was very happy with my performance, and they could tell I was passionate about their school. I was strongly influenced by a number of leadership books I read, as well as the leadership seminars that I attended, which helped me to better handle students, parents, and teachers. I always believed that leaders are readers, and that was what was needed to lead children and teachers toward educational goals. I guess I was naïve then, and I realized there was a disconnect between the ivory tower of the central office and the schools within the system. This was a lesson I was not prepared to learn.

We were going through changes in the physical education department as well as in the athletic department. My old supervisor, Marsha, took on a health program grant, which brought $5 to 6 million into the school system. Marsha ran the grant, so she left her professional duties to someone else. Also, the second athletic director, Raul, was about to retire in August. For me, it was another solid year, and I was tight with the teachers and administrators on my team. The school year ended, I gained more experience, and I was one step closer to becoming an administrator. I was ready.

I wanted my mentor's last year to be smooth. I respected all the effort he put in to make me an effective school leader. In the beginning of the 2004–05 school year, I was told by administration that I would have more responsibility and my class load would be reduced. I was fine with that because I knew they were training me to take over Bill's position. It was Columbus Day weekend of that year that changed my direction in life and my career. I was about to experience something I wasn't prepared for.

As I arrived at the Urbanville Stadium—the showcase football stadium in the city—to officiate a high school football game, I bumped into a grounds crew member, Jay, and he told me that there was going to be trouble that night. I was confused. All I knew was that it was October 4, 2004, it was a long weekend, there wasn't a cloud in the sky, I was going to officiate a sport I love, and I was certain nobody was going to ruin my night. I also believed they were exaggerating like they always do. If you work for a municipality, you know what I am talking about.

As I was walking to the locker room with my officiating crew, I saw a physical education friend of mine, Henry, running around like a chicken with his head cut off. His best friend was the new athletic director, Hal.

"Why are you working tonight?" I asked Henry. "Where's Hal?" I was bracing myself, because given what the grounds crew member told me, I was now putting two and two together. I did know that Hal was at the end of his career and close to his retirement, but I also knew he had health issues. Henry told me that Hal was sick and in the hospital. The news hit me like a ton of bricks.

I was shocked and confused as to why Hal wanted to take on such a large job. This job was called the director of physical education, health, athletics, and intramural sports, and to hold this position, a person must possess licenses from the state in physical education and health as well as have experience as a supervisor or director. Unfortunately (you will see why soon), I had all three. Seven high schools, five middle schools, thirty-eight elementary schools, more than forty physical education teachers, twenty health teachers, multiple coaches, and multiple student athletes were all overseen by just one director and his secretary. No wonder Hal ended up in the hospital.

"John, after the holiday, call the deputy superintendent, Marv. We need you," spouted Henry.

"What? Are you kidding?" I answered quickly back.

"No, I am not," Henry insisted. "You'd be great at this job, and you're qualified." He was not taking no for an answer.

I knew that, but I had wanted the assistant principal's position at my school. Plus, I had heard so many horror stories from central office that I didn't want to experience firsthand. I called it the EVIL EMPIRE, just like the *Star Wars* movie called the Death Star. I just wanted to officiate my game and go home to enjoy the rest of the Columbus Day weekend. The problem was, I couldn't. This conversation was on my mind all weekend and I got zero sleep.

I discussed what I heard at Urbanville Stadium with my wife and my children. The sound of more money and the prestige of being the athletic director of the second-largest school system in New England were appealing. My oldest son played football at Westly High School, which was one of the schools I would be in charge of, and he wanted me to take the job. After many hours of thinking about it and going over the pros and cons, I concluded that I would be too close to the central office, which made me believe that it was not the right fit. I decided not to call the deputy superintendent on Tuesday. I was going to stay on course for the assistant principal job.

Tuesday started like any other day. I watched the children at breakfast then went down to my academy to get some paperwork done. At about 10 a.m., I had my first class in the gym. I saw John, the principal of the school, come across the gym as I started my instruction. He moved as if he was on a mission, and he had a look on his face like he had lost his best friend. Without pardoning himself to the class for the interruption, he started to speak to me about the position. I stopped him for a minute to ask if he could wait while I let out the basketballs for the students to shoot (since instruction was not going to happen). I felt this was an important conversation and I didn't have time to organize a class activity. Besides, if you are not in tune with this age group, they will be hanging from the rafters.

Before I was able to say hello, the principal proceeded to let me know that the deputy superintendent, Marv, called him and asked if I was to report to Urbanville Stadium to be the acting director of physical education, health, athletics, and intermural sports until the other athletic director came back.

"I don't want the job," I told him.

"You don't have a choice, and it's not up for discussion," warned John. "If you don't take this position, you will not be given any other administrative job in the future."

"Wow, I can't believe it," I said. "But okay, I will report there tomorrow." As soon as he gave me the news, he was gone, which left me in a fog. I was done for the day both physically and mentally. Now I was going to find out how the central office operated firsthand.

"I thought we decided no," my wife said when I told her about the conversation later that evening. I told her the situation and asserted that

I had no choice. I guessed it was a "get out the shirt and tie and let's go from there" sort of thing. The positive part was that I have been involved in sports all my life. Maybe I was overreacting. It couldn't be that bad, I thought, or could it? Only time would tell. The other dilemma I faced was not working football games, coaching basketball, and teaching at the summer sports camp. I was hoping this position would work out, because I was losing money.

It was Wednesday, October 13, 2004. I walked into the side door of Urbanville Stadium's office.

"Oh no! Another physical education teacher who doesn't know what they are doing," was the greeting delivered by Terry, the secretary for the position. Who? Me? I already had bad vibes about the position, and this was a bad start. You see, the swamp was deep with political appointees who had been sitting in these positions for more than thirty years, and the secretary was one of them. She was in her seventies and should have retired years ago except she had no place to go. Her husband passed away, and she felt safe going to work every day—and I mean every day.

I didn't feel the need to explain my qualifications to her, and all I asked her was where the schedules were. She then proceeded to point to three different rooms. "Great," I said as I proceeded to one of the rooms. I was greeted by two physical education teachers, Henry and Kibby. One was my friend who I saw at the football game the previous Friday, and the other was a female teacher who was very technologically savvy. My first line of duty was to bring the department into the twenty-first century.

When I first saw the schedules, I couldn't believe my eyes. The method had clearly been passed down from one athletic director to another over the course of thirty or so years. The system was not only a dinosaur, it was also very tough going from one room to the other. When a game or practice was postponed, the athletic director would run a red line through the event and then a green line when it was rescheduled. I did not have time to play red light green light to keep up with game schedules. Plus, the phone, oh my word, the phone. It never stopped ringing. From 8:30 a.m. until 4:30 p.m., it was one call right after the other.

Now, remember the secretary? I could not leave her alone for one minute because she made more mistakes than anyone I had ever seen. I don't know if she did it on purpose or if she was not up to the task. Whatever it was, her incompetence reflected poorly on me, because mistakes simply could not be made. If I told you some of the things she did, you might think that I was making them up. But no, these things truly happened.

For example, I asked her where the swim team practiced. Now mind you, swim team is considered a winter sport, and she told me Lake Profondo. I said, "Wait, what?" I asked for the schedule from last year, and sure enough, I saw "Profondo CC," which means Profondo Community College. It was funny at first, but when two teams that are supposed to play each other are both listed as away teams, it's very embarrassing to have the two buses pass each other. It becomes expensive as well. The worst mistake she made involved an outside school that was coming into the city. A parent called the office about an upcoming tennis match at Urbanville Stadium. Terry was arguing with the parent and kept insisting that there were no tennis courts at the stadium. Fortunately, I was listening to this exchange from the other room. I ran over and took the phone from Terry and gave the parent directions to the stadium. Terry proceeded to tell me that I just lied to the parent. I asked her to follow me as we went out the back door and I pointed to the tennis courts. "When did they build them?" she asked. "1934," I told her.

The next swamp creatures were the grounds crew. There were four of them. Two were very helpful, Phil and Sam, and I felt bad for them because they were picked on and bullied by the other two crewmembers, Bill and Jay. The bullies were political hacks and they could do no wrong. In fact, they would plow the private driveways of many politicians and central office employees during snow storms. One owned a doughnut shop, and he would often skip assigned overtime work at the stadium to work at the doughnut shop instead. The other would ditch work to go to see his son's hockey game.

Since I saw value in having a good work ethic, I did not like how they would take off during football games and not hang around in case I needed them. One time, the stadium patrons were complaining about a clogged toilet. Neither Bill nor Jay was around, so I unclogged the toilet myself. I confronted them after and reported them to their superiors, but nothing could be done, and the two of them continued to harass me. Every time I would ask them to line a field or get another field ready, they would laugh at me and walk away. I had to do the work myself. Games were sometimes cancelled because Bill and Jay were unprepared. The worst part of the whole ordeal was the two of them would team up with the secretary—a lethal trio.

Every time I would have a meeting with my superior, Mary, who was the director of student and staff support services, or Marv, the deputy superintendent, they seemed uninterested in my complaints about the staff. One time, Mary told me to give Terry a poor evaluation, but by the time I was ready to give it to Terry for her awareness, she had already filled out her own and told me to sign it (obviously, she marked her performance as "excellent"). I refused to sign the evaluation. Mary became angry with me, and she accused me of picking on Terry. It was a no-win situation. This was my first administrative job, and I felt alone, without anyone in my corner. I was starting to have my doubts about this position, and I was only in the first three months.

With the extracurricular activities going on between the grounds crew and the secretary, the job was unbearable. The director's position was difficult as it was, having to manage schedules of buses, games, officials, and game management, but now I had to worry about the swamp.

My focus was on digitizing the schedules. Getting them online would allow me to be on the same wave length as the other athletic directors. I was very fortunate that I had two physical education teachers around to help with that. The only bright spot was the school year was already in motion, and the physical education and health teachers were off and running. I had meetings with them once a month to keep them on task.

The schedules were hard to follow in paper form, but as I uploaded them to the computer, the program worked itself. The only problem I faced was that I needed to make sure that the schedules were complete before I posted them. If I didn't, they would lead to more phone calls. I often wondered if parents intentionally sat by the computer and thought, *A-ha, I got him*. Anyway, having moved the schedules online, I realized that I had created another dilemma. The secretary and grounds crew were stuck in the 1700s, and I was in the twenty-first century with the schedules. I quickly learned that you can't mix the two, and it was clear to me that they were not going to change.

For my sanity, I left Terry out of the equation and talked directly to the grounds crew (who would still throw me under the bus by using the old schedules). I mentioned to student athletes, coaches, and principals to always go online to look at the schedules. Everything seemed to work, but clearly the secretary and the grounds crew worked for the swamp, and they attempted to sabotage my department at every turn.

One of the other problems that haunted me for my entire tenure in this position was the lack of money. I had to run my own fundraisers to help offset the everyday cost of running the athletic programs because I wanted to run a top-notch department. The student athletes deserved it. I worried about Bill and Jay stealing from the till, so I approached the CFO, Bobby, for a safe and a secure, locked closet to which only I would have the key. That aggravated Jay and Bill because I never gave them the key.

I did learn how to live with the hand I was dealt, and I was going to go above and beyond my job title. Remember, if it's for the kids, you can never go wrong. I remember the first Saturday in December 2004 as a time when I went above and beyond the remit of my position. Two of the major high schools, Westly and Streeter, had qualified for the Super Bowl that was to be held at Urbanville State College. The two teams would compete against two of the top schools on the other side of the state. I was very excited because this has never happened before in the city's history. Plus, my son was the running back for Westly High School.

My son's team would play first at 10 a.m., and I made sure to be at the game site at 9 a.m. The day before, there was a lunch for all the teams at the Student Union building at the college. As a new athletic director, I was able to attend, but the biggest thrill was when I was able to stand on the sideline for the big games. People were coming up to me to talk sports and to talk about the job, which was awesome.

It would have been a perfect day until I saw this person coming onto the sidelines. He was dressed in a Yankee coat all bundled up, and I only could see part of his face. He had sweats and sneakers on, and I noticed the look on his face. I will always remember that look. This person looked at me as if to say that I was the problem. I just ignored him because I knew it was Antonio, a bully, and there wasn't anything I could do to change that. I couldn't get away from him to enjoy the day. I know he was the secretary of the union but really, did he have to stand next to me? He was there to torment me, but I carried on like he never existed. I was around friends, other coaches, and the athletic directors. I never acknowledged him.

As the first game was coming to an end, I reflected on the all times I coached, officiated, and worked at sports camps with giants in the industry. *Now I am here,* I thought. *My son a victor, and I'm on the sidelines as the new athletic director.* It was so surreal even though I was just in the acting role. What made it an even better day was that my son's team won. My friend Tim, who coached, had his second Super Bowl win in four years. I especially was proud of my son, who had scored a touchdown. He played great. It was time to celebrate.

As the crowd started to disperse from the first game, I was approached by many parents and friends who came to watch my son. Many of these same people had followed my son's games when he played Pop Warner football and Little League baseball. As they talked to me while leaving the stands, I stood at the fence and looked onto the field to see the second city team enter the playing area to prepare for the next game. "You must be proud of the city having two Super Bowls on the same day," one of the parents said to me. I acknowledged him with a nod and a smile. Yes, I was very proud.

I told the parents that I needed to get back to the sidelines because the next game was about to begin. As I made my way back to the area where other athletic directors were standing, I saw Raul, one of the former athletic directors who also happened to be the father of someone on my football officiating crew, talking to my cousin. I knew where not to go.

I don't know why, but I kept glancing over to where the two were standing and talking. Every so often my cousin gave me that cold, icy glare. I did not even give him the satisfaction of reacting. I decided to keep my back to him throughout the whole second game. With bullies, you don't want to confront them in front of others. With Antonio's loud, demeaning voice, he would have made me look like I was attacking him. I just didn't want to give him that satisfaction.

It didn't matter anyways because I had my best friend Robert at the games and all of the other athletic directors stopping by to talk to me. I asked Robert to hold the football chains during the games, and he jumped on the situation immediately. At halftime we were joined by my son, who had played in the game before this one. I was proud of him for what he had accomplished. He was only a junior and he had already played in two Super Bowls. In a way, I knew he was proud of me, even though he didn't say so. We both watched the second half to see the second city team win a Super Bowl for the first time in the city's history. My mind was going a mile a minute. But I knew one thing, we need to celebrate this accomplishment with a banquet. I knew exactly what was needed but my question was, How was the swamp going to like it? The answer to that was simple. *I don't care*, I thought. *What is good for the student athletes is good enough for me.*

As the weekend came to a close, I went back to my office and started the planning stage of the celebration. I first wanted to clear it with Marv, the deputy superintendent, and I needed to secure funding from other sources so that it would not come out of my budget. As I walked into

Marv's office, I presented my plans to him. He was excited and thought it was a great idea. He said he would get sponsors for me and that he wanted jackets instead of plaques. I knew that jackets were much more expensive than plaques, which I told him. He was convinced that he would raise enough money to cover the cost of the jackets. My gut told me differently. I decided to raise my own money.

My gut was right. Marv never raised a dime, and if it wasn't for my efforts and that of my family, it would never happen. The dilemma I was in meant that I had to keep track of the banquet, which was scheduled for January, as well as the ongoing work of running schedules of the basketball season. Fortunately for me, I had hired assigners for the officials, whom I thought I could trust at the time. One happened to be the former athletic director's oldest son, who assigned all of the basketball games. I was still running the athletic program using the old, paper method, which was frustrating because my secretary was making too many mistakes with buses and games. Maybe I was biting off more than I could chew, but again, the kids deserved it.

I needed this banquet to be the best it could be. Since I felt a lack of support from the central office, I decided to wield my influence among my friends. I recruited one of my childhood friends from my neighborhood, P.J., to be the guest speaker. At the time he was the general manager of a major league team and one of the most successful people to ever come out of Urban Hill. I knew he would come through for me. I asked a sportscaster from a local TV station to be the master of ceremony, which he agreed to with excitement. Both P.J. and the sportscaster told me they wanted to do it for the kids and refused any money. These two men were giants, and I couldn't begin to express my gratitude toward them. The final piece was getting money for the hall, the spaghetti dinner, and money for the jackets.

Two large companies in the city donated a huge amount of money, and all I had to do was send them the bill for the hall, dinner, and jackets. We had the banquet at a church hall, catered the spaghetti dinner from a local restaurant, and the jackets were also printed at a local business. Not only was the whole banquet paid for, but I was able to support local businesses, and that was important to me.

Sure enough, you can never rely on New England weather. As the night of the banquet rolled around, we were in the middle of a snow storm. People were calling me to see if the banquet was still on. I knew I had a lot riding on this night, and I couldn't cancel or risk losing money. We ended up with four to six inches of snow that night, but as crazy as it was, we made it work, even though the guest speaker poked some fun at me during his remarks. We both laughed, but what a successful night it was. I was also proud of my son for being part of one of the winning teams. How many fathers could say that in their tenure as athletic director, they saw their son receive a prestigious award?

The student athletes, coaches, the central office, and the Master of Ceremony along with the guest speaker didn't have to pay to attend the event, but the rest of the adults did, including my family and myself. I needed to cover some of the cost beyond the donations. Again, this event was for the kids, and I wanted them to have an experience. I found out later that this has never been done by any other athletic director. We had two schools from different parts of the city come together to receive jackets for Super Bowls that they both won on the same day. This night we felt that we were one school under one roof that had accomplished a great feat. That was worth celebrating.

Again, I could have done without the swamp (central administration) coming, but being a good administrator, I invited them. They had their own table, which I tried to stay clear of. The deputy superintendent was there. Remember, he promised to raise money, and he suggested jackets instead of plaques. No money ever came from him, and he got a free meal out of it. At this point, I didn't care, but I should have opened my eyes and seen the hidden agenda of the evil empire.

I was in the zone that night, and I felt my passion for the job grow, especially in the week that followed, as I received thank you letters and cards from parents and student/athletes. They definitely outweighed the suggestions and criticisms from the swamp that I should have done this or that. Even P.J. told me this job fit me perfectly. I was now a name that spread throughout the city of 185,000 people.

This high was short-lived, however, because I had to get back to the grind of making sure the schedules would not be sabotaged by my secretary and grounds crew. As I looked over my secretary's shoulder, I got that uneasy feeling I had every time I showed up to work. Nobody from the central office seem to care except me, but I figured that if I continue to do the work and get the sport teams and physical education department running like a well-oiled machine, it would not matter what downtown said. I took a program that was stuck in the 1930s and brought it into the new millennium.

Every so often, somebody from our athletic program—be it a team, an athlete, or a coach—would be honored at the school committee meeting held on Thursdays. These meetings were televised, and my family could watch me on TV. I would get up in the front of the superintendent and school committee members to honor the recipient and say a few words. After the team or individual was presented with an award, we would go around the room to shake hands with all the mucky mucks. They would say to me, "Great job, John," "Keep up the good work, John." I thought to myself, *Yes, they like me. I am going to get along just fine.*

One particular school committee meeting, the two football teams from the banquet were honored. All I heard that night was, "What a great job," and "This is what I am talking about in the athletic director's job." Now, wouldn't you think that this was good? Between my friends and my family, this was it, the ultimate job. I am not saying that it didn't come with problems, but I WAS GOING TO STRAIGHTEN THEM OUT!

One of the biggest hurdles that I had to overcome was dealing with the principals in the elementary, middle, and high schools. I didn't really interact much with the principals of the middle school, because they hired their physical education teacher and they didn't have team sports. The elementary principals would comment on physical education teachers because these teachers were assigned to one of their schools. Some of them were assigned to as many as two or even three schools, depending on the size of the school. Some schools had gyms and others barely had a schoolyard, especially if the school had been built in the late 1800s. The problems at the elementary schools were minor and could be fixed with a phone call or a brief meeting.

Basketball season was a lot of fun because this was the first opportunity for me to test my online scheduling system, even though I believed that the spring sports would be the telltale sign of the system's success or failure. The season was intense, and as the athletic director, I believed I should show my face at both the girls' games and the boys' games to support the student/athletes, coaches, and the school community. Plus, it was a lot of fun, because that was my thing, basketball and football. I had all of the site administrators, who were responsible for the collecting of money, making sure the police were present, and submitting the money into the school system's bank account, set up at all of the game locations.

The season went so well that for the first time in many years, two city schools competed in the district finals at UPI an engineering college on the west side of the city. One of the schools was called Eastly High School, from the Eastly side of the city, and the other school was called Westly High School, which was also from the east side of the city (go figure). It just so happened that Westly High School had just won a Super Bowl, the same one we celebrated in January, and it just so happened to be my son's school, even though he didn't play basketball. The game was scheduled for a Friday night, and tensions were high among central office administrators who feared the worst. Of course, that day I was called to the deputy superintendent's office I felt like a child being called to the principal's office.

As I walked in, Marv congratulated me on having two schools in the finals. I thought to myself, *It wasn't me, the coaches and athletes did the work.* I still accepted his congratulations. He told me that he was going to send staff to the game to make sure that nothing went wrong, and that I was not to tolerate any problems. I assured him that it was all set. The coaches of the two teams were both African-Americans, and they were great role models for the athletes they coached. I was very proud of them.

At the time of the game, I wanted to show I was not favoring any team. Since I was the athletic director for both schools, I was supposed to show no bias. So I figured during the first half, I would stand next to the Westly High School bench, and I would stand next to the Eastly High School bench in the second half. The first half went off without a hitch, so I went to the other side to stand during the second half. Sara, the principal of Eastly, said to me, "Why don't you stay on the other side since you favor them? Your son does go there, right?" I ignored the comment, but I knew that Sara and my cousin Antonio's sister were friends, so I didn't expect too much from her.

The final score was very close, but Westly High School eked out a win, which made them a Super Bowl champion in football and a district champion in basketball. The school was on a high. After the final tick on the clock, the players ran into a big huddle with students and fans coming on to the floor to celebrate. I immediately went over to the losing side to shake the coaches' hands as well as the players' hands to let them know I was proud of their efforts. Then I turned to watch the big crowd in the middle of the floor. It was great to see the celebration going on. Then I saw my supervisor, Mary, the director of *students and staff support services* (amazing what titles municipalities come up with), and Beth, the director of *curriculum and teacher accountability* (should be administrative accountability), coming out of the stands. Both women were principals before their $50,000 promotion, and they came over to tell me how awful the scene on the court this was.

As I stood there with some of my friends next to me, I didn't know if they were joking or if they were serious. "What do you mean?" I asked.

One of them said, "The players and their fans are jumping on one another, and this will make the other team upset."

"They just won a championship. How else do you want them to act?" I said.

They jumped right down my throat. "Not like this," one said. "Stop them now!"

I told them okay and went to the other side of the crowd and continued to watch them celebrate. They didn't do anything wrong, but in the eyes of this administration, it wasn't politically correct enough for them. I did come up with one nugget from the night. I was clearly in for a long tenure dealing with principals and other vampires who wanted to suck the life out of me.

I dealt with high school principals 80 percent of the time, and believe me, it was not easy. As I mentioned many times in this book, the students were my first priority, and I very rarely listen to a parent unless it affects the child physically, emotionally, and mentally. If a parent approached me on playing time, I told them I supported my coaches because they knew best for their team. If the coach was abusive or acted unprofessionally in front of the student/athlete, I didn't tolerate it. This led me to my first problem with a coach in the spring of 2005.

I was not looking for any problems with my coaches, but in this situation, I had to act because it affected the wellbeing of the students in his care. The varsity baseball coach at Sage High School had been the subject of numerous complaints from parents. He would call his players inappropriate names, and players were becoming so miserable, they were quitting. Parents wrote me letters, and some went directly to the deputy superintendent. The letters also mentioned that the team hadn't won more than five games in a season. Like I said, wins and losses don't bother me, but what did bother me was how the student/athletes were treated. Someone had to be held accountable, and I knew who that was. The problem was that the law didn't allow me to fire offending coaches because the *Commonwealth of Massachusetts Educational Reform Act of 1993* stated that only the principal has the authority to hire and fire.

At least I thought that was the case when I sat down with the deputy superintendent. This was a lesson I learned quickly—who knows who is Politics 101. The swamp was bigger and deeper than I thought. Especially when Marv, the deputy superintendent, told me to fire the varsity baseball coach. I recited the law again, but Marv raised his voice so loud that I thought the coach would be able to hear from the other side of the city. "YOU ARE THE ATHLETIC DIRECTOR," he said. "FIRE HIM!"

*Now, what do I do?*

Before I made any move, I decided to go to the human resources department and do a little research on the coach. The director of human resources, Aisha, was an African-American woman who was very easy to deal with at the time. So our relationship seemed positive, but I knew she was political because she had left the city council as an elected official to take the director of human resources position. Anyway, I wanted her thoughts on the situation.

As I entered the human resources department on the first floor of central office, I forgot how big the room was and how many secretaries worked there. One of the assistant directors greeted me and asked if he could help. The assistant director, Walter, was a bearded, heavyset man who was about my age. He had come to the department after his term was completed as the president of the teachers' union. I couldn't help but think, *Was that a conflict of interest?* I also thought, *What teachers did he sacrifice to get into this position?* This was the topic I will address later in the book. The other assistant director of human resources will also be addressed later as part of the "Bonnie and Clyde" team.

I did ask where Aisha was, but he avoided the question and just said, "She's not here." I didn't pry, but I did want my question answered ASAP. We went and sat in his office and looked up the laws and the coach's contract to see what he could come up with. I already knew the law and the contract. When I went for my master's degree, one of my instructors, who was a principal in a school in Connecticut, told me, "Always follow labor laws and contracts. A grievance against you wastes *taxpayer money*." That was what I aimed to do, except I also didn't want to go against the deputy superintendent and become insubordinate. As I waited, the assistant director said that coaches' contracts are year to year. I knew that, but my problem was that the principal hires and fires by law.

My frustration grew, but what really put me over the edge is when Walter asked, "Who told you to fire him?" When I told him Marv, his immediate reply was "There is your answer." At this point, I started to believe that the Commonwealth of Massachusetts has its own laws and this school department has its own. I was stuck between a rock and a hard place, but I knew the only choice I had. I had to fire him.

I called the school the next day to have the coach call me at his earliest convenience. He called after school hours. I asked if he could come in today to discuss the upcoming season. The state finals in basketball was ending Saturday, and it was already Wednesday, which meant that high school baseball would start on Monday. I wanted to meet with him to give him a chance to tell his side of the story, but ultimately, I knew what I had to do. His reaction toward me was surprising, since I had never met him in person. He was hostile, and it suggested to me that he already knew what was coming. His unprofessional behavior made me realize that he had to go, but it was the protocol that bothered me.

Since he didn't want to come to my office, I went to him. I pulled him aside and told him I was not going to renew his contract. After hearing out his vulgar response, I knew I had to find his replacement and quick. I turned toward his assistant, who I already knew was very well qualified, even more so than the person I was letting go. I stood firm on my decision but never anticipated the fallout that would follow.

My secretary and the grounds crew harassed me, asking me after they heard about the firing, "How could you do such a thing?" What really angered me was that the secretary didn't know the difference between a volleyball and a baseball, yet she insisted on insulting me. The grounds crew, too, stole taxpayer money by putting in for overtime and not showing up, yet they were going to tell me how to run my department. I turned around, walked into my office, and shut the door. I needed time to wrap my head around this.

I began to hear rumors that I was hired to clean house and that I was the worst athletic director in the city. I ignored the scuttlebutt, but what I couldn't ignore were three incidents that indicated that I was being set up by the deputy superintendent. The first was a call I received from our state representative, Cal, who wanted to know why I fired his cousin (the baseball coach). I refused to answer. I only told him that it was a personnel issue. After he hung up, I knew this situation marked the beginning of the end for me. I was not in the municipality's political clique, but then again, to quote my facilitator, "When making decisions, if you keep the children in mind, your decision is NEVER wrong."

The second phone call I received was from the coach, who told me that he had filed a grievance against me. I told him that it was not a grievance situation because coaching contracts are year to year. He then said that he wanted an appointment with me, and that the executive secretary of the teacher's union was coming with him. We made up a time and I hung up. I said to myself, *Oh boy, Antonio is coming to rip me apart.* I had to get ready.

I needed to establish the upper hand even before they showed up. I promised myself that I would not be intimidated by my cousin. Antonio is loud, but the coach did not have legal substance to this grievance. I was going to stand my ground. I went into the conference room and replaced the two chairs in front of my desk with kindergarten chairs that were stored in the conference room. As the two of them came into my office, I sat behind my desk and they sat on the other side of my desk in the two small chairs. I had a row of books between book ends on my desk, so they had to crane their necks to the side to see me sitting at my desk. It was a good thing I was a psychology major in college, because it worked like a gem.

Before Antonio pleaded his case in his booming, obnoxious voice, he said to me, "Aren't there any other chairs in your office?"

"No," I said. "Budget cuts," and laughed to myself.

Antonio proceeded to agree with me that coaching contracts are year to year, but he said, "Traditionally, we don't let our coaches go unless they leave on their own." Traditionally? Give me a break. I then proceeded to tell them that I was firm in my decision. They left unhappy.

The third phone call was from the principal of Sage High School and her assistant. They ripped me down one side and up the other. They didn't believe that the deputy superintendent wanted me to fire the coach. They were not hearing it and wanted my head. This made me think how much they cared for their children or were they for the "good ol' boy network." This was a discouraging sign of what this school system stood for, or better yet, what they don't stand for.

The grievance did pass all the way to the superintendent's office, but the season was three-quarters of the way finished, and the new coach did such a great job and that the team qualified for the districts. The team won two games in the districts for the first time in ten years. When the superintendent received the grievance, he wanted me to reinstate the baseball coach, but since the season was in full swing, the principal told the grieving coach he was out.

I learned so much that year how political hacks use their influence to get the job they want, which means that nobody is held accountable. This discouraged me, and I couldn't wait for the other athletic director to come back to work. Until that happened, I would not rock the boat anymore. I just wanted to last the rest of the school year. One thing was for certain, I would not challenge any coaches and their principals. If those coaches were unethical, the blood was on the hands of the principal.

In mid-April I received some information that made me rethink everything. Mary, my supervisor, called me to say that the athletic director was coming back—but as a teacher, not in his old position. Mary told me that I needed to stay in the position and that they would look into making me permanent. As I contemplated the situation, I went home to discuss it with my wife and children. I thought that on the bright side, I would at least be getting a huge pay raise.

I went to work the next day, which was the Friday before April vacation, and I did some deep thinking as I sat in my office. If I was going to survive this job, I needed to organize the department and make it easier to manage. I needed to make changes to benefit the children. I managed the rest of the spring season and I waited until school let out. The only event I was part of as the director of physical education was the Mini-Olympics, which went off without a hitch. It was even a nice gesture that the quadrant manager wrote me a nice letter for a job well done.

# 6

# YEAR TWO

The summer of 2005 was a time to relax. At least that's how it began. But when two football coaches and three field hockey coaches approached me for uniforms, I had to act. When they showed me the ratty condition of their uniforms, I knew I couldn't have them represent our school system with disgraceful-looking uniforms. I figured it was time to start locating estimates from different vendors to see what I was dealing with as far as price. Since school was out of session for the summer, I had the time to decide, but I could not make any purchases until the new money came in at the beginning of the fiscal year, which would begin on July 1. This was my first time ordering uniforms, and I felt I needed some help. I turned to the purchasing director, Barb, for advice.

After sitting down with Barb, she gave me some pointers on what to do. She told me that I needed to send out a bid to several vendors that were approved by the city. Each one of the four vendors came to my office, took down the specs, and said they would write up a formal bid. Each one knew the drill, and I would purchase from whoever won the bid. I would then write up a requisition and have it approved by the purchasing department to create a purchase order. Once that was done, the work would start. I would then have to approve the order when it arrived so that the vendor would get paid. Simple, right? Well, guess again.

The field hockey uniforms were approved as the best bid, which means it came in as the lowest cost. The uniforms would be produced by a local company and delivered in August. I told the football coaches that ordering sixty-five uniforms for each team would have destroyed the budget for the year. They understood, but I was soon blindsided by a large company out of Illinois, which made uniforms for many NFL teams, including the professional football team in the area. Out of all of the companies, this one should have known better. The worst part of this travesty was that I didn't know that they stuck it to me until the start of the football season (I was not physically at any one these schools).

A week before the season started, I received two phone calls from the football coaches who had requested uniforms. They both left messages on my answering machine to the effect of, "I thought you weren't getting us uniforms this year, but thanks." I stopped in my tracks once I heard the messages. *Wait, what?* I thought, *What uniforms?* I called each one immediately. They weren't around, and I knew they were at practice. I decided to take a trip. One of them coached my son at Eastly High School, the school that just won the Super Bowl. I went to my son's coach first.

As soon as I saw the coach, I asked him, "Who dropped off these uniforms?" He told me about the gentleman who represented the company from Illinois. I told the coach these uniforms had to be returned because there was never a requisition or a purchase order, and it would be illegal to proceed with these uniforms. I didn't even bother going to the other coach, because I knew he would have the same story, so instead I went back to my office to call the representative from the company. Fortunately, I had his cell phone number, and he answered the phone almost immediately. After I told him he had no right to purchase these uniforms without my approval, he proceeded to tell me not to worry, that I could just use an old P.O. just like the former athletic director did. I was not too pleased with his answer, so I decided to call the purchasing director to get this straightened out.

After explaining my situation and telling her how distraught I was, she assured me that it would be taken care of and not to worry. The best thing I did through this ordeal was to create a paper trail with her. We exchanged multiple emails, and in one of them she even wrote, "You did nothing wrong." Even though she said that, I still had that uneasy feeling that somehow, someway, this was going to come back and hurt me. I'm glad I had the foresight to print all the emails out and save them in a folder for future reference.

Barb kept on communicating with me to let me know that she told the company we were not going to pay for the uniforms. The company claimed that they were going to sue us, but since there was no P.O. signed by me, they had no chance of winning their case. The department was clearly in continuous mayhem. During my tenure, I found more examples of illegal and unethical activities that were done in the past.

I tried to make the department run the best I could. I held a few fundraisers to pay for baseballs, softballs, and other spring equipment. There was never enough in the budget for this equipment, and it didn't seem that administrators or school committee members cared. They didn't even want to replace my secretary, who still made many mistakes and caused more headaches. I felt very lonely in this position.

My only saving grace was when I would talk to student athletes and got to see games. In a short period of time, I coordinated homecoming games for all the schools that had football teams. I believed that what was good for private schools and suburban towns would be good for the inner-city children as well. At my homecomings, I scheduled soccer and field hockey games in the morning followed by a football game as an evening event. Some schools got into it more than others with dunk tanks, pie-eating contests, and pep rally bands. Even though I would get a lot of grief from the grounds crew, because obviously it was too much work for them, I ignored them and continued with the events.

Another new event I put on for the athletic programs was an MVP award ceremony following the Thanksgiving Day football games, which all of the other school systems around the Commonwealth already had.

These awards were traditionally named after former coaches who were successful in coaching football at each of the four major schools in the city. We would have either the spouse of the former coach if they were deceased or the coach themselves give out the award.

I also would have orthopedic sports medicine doctors volunteer their services at all of the home football games at Urbanville Stadium, which helped to prevent injuries during the games. The doctors and I negotiated to be present at all football games. This increased the safety for all players. Since I had a strong police presence plus the doctors at the games, I felt certain that these events were safe. My number one accomplishment for the department was the creation of the school system's Hall of Fame, which celebrated former athletes who hailed from the area. (I will discuss the Hall of Fame later in the book.)

As I worked on going to various conferences, meetings, and other important events that pertained to the athletic department, I would still be harassed by the principals, my secretary, the central office, and the grounds crew. I also had to send back any package sent to my office by vendors trying to coerce me into buying their product. Even though I sent the products back, one vendor continued to claim that I should pay for their product. It was amazing that one distraction after another didn't affect my goals for the department.

I had my problems with principals, but the principal from Eastly, Sara, did more harm than the rest. She would try to drive a wedge between the coaches at her school and myself. During the fall season, the volleyball coach slipped up at an away event, using vulgar language and unprofessional behavior. After I was forced to fire that baseball coach, I vowed that I would not get involved in firing another coach. I thought it was more important to teach coaches, so they could be successful. I asked for a sit-down meeting with the volleyball coach, but the principal told me it was none of my business what happened at the event, and she would not allow me to speak to her. Even when I approached my superior, Mary, she warned me that Sara gets emotional and she would never be corrected. I learned in this position how to pick my battles, and that was not a battle I was about to have.

As November approached, toward the end of the fall season, I received an email from the director of human resources, Aisha, telling me that I needed to apply for the permanent position. I was reluctant, but I figured one more year couldn't hurt, and I could leverage this experience to find another job. So I rounded up my resume, filled out an application, and handed the documents to Aisha.

The interview process was really embarrassing. I could tell by the way they conducted the interviews who they favored. Why? The only reason they were doing this was that they had a hidden agenda, but I didn't know that at the time. It was ironic that I did receive the job, and I became permanent on November 5.

As Thanksgiving approached, I started to make noise about replacing the turf at the stadium with artificial turf. The new turf looked like grass and it was softer than the old artificial turf that was used in the 1970s and 1980s. I knew this was going to be expensive, but the orthopedic doctors had told me that somebody would get hurt because of the rough shape of the field. By the time the last game of the fall was completed, the mud would freeze on the field, which made the surface feel like cement. Once I made it public that I wanted to fix the field, every vendor started to serenade me to pick their company to replace the turf. The question was, how were we going to pay for it?

I ran fundraisers to promote the refurbishing of the old stadium, and I developed a five-year plan to bring the old, rundown stadium into the new millennium. I held a fall raffle drawing in which I gave away a TV and other items that were donated from stores around Urbanville County. The money I collected I sent downtown and instructed them to have the money itemized under the stadium remodeling fund. The central office wouldn't do that and said it would have to go in my budget under miscellaneous. I disagreed with how it was handled, because it was used against me to reduce my budget again. The harder I worked raising money for the stadium, the more they took away funds from my budget to use in other departments.

I then came across a professional promoter who helped organizations raise money, and we decided to have a concert at the stadium. They were promoting a local country singer who had released her own CD and performed in Nashville. I was excited.

I received permission from Marv, and the event was set for April. The principals all agreed to promote the concert and sell tickets. One thousand tickets went to the seven high schools in the city and the schools were to put up posters. Marv agreed to orchestrate all this to take a lot of the pressure off me running the athletic program. It was all set. I was excited, but I did not plan for what was about to happen.

A month before the concert, I took a tour of all of the turf fields installed by each of the vendors we were considering for the stadium project. I went to college stadiums, Gillette Stadium (home of the New England Patriots of the National Football League), and other high school fields to see the difference each company had to offer. I really liked what I saw, and I knew what I was trying to accomplish was the best for the student/athletes of the city. When I got back to my office, I started my five-year plan for the stadium with many details that would make the stadium a state-of-the-art facility. The next day, I gave a copy to Marv, who loved the projection and the plan for the future.

As I was trying to plan a way to raise money to remodel the stadium, I still had basketball season finishing up. The same school who lost in the district finals last year was in the final four this year. The problem with this basketball team, Eastly High School, was that I had no access to the coaches at the school because as I said, the principal, Sara, would not allow it. Even to help them with their program, I was isolated from doing my job as athletic director. This became a huge problem when the men's basketball team made the final four. It was a terrible situation because I loved the student/athletes as well as their coach, who was very talented.

As I normally did every year, I sent out paperwork to see which officials the coaches wanted and who they didn't want. Well, obviously, I didn't receive any response from this coach. I called Sara, and she responded to me, "You figure it out, but you are not talking to my coach." I mentioned to her that without this coach's input, I might end up submitting the names of basketball officials that the coach may not like to the commissioner. She held firm, so I submitted the same officials that other schools in Urbanville had.

Now that this team had made the final four, I didn't realize this coach didn't like the officials I chose. The game was scheduled for Sunday, March 5, 2006, and the winner would play the championship game on Friday. I stood next to the team bench, and I thought the game was well played. The other team was Holy Faith CCHS, which always had a good basketball team. It was a close game right down to the end, but the finish was not favorable for Eastly High School. As I left the college gym, I felt everything was going well and there were no problems.

The next day, I grabbed a coffee, the newspaper, and headed to work. When I started to read the paper, I couldn't believe it. There on the front page was the basketball coach from Eastly claiming discrimination on the part of the officials. He was African-American, as was the majority of the team, but I didn't see any problems during the game. I was confused. The coach claimed that the reason they lost the game was because of two racist officials. The worst part about it was that there were three officials and they were all white. As a former coach and as someone who also played the game, I know firsthand that officials do not win or lose games, players and coaches do. I even mentioned that to a reporter not knowing the firestorm that was about to happen.

Every person who had some encounter with racism in the past called my office telling me that I was racist and should do something about the result of the game. I was alone fighting the situation and waiting for the superintendent to contact me and guide me through the fire. I even called him. No response. The end of the week came, and finally he called me. We had a meeting with the superintendent, the deputy superintendent, the principal of the school, all the assistant principals at the school, and me. Right off the bat, it wasn't good.

People in the meeting agreed that it was my fault that this

happened, that I should have spoken to the coach, and that I turned in the wrong officials list. Even though I told them that Sara wouldn't let me speak to any coaches at the school, it landed on deaf ears. I was a racist, and I was the reason they lost the game. I knew this was unfair and it didn't look good for me. This was the longest month I ever experienced. We had meetings at the state office of the American Interscholastic Athletic Association (AIAA) and with the school committee. I ultimately lost, even though I was set up by Sara. She knew what she was doing, and her goal was to destroy me. I needed to get through March with the least amount of battle scars. I needed some good news and it came sooner than expected.

I was working on a grant during the fall from a professional foundation to get new baseball and softball equipment. I was informed by the organization that I won the grant, and on April 1 they were going to deliver the equipment. I showed the letter to Marv. He was so excited that he shared it with the school committee. I was proud that I was able to get a grant worth $20,000 of equipment as well as having a concert in April that would help fund the new field. Even after the problems I was having with my secretary, grounds crew, and principals, especially Sara, I felt I was in a good position with central office, and that's all that mattered.

I would approach Marv weekly to ask how the ticket sales were going, and he would reply, "Great." So I thought there was nothing to worry about. Right? Wrong! Rain was in the forecast for the day of the concert, and I couldn't change the date because of the performer's schedule, so Marv told me that we would move the event to Eastly High School. He claimed he posted the change so that everyone knew, but I was still concerned. He hired a bus to go between Urbanville Stadium and Eastly High School to pick up concertgoers. I was ready for the concert.

I went early to the high school to help set up the concert and introduce myself to the performer. School committee members showed up along with Marv telling me how great the event was going to be. The first bus showed up empty. The second run came up empty. The third run came up empty. After ten runs of empty buses, my stomach sank, and I felt embarrassed. My secretary and the grounds crew showed up not to support me, but to insult me. They made it a joke. My family was there, and a total of ten people were at the concert. I apologized to the performer and the promoter. I told them if they want to leave, I would understand, but the performer told me she would perform no matter how many were there.

I went up to Marv as well as a couple of school committee members to ask what happened. They were not even phased and told me that things like this happened. "Don't worry about it," Marv told me. Well, it wasn't until a week later when I asked the coaches and student/athletes why they didn't attend the concert—because, after all, it was for them. They told me that they never knew about it, and that their principals never announced it or sold tickets. Maybe for one school, this was plausible, but for every school? Something didn't add up until Marv's secretary called me to let me know that he wanted to speak to me.

When I went to his office, he told me how disappointing the concert was. I stopped him in his tracks. "The principals never promoted the event or sold any tickets," I told him. Marv proceeded to tell me that this wasn't his call, and I should have promoted it better. He then told me that he was taking over the remodeling of the football field. Now it all clicked! This was his hidden agenda all along. He was going to take my five-year plan for field improvements and use it as his own. It seemed to me that he realized the field would be a moneymaker, and his ultimate desire was to be superintendent. It started to make sense. I figured it out. This would be his calling card for a promotion, and since he planned to take all the credit, his relationships with the mayor, Jim McMurray, and the US Congressman Tim Jones were also a factor because the project quickly turned political.

This meant that all the work I had done to promote our programs was all for naught. The orthopedic doctors who donated their time at all football games didn't matter. The homecomings and award ceremonies named for former coaches didn't matter. The increase of ticket sales for games that exceeded $30,000 didn't matter. It was all for not and politics rule over children, which left me with a sick feeling in my stomach. I knew deep in my heart that I could not last in this position. I needed to keep my eyes open, use this as valuable experience, and look for another position outside of the system.

As the school year came to an end, I decided to start revisiting my career and look to add to my resume. I knew that if I was going to survive as an administrator, it would not be with the Urbanville Public Schools. My family began to worry about my health and all the hours I spent working. Friends approached me to say that I needed to leave this position because of the lack of support I was receiving. At this point, I could see where the school department was coming from, I started to look elsewhere. The problem is, it was too late for this year because education positions start opening up in January. I knew I would have to do one more year, but could I survive?

# 7

# THE CON JOB

I named this chapter "The Con Job" because after I explain the situation, you will understand what a con job this was. Remember when I said earlier in the book that my goal was to make a difference in young people's lives? I also stated that, as an administrator, "As long as I keep the children in mind, I can never go wrong?" Well, this is where the con came in. I had to learn a hard lesson during my third year as the director of physical education and athletics that IT'S NOT ABOUT THE CHILDREN; RATHER, IT'S ABOUT THE SALARIES AND RETIREMENT PACKAGES FOR THE CENTRAL OFFICE ELITE. IN OTHER WORDS, IT'S ABOUT MAKING SURE "THE CASH COW" IS DOING WELL.

I found out it was never about the children or the taxpayers who pay over and over again for the central office staff. They are well funded and have endless resources to control teachers and the power to destroy them. If you don't believe me, look at the public school system in your city or town. Some are run well, but others, especially large urban areas, are not. In this chapter, I will explain and show you how the central office protects their own.

As I prepared for the new school year in August 2006, Mary called me to her office. When I arrived at the central office and sat down with her, we went over goals to accomplish for the 2006–07 school year. This was normal and raised no red flags for me. As a team player, I always looked for ways of running my department with as much efficiency as possible. The only topic I didn't mention was my secretary or grounds crew because I knew I was going to lose that fight. I then sat there and listened to what my supervisor considered to be efficient.

The administrative documents she wanted me to create were unbelievable. I would have to check each team from each school and their equipment as well as perform my normal duties of scheduling. I had to do this by myself, which no other athletic director had to do in the past, let alone after I left the position. Again, I asked her for an assistant. She then said to me, "Oh yes, by the way, Marsha is going to take over the physical education and health responsibilities to help you."

My response was to give her some facts. "Marsha has a huge grant plus she is not licensed in physical education or to be a supervisor/director," I said.

Mary snapped right back in a huffy voice, "How did you know that?"

"She told me," I replied in a confident manner.

"MIND YOUR OWN BUSINESS," she yelled back at me and told me to leave. I knew something was up, and it wasn't good.

As I left the office, I couldn't help but wonder, *What is going on here?* As August was ending, Mary was putting more and more pressure on me to get the documents to her so she could implement them. I was stressed from the last two years with scheduling and the overall day-to-day task of running my department, but this was a different kind of stress. The worst part about this stress was that I didn't know what her agenda was. I was told that this unqualified woman was coming in to "help" me by TAKING OVER physical education and health, as Mary was overloading me with documents I had to prepare. This seemed wrong in so many ways.

The first day of school came pretty quickly, and even though I was under a lot of pressure, I didn't finish all of the documents. I had other preparation work that needed to be completed, such as the binders each coach needed to receive before the season began. These binders were very time consuming to put together, but the information included in its contents would save me numerous phone calls about schedules or equipment.

The first physical education meeting of the new school year was held at 8 a.m., and I was in the office at 6 a.m. to get ready for the day. I was ready to begin the meeting, but Marsha, who was "helping me," decidedly took over. As she put it, "This is my meeting." I looked at her in disbelief. Knowing her history—she was a health teacher who was promoted to administrator without a master's degree in educational leadership or a license from the Massachusetts Department of Education—I was taken back. I called my supervisor, who basically told me, "Do as you're told." I walked out to the playing fields to get away from this embarrassing situation. How were the teachers going to react? I thought, *Are they going to feel that I couldn't control my department?*

As I sat in the empty bleachers at the stadium, I kept thinking. Every one of my friends that I spoke to told me to ask for help. I did, and this happened. I had been supplanted by someone who should not be in administration. Especially if she was not licensed. I tried to replace the secretary who made plenty of mistakes and made my job harder, but she had too many political ties. So I lost that battle. The two grounds crew members would sabotage the markings of the field and were never present when I needed them at the football games, but I was the one the school department blamed when things went wrong. Image that, the taxpayer's money was going to the crew for work, and they were not even there. Later I found out that one of them would plow politicians and central office administrators' houses. I started to connect the dots.

My heart was in my throat because I loved this job, even though it was a lot of work. But after learning the realities of the political landscape, I knew it was time to leave. I did know one thing, I couldn't get a job in the city. As I left the bleachers, I had to rethink my goals and strategies. It was clear that I needed to look for a new administrative job and survive the year. I didn't think that would be too hard. I was forty-seven years old, had a master's degree in educational leadership, was just six credits shy of my Certificate of Advance Graduate Studies (CAGS), licensed as a supervisor/director, and I had a lot of experience under my belt. At least that is what I thought, but the swamp creatures started to come out to show their ugly heads.

Three major situations came to a head in the fall of 2006. We started to have meetings with engineers and other turf companies to make presentations to the administrators for the new turf field at Urbanville Stadium. I was involved with that process. This would last until February 2007 before the groundbreaking that was scheduled in April. That wasn't a big concern of mine, what I did have to handle was the field opening up across the street from the new vocational high school. This school was the pride of the city, and the Department of Education made it a Blue Ribbon School. Years later, President Obama gave a graduation speech for the graduates. Throughout the years, other luminaries like Dr. Ben Carson and other motivational speakers addressed the student body. The school had received major donations from companies from all over the country to help set up the numerous vocational and technical shops on campus.

To give you a little background on the school so you fully understand how the city operates, I would have to go back a few years. Like other vocational schools around the country, this school had its own budget, its own superintendent, and its own pay scale for their staff. The building was very old, almost beyond repair. The city wanted the vocational school to merge with the rest of the public schools. The superintendent and principal, along with the staff, fought the takeover, but as politics goes, they forced the administrators out and the schools merged.

When I was the director of physical education and athletics, I had spent a lot of time at the vocational school because basketball games were a challenge. It wasn't because of the students or staff, they were great, but the clock for the basketball games was always breaking down. We didn't want to replace the clock because the new school was already in the process of being built. The principal at the time was once a shop teacher and was a down-to-earth person. He was a great guy, and it was his leadership that led to the building of the new school. He would also invite me to banquets held to celebrate athletic seasons. I loved it up there. I don't know if it was the hospitality or the food. I know it was both.

He and I had a great working relationship, and everything was going well until he wanted to change the school's team name from the Bulldogs to the Eagles. His reasoning made sense. About two months before construction on the school was completed, he took me up to the conference room. We looked out the windows that surrounded the whole room. Because we were on a hill, on a clear day you could see the skyline of Boston. He turned to me and said, "It's like flying with the eagles. It's important to show students that you can accomplish anything if you put your mind to it." Wow. This principal was a simple man but a great visionary.

I also understood his reasoning. There was another school in his league that was called the Bulldogs, and the girls were complaining that they didn't want to be called the Lady Bulldogs. This vocational school was once an all-boys school, and the girls had their own vocational school called Girls' Trade. Their name was the Falcons. I told the principal, "I like the name, and you need to push it through." I was all in, but I didn't think he was going to pay the price.

The mayor at the time, Tim McMurray, who later became the disgraced lieutenant governor, argued with the principal that he didn't want the name changed. First of all, why should he care? He went to a private high school, and furthermore, he shouldn't get involved in school matters. That's up to the superintendent and the principal. The mayor then started to harass and torment the principal. You can see as plain as the nose on your face that this was an ego-driven power trip, and HOW DARE ANYONE question his authority. What made matters worse, during the vocational graduation, the last of the old school, Mayor McMurray brought his bulldog to lead the graduates down the aisle. The only funny part of that evening is when the dog went to the bathroom in front of the stage after leading the procession.

Just picture this, all the family and friends as well as graduates and staff members watched while the mayor was on his hands and knees cleaning up the feces.

After that, the principal decided he would retire. After all of the work he put into the new school, he never got to see it open. He saw how bullies operate, and I could see his point that he didn't want his family to go through this torment anymore. Of course, the school system didn't have to look far to find a new principal who had other political ties within the system. I am not saying the new principal wasn't qualified, because she was, but so were others who didn't know someone in the inside track.

Now that you know a little history of the school, and you understand it is a state-of-the-art building, you might assume that the athletic fields should be of the same caliber. Well, like they say, "We ran out of money." The new school received a reimbursement from the state plus more money from the federal government, not to mention the donations from various companies. I even had to buy a wrestling mat for the wrestling team, which had never had a mat to practice on. Imagine that. A wrestling team without a mat is like a basketball team playing without hoops. The problem with the new school was that I had to buy used mats that another school was discarding.

I was at a football team practice at one of the schools when I received a phone call from the coach of the vocational school. He asked me when I was going to sign over the fields so that the school could use them. Sign over the fields? I called the central office and spoke with the deputy superintendent. He told me he would get back to me tomorrow. I guess he didn't know, either.

The next day I received a return call and was told the mayor wanted me to sign the field over at his office. I didn't feel right doing that unless I inspected the field first. As I explained that to the deputy superintendent, he got huffy.

"You never leave the mayor waiting," he said.

"With all due respect to the mayor and you, I don't sign anything unless I inspect it," I said. I stuck to my word.

I grabbed one of the grounds crew (my thorn, Jay) and headed up to the field. I was met with the Parks Department assistant to the assistant (you know how that works). I had no idea who he was. He handed me the key and we went onto the field. As I turned back around to say something to the Parks Department representative, he was gone. Wow! As I walked the field, it didn't take too long before I noticed a huge problem. There was a deep hole in the end zone. Before completing my inspection, I decided to call the new principal who was on the job for a month. She came up to the field within five minutes.

Once she approached, I mentioned to her that we had problems with the field. As we inspected the field together, we found huge holes and other dangerous areas that raised red flags for me, and I told her I could not approve the field. Immediately, the principal called the superintendent and talked to him about how dangerous the field was. I knew she was upset, and I felt we were all on the same page. I followed up with a letter to the superintendent, and I sent a copy to the principal outlining all of the problems the field had.

The following week, we decided to have a meeting at the new school to discuss the issues with the field. As I walked into the meeting, I could not believe who was in attendance. There were four engineers, the mayor, the city manager, the superintendent, the deputy superintendent, and the principal. I felt I was going into the lion's den. It was not pretty because I was more or less defending my stance and emphasizing how I was there to protect the children. Their objective was just to open the field.

I left upset. I got into my car to head back to the office, but before I got to the end of the driveway, my school cell phone started to ring. I picked it up and it was Mayor McMurray. I tried to be cordial, but the conversation started to get heated. He told me I needed to sign off on the field. When I refused, he started spouting vulgarity.

He said again, "You are going to sign off this f—g field."

"With all due respect, Mr. Mayor, if you want to sign off on the field, be my guest. But I will not jeopardize the safety of the children."

Obviously, he did not like my answer and abruptly hung up the phone.

I received no support on this field issue, and my job was becoming more impossible than ever before. The next phone call I received, which was from the youth football league headquartered across the street from the stadium, was the icing on the cake. The Pop Warner Football League was in the middle of construction for their new field at Wolf Park, and they asked if they could use our facilities for practice and games. I had no problem with that because I opened up the field to other schools, adult football leagues, soccer leagues, and many other venues. This was not a problem to me, and in fact I love giving back to the community. I figured this would be the last year with our old field anyway, because in the spring we were going to put in the new field turf.

When the league president of youth football came to me, I made sure to let him know that there was a cost to renting the field. This was not my cost—the fee was set up by the superintendent. I told the league president that if he wanted to approach the superintendent to waive some of the fee, he would be the only person who could do that. That seemed to me to be a fair remedy of the problem, except he decided to approach city politicians instead of going through protocol.

One evening, I was heading out of my office to go to the field for a football game. As I stepped out of the doorway to my office, I was approached by a TV cameraman and reporter from Channel 8. The reporter approached me and asked, “How could you charge children to use your field?” I was stunned, but feeling under control, I explained to the reporter that it was not my call because the superintendent sets the fees. This exchange got me angry, especially because I did not hear from the superintendent to help clarify the rental fee structure. This reminded me of the fiasco with the basketball coach. Again, I was left hanging.

When I went home that evening, I decided to turn on the news, and lo and behold, the superintendent was blaming me for the fees at the field. It was not just him who threw me under the bus, but three other politicians with whom I thought I got along. Not one of them gave me the common courtesy of a call to let me explain my side of the story. Instead, they fed the media a bunch of lies and fabrications.

It wasn't even winter yet, and I had already experienced the fallout from untruths, manipulation, and fabrication. Adding to my job, difficult as it was, I was now dealing with a more underhand agendas just beginning to surface.

No matter what happened during that fall, I was going to be contradicted by administrators and politicians. I was happy that it worked out and the children were able to use the big field. I also apologized to the league president because I thought he went behind my back, but it was the superintendent all along. I just tried to maintain my sanity and ride out the storm without any more issues. Of course, that wasn't me, and if the safety of the children was in jeopardy, I felt I had to speak out. I just didn't know it was going to happen again in the winter. "When it rains, it pours."

After recovering from the major field problem in the fall, I was hoping for a quiet remainder of the year. That is, until the safety inspector, who inspects all of the gyms in the city, came back to me with his report. One of the larger schools in the area, Eastly High, came back with an inspection report that stated that the bleachers only could hold 400 pounds because the crossbeams that were holding up the seating were missing. This was very crucial since each bleacher holds 1,500 people, and they were very high off the ground. If the bleachers collapsed, it could not only injure, but possibly kill somebody.

Looking to fix the problem, I had to change the venue of the basketball tournament that was going to be held at the school the week after Christmas. Moving it to another school within the district was not the problem. It was the principal, Sara, who was my thorn throughout my tenure as athletic director. She played the victim card again, making me look like the bad guy in the public eye. She made others believe that she owned the tournament and that I was picking on her school. You see, bullies do not care about facts. They just want to keep the pressure on the target and embarrass them.

The only reason the tournament was held at her school was because of the size of the fieldhouse, which would hold many people at the same time. She argued with me and brought it up to the superintendent, and again, I received no support. I was not too happy about the situation, and she ridiculed me by saying that I favored my son's school, Westly High School. She had no trouble trashing my name around the school system. When I approached Mary, all I got from her again was, "Don't worry, she gets emotional."

These crises I had to endure started to wear on me, and I started to second guess my authority and my ability as the director of physical education, health, and athletics. I would come home at night and would be agitated about dealing with these bureaucratic snakes. I knew I had to keep going, but the first thing I needed to do was not let these principals control me. It's easier said than done, since I received no help from the superintendent, deputy superintendent, and my supervisor. They all had an excuse for this inexcusable behavior within the school system.

I stuck to my word and made sure that the tournament location was changed, and I felt certain that I was doing the right thing, no matter what they said. I knew Sara was well-connected in the swamp, but it still didn't make it right. Reading the newspaper a week later, I saw a parent had been quoted in an article, and they ridiculed me about shutting down the gym for safety reasons. I figured out that the principal put her up to that by telling her lies. The article was very small, but if I didn't have the bleachers fixed and they collapsed, it would have been on the front page. I could see it now.

In mid-January, I started to apply for positions in other school systems. My friend Robert's wife, Cindy, fine-tuned my resume so I could promote myself as a leader and highlight all the programs I had instituted when I was the athletic director. I used the job-application process as my sanctuary among the craziness of my hostile work environment. Even though this was a new experience, applying outside the Urbanville Public School system, I didn't have a choice. I had witnessed people stealing, being abusive to children, and neglecting public safety, all of which was brushed under the rug, and they didn't have any problems to covering up each one of these issues. I knew it was time to go.

It was early in the year to apply to schools, but I wanted a jumpstart to get ahead of the application process. I still saw five excellent positions available, so I started to apply. This gave me the opportunity to reflect on all the programs I implemented over the two years as athletic director. There were two more accomplishments that had yet to come to fruition before the end of the school year, which was holding the Hall of Fame ceremony and replacing the field turf in the main football field. Once these happened, I would have felt I had done what I had set out to do.

I was now in survival mode. My feeling for the job changed because I was physically, emotionally, and mentally beaten up. With the principals, my bullying cousin, and the direct relationships I had with my secretary and grounds crew, I was getting it from all angles. What added to the negative situation was the lack of support in the central office, which made it seem like they were in on it. Boy, my instincts were right.

It really started to hit me during a meeting about the field turf project. All of the bidders had come to showcase their product. The one I liked the best was the same company that installed the turf at Gillette Stadium where the New England Patriots played. The dilemma was, they were the most expensive. Of course, it was the best on the market. I knew we couldn't afford this turf because state law only allowed us to purchase from the lowest bidder. I mentioned this to the committee and to Marv, and afterward he did not allow me to attend any more meetings. I knew at this point that it didn't look good for me.

What was going on here? I was not getting any support, like the concert that would have brought in money for the turf. They wanted me to fire teachers and coaches for no reason whatsoever. Even if they deserved it, they were teaching for so long, but if the administrators dropped the ball, they threw the ball in my lap. They figured I would be the fall guy in case of any lawsuits. How about safety on the field or the gyms? That didn't count because I was "picking on the school." That same school with the dangerous bleachers was also the school where I caught the ticket manager stealing money; $4,000 was missing from the ticket collection. Sara would tell me, "Not him, you misunderstood the ticket manager. You are picking on the school." That's all I heard over and over again. I started thinking, *Is it me? Am I just imagining this?* I started to second guess my ability to perform.

After applying for the five positions listed on multiple websites, it was a never-ending wait. I could not help thinking that the city was going to sabotage my job opportunities. *But why was I thinking that way? I was a team player, wasn't I?* It was a loaded question. *Yes, I was a team player, but for what team?* Then it entered my mind: *Is there an ulterior motive? Am I now thinking that there is a conspiracy here? Wait, what? Nah, those are only in the movies; or are they?* My wheels started to turn, and I started a period of sleepless nights.

One night, I thought of how, when I first accepted the director of physical education and athletics position, human resources played with my pay. I was getting paid less than my teacher's position, plus I was doing more work. This was another battle I had to fight. There were items that were shipped to my office, such as "terrible towels" and preteen tampons. I didn't order those! I went up to my secretary then, and of course, she knew nothing about them. The towels didn't even spell "Urbanville" right. Then it came to me. *Where was my signature stamp?* I realized I was being set-up. They wanted me to fail or catch me doing something illegal so that the politically connected person, Marsha, who was "helping me by taking over the physical education department," would step in and save the day.

Despite my lack of sleep, the next day I confronted my secretary. "Where is my signature stamp?" She snapped back at me, "I don't have it." When trying to figure this out, the door opened, and two young ladies from the nearby city high school showed up.

"Hi, Mr. Pepi. Could you do us a huge favor?" Before I was able to reply, one of them continued. "Could we do our internship here with you? Nobody will accept us." I knew the two young ladies. One was the daughter of Marv, the deputy superintendent, and the other was the sister of the boy who was being picked on by the baseball coach. Her father, Steve, ended up being a union president. Without hesitation, I accepted. The good part of this was, they were excellent help.

My day was supposed to end at 4:30 p.m., but for me, it never ended, and I would get more work done after 4:30 p.m. because the phone would stop ringing. One evening I was alone in the office, and I was trying to staple some papers together, but I had run out of staples. I went to my secretary's desk and found more than staples. There was my signature stamp, and under the stamp was a copy of an invoice for the "towels." *So this is what they are up to*, I thought. I made a copy, and I brought the copy home for safe keeping. In fact, I made binders, the same one I handed out to coaches, but this time, I used each binder for every administrator and school committee member. I placed whatever documents they sent me in the binders with their name on it and placed them on my shelves. Now, I was on edge. They had crossed the line, and I had to prepare myself for anything.

# 8

# CONSPIRACY THEORY, OR CONSPIRACY REALITY

I was never one for conspiracy theories, nor was I ever a believer in coincidence. But given the situation I was currently in, something just didn't add up. Going to work looking over my shoulder or waiting for the shocker from my superior was something I had to live with the rest of the school year. All I wanted was to get through the year and leave on a positive note. I was looking for a position where I only had to deal with one school and not several. All I was asking for was a good, trustworthy secretary and a grounds crew that could do their job. I was looking for a team atmosphere and not a "gotcha" environment. Was I asking for too much?

I knew at that time something was up. I knew that the attitudes changed toward me. I wasn't getting "Great job!" notes anymore, and I felt I was about to be hit by a political freight train, but I was too naïve to anticipate it. My oldest son would join me for lunch every day since he went to Urbanville State College, which was near my office. One day in January he even said, "Dad, what's wrong?" I couldn't even tell him because I couldn't put my finger on it.

If I didn't need another questionable situation, what happened next started to make me paranoid and believe I was subject to a conspiracy. I was at my office late with nobody else around except for me. I usually don't answer the phone after 4:30 p.m., but this particular time I did. It was my brother-in-law. I wondered, *Why is he calling me?* He started, "What's up, John?"

Cautiously I answered with, "What's up with you?" He then proceeded to tell me that a group was going to bid on the stadium's excavating job, and he wanted the plans from me in order for them to give the proper bid. I told him they would receive the plans like everyone else. I also asked him who the group was. He wouldn't say, except he told me that they were willing to pay $10,000 for the plans. I told him, "That's a bribe, and once again, they will get the plans when everyone else gets the plans." My brother-in-law was adamant and told me they don't like people who say no. I stated again in a sterner voice, "WHO ARE 'THEY,' AND I DON'T TAKE BRIBES." When he continued to persist on the $10,000, I told him that I had to go and hung up the phone.

As I left the office, I thought, *What was that all about?* Going home I was confused about what had just happened, but I decided to pass it off as nothing until the family holiday party scheduled for that Saturday. After about an hour at the party, my brother-in-law approached me again and asked if we could meet outside. He then said, "They need the plans, and they will offer you $15,000. Imagine what you can do with that kind of money." I was then very angry that we were having this conversation at all.

"Yes, I do know," I replied in an irritated voice. "I will lose my job and spend time in jail. It's a bribe, and I don't take bribes." I abruptly walked away from him and told my wife and my children that it was time to go home.

On the way home, I was quiet. *How could anyone, especially my brother-in-law, do this to me?* I thought, *What is going on?* All of these thoughts were running through my mind. This was my career, my future. I never was so upset. It was bad enough to have to deal with the swamp creatures at my work, but my family? Unbelievable! When I got home, I told my wife. She was beside herself. But we decided to let it go. Maybe it seemed like nothing, but I knew it was something.

As the basketball season came to an end, I was planning on my annual athletic directors' meeting the American Interscholastic Athletic Association (AIAA) to be held on Cape Cod. I always looked forward to the week because I was able to talk sports and shop with the athletic directors from all over the state. I also learned a lot from the experienced athletic directors who were legends. That year it happened to fall on my son John's spring break from college. He asked if he could come with me. I thought it would be great, especially if he wanted to get into teaching.

When the meeting started to get closer, I got a memo from Mary that the city was not going to pay for the trip to the conference this year. For the first time ever. If I was going to go, I had to pay for it myself, so I did. I was angry, but I had promised my son, and it was a learning experience for me. I was not going to miss this trip. I paid for my hotel room, but I knew that I as a member of the Athletic Directors' Association, my food would be taken care of. I just had to make sure my son ate.

Another significant event also happened before I left. My wife and her sister went out for lunch in the city and ran into a person that her sister's family, as well as many others, knew. This person, Sonny, wasn't a good person and spent time in jail on a drug-dealing conviction. I knew all about him. He was considered by many to be a street thug with a nice suit.

He saw my wife and asked, "Isn't your husband the athletic director of the city schools?"

Of course, my wife beamed because she was very proud of me in my position and replied yes.

"Great," he answered back with confidence. "Tell him I will stop over to see him."

My wife didn't know why, but she told him sure with a puzzled look on her face. When she came home, she mentioned it, but the two of us didn't make anything of it.

That year at the conference, I was getting my name out there.

Instead of my usual line of questioning to athletic directors on how they ran their programs, I was looking to see if any of them were leaving so I could apply for their jobs. You also have to look to see if there are any insiders looking at the position, so at least you know where you stand. I did know the athletic director position in Seatown was available, and even though it was forty minutes away, I still wanted the position. I decided to apply for it, and I knew that no one was applying within the school system. The position was wide open.

On my way home, I felt great, and I was ready to put my plans into action. I was hoping for that break, but I needed the school year to end on a strong note. There was the spring season, the first annual athletic Hall of Fame banquet, and setting the budget for next year. I was focused and ready to go, but when I got back to the office, I felt the same polluted environment kept dragging me down. Every day I played and said to myself, *Focus John, focus*. Easier said than done.

The beginning of the next week, just before Easter, I had an unexpected visitor, Sonny, come to my office. He looked like the stereotypical "Italian Stallion". I smelled his cologne before I saw him, and the odor stayed in my office for the rest of the week.

"How you doin', John?" he said when he came through my door. "I have to axe you a question. Why you not taken money from my boy?" I knew right off the bat who his boy was. My brother-in-law offered me $10,000, then $15,000, to get the plans for the field. Now at least I knew who was funding him.

"I will offer you $20,000," he said.

"No." I came right back at him, "That's a bribe, and furthermore how dare you come into my office to offer me dirty money?"

"This isn't dirty money," he countered. "My offer is $25,000."

I responded firmly, "Listen, I don't care if you offer me a million dollars. I don't take bribes, and you need to leave my office." As he started to leave, he asked me who was running the project, and I responded that Marv, the deputy superintendent, was. I don't know what happened after that, but what I do know is I ran my department clean. Right after he left, my secretary asked me, "Who was that?" I sidestepped the conversation by saying a parent.

The next Sunday was Easter, which was excellent because I tried to forget the stress at work. I just couldn't help thinking, *Was it me? Did I do something wrong? Why am I being treated this way?* I started to question my own ability as a professional and as a person. But on this day, I was going to enjoy being with family. Easter was a special time for me because I believe that Jesus had risen, and through his resurrection and power, he was going to lead me toward righteousness.

Monday was a normal day spent organizing spring sports, and the season was underway. It was the next day that changed my life: April 10, 2007. It started off as a normal day. I walked into my office, tried to make light conversation with my secretary, and proceeded to follow the agenda for that day. Around 9 a.m., my phone rang. When I answered the phone, Mary greeted me and stated she wanted to meet with me at 11 a.m. I said fine and told her I would meet her at her office. She interrupted me. "No, I will come down to see you," she said. My heart started to pound through my chest, and many different thoughts ran through my head. None of them good.

I came walking out of my office to let my secretary and the two grounds crew people know that she was coming. My secretary said right away, "That's not good. She never comes to the office unless it's important."

The two grounds crew members yelled out, "She is going to FIRE YOU!" They started to laugh in a sinister manner. The grounds crew and the secretary alluded that Marsha, the woman who was not licensed or qualified for the position and who also happened to be my supervisor's friend, would be the one to take over. *How did they know?* I thought. I could feel my blood pressure soar and I started to break out in a cold sweat. *What if they are right?*

The 11 o'clock hour seemed an eternity away, but sure enough she was five minutes early. She came in very confident and said hi to the secretary like she was a long-lost friend. I said to myself, *Of course you were not going to let me fire her, she was a friend.* Even the grounds crew came over to greet her. Right then and there, I saw that the cards were stacked against me. I knew then that it wasn't going to turn out the way I hoped for. After the kiss-up session was over, we both walked into my office. My feet were like cement blocks, and everything slowed down like I was in some kind of time warp.

I offered her a water, but she said, "No thanks, this is not going to take long." *Wonderful, I thought, What does that mean?* Right off the bat she stated, "I don't know how to put this because you did so much in this position. You are having the first Hall of Fame banquet next month, but I have to tell you that Marsha is taking over your position. You will be demoted back to being a physical education teacher." My face dropped. She continued, "The reason why we are doing this is we are reorganizing the department because of a huge budget shortfall." I thought, *OKAY, REALLY!* She went on, "The good news is..." *WAIT, GOOD NEWS?* "The quadrant manager, Dan, told me that you are licensed as an assistant principal."

I responded, "Yes, and it just so happens there is an opening at the same middle school that I left." *AT LAST, HOPE!*

"No," she replied, "That's for—" *OH, THE CITY COUNCILOR'S WIFE, I SEE!*

"She is not qualified," I replied. "And neither is the person taking my position."

She then jumped down my throat. "DON'T QUESTION ME. YOU ARE OUT, AND SHE WILL BE TAKING OVER YOUR POSITION!" She then got up and walked out.

I didn't even get out of my chair as I watched her walk out the door. I might have stayed in my chair for at least an hour, but I was interrupted by my secretary entering my office. "What did she say?" *Like she didn't know.* After I told her, I started to get aggravated, and the secretary only added to my frustration.

"You have to take it like a man," she advised me. *Oh sure,* I thought, *am I going to take advice from an incompetent person who should not even be in her job?*

I was very harsh in my response to her. "Please leave my office. I don't want to see you for the rest of the day." In fact, I didn't see anyone for the rest of the day.

I spent the rest of the week trying to find out information. The good thing about me is I can always find the inside scoop—"if it smells like a fish, it is a fish." I thought it would be wise to start with the union, but I was nervous because Antonio worked for them. After calling the union, I found out my cousin had left for another office, and the person from that office, Pete, had taken Antonio's place in Urbanville. I didn't make a big deal out of it, but I thought to myself, *They planned this and must have known that I was going to lose my position.*

What made matters worse was the union president, Claire, wouldn't talk to me and referred me to Pete. The other part that bothered me were the letters sent from the school department to the union, and vice versa, that indicated the union already knew what was going on for weeks in advance. When were they going to call me? If I didn't approach them first, were they ever going to call me? Furthermore, the letters I retrieved stated that the person taking my position was not going to be alone. They were planning on hiring an athletic liaison, a physical education liaison, and a second secretary—something I never had in the three years I was there. My staff had one so-called secretary and me. This was a budget cut? How?

I told the union right away that I wanted to file a grievance. They said to me, "We have to see why they are getting rid of you." I told them to forget that and file it anyway, and that we would figure it out then. They still would not, even after I reminded them that it was in my contract that I only had ten days to file a grievance. This frustrated me, and it made me feel like there was underlying collusion between the union and the school department. It was almost like they were told not to file.

The next week after I was told I would be demoted, I attended the last Hall of Fame meeting with the committee in my office. I didn't share the news with them, and I was happy that I didn't because I had my reservations with two of the committee members who were placed on the committee by my secretary. I believed that they were spying on me and were part of the swamp. One of them was family friend of the secretary. He was one of those name-droppers, and I had my reservations about whether he actually knew anyone. The other was a former judge in the Urbanville Superior Court. Imagine that.

We discussed the Hall of Fame ceremony and how we were going to set up Union Station in downtown Urbanville. The food was set. One of the spying committee members, who happened to be on the committee for Union Station, quoted a cost of eight dollars a head. I thought that was a great price since we would have more than 400 people in attendance. The problem was that the committee voted to hold the ticket prices at twenty-five dollars. I was totally against it because the price of the hall, the food, the plaques, and other decorations would not add up financially. It didn't matter—I was a lame-duck administrator, and this fact was thrown in my face throughout the meeting. I was getting it from everywhere, and I was bothered by the nagging question of who told them. It had to be my secretary.

I was originally going to cancel the Hall of Fame ceremony because I was sick to my stomach between being demoted, which would see me lose $40,000 of my salary, and the committee at the Hall of Fame trying to undermine my decisions. My wife, my family, and my friend Robert told me to stick with it and show them, so I did. Two of the committee members of the Hall of Fame I was closest to felt bad for me. I had known them for years through coaching basketball, and they couldn't believe what I was going through. I started to sink into a deep depression, but I had to be strong for my family. My daughter, who was my youngest, in the sixth grade, my son in middle school, my other son in high school, and my oldest son, who was then in his sophomore year at Urbanville State College, were all depending on me. I couldn't give up now.

The stress was building because I knew that each member of the committee had a role to hurt me. This is a great example of "mobbing." This led to mistrust within the system. Who could I trust, and who could

I talk to? My career was sinking fast, and I knew I couldn't give up. I had to seek all of my options, so I decided to connect with politicians from both city counselors and the school committee. I went through every one of them. Some came to my office, some I talked to on the phone. All they would do is yes me to death or say that they would get back to me. It never happened. One school committee member, Cal, in particular, screamed at me on the phone and said, "HOW DARE YOU QUESTION THE SCHOOL DEPARTMENT?" This is called elitism. The positive that came from this phone conversation was a touch of Karma. He lost the reelection, and in my mind, it couldn't have happened to a better person.

This continued through the Hall of Fame banquet. Mentally, I had to prepare for the big night at Union Station. One of the principals, Katie, who became very close friends with my wife and I, helped out that night to set up the banquet. Her son played football with our son. She was great, but unfortunately, she died a year later. She was a big supporter of us. It was a shame. You know, she was one of the few that I could trust. I knew I could trust Robert and his wife, Cindy, who were my rock when I needed it. Then it was my son's football coach, Tim, who supported us through the tough times. They were all at the banquet, and I felt secured in the face of evil.

I really didn't do much except sit at the head table overlooking the more than 400 people in attendance. The only administrator there was Aisha, who positioned herself at the back table watching my wife to see how much money was taken in. The interesting part was that all tickets were bought by check before the event, so only we could trace the purchase. All my wife did was collect the tickets, put boutonnieres on the male inductees, wristlet flowers on the female inductees, and escort them to their tables as they came in. There were **no politicians** at the event, almost like they boycotted it, but as far as I was concerned, I loved it.

As the night began, people were coming up to me congratulating me on such a successful night. Then the questions and comments started rolling in. "Why are you leaving?" "Were you fired?" "You did such a great job." The more I heard, the more depressed I became. I knew they didn't mean anything by the comments, but the facts were facts. After all of the hard work I put toward the position, I was kicked to the curb. Even the sports reporter, Dick, who was receiving the Contribution to the Urbanville Public Schools Athletic Award and the priest, Father Pete, who gave the invocation before the banquet's meal was served, asked me why I was leaving. The only answer I had was what they told me at the time, a budget cut. Both of them looked at me like I had ten heads. "That's a bunch of BS," said Dick. I couldn't have agreed more.

As the evening concluded, more people came up to say thank you to me than I had ever received in my professional career. I was proud and blessed that I started such a tradition that has continued years after I left. It still didn't change the fact that on Monday I had to continue the fight to find out the truth. The good thing was at the end of the week I would be going for my interview in Seatown. *Maybe things will work out*, I thought. *Only time will tell.*

As I stayed around after the Hall of Fame ceremony to clean up some loose ends, I went to pay for the food, which a Hall of Fame committee member had arranged. The fact that he had been placed on the committee by my secretary should have raised some red flags. Paul, the owner of the restaurant that was located at Union Station, gave me the bill. My mouth dropped: the bill had come out to twenty-five dollars a head. I had been told eight dollars a head! The ticket price was only twenty-five dollars. I couldn't pay that! I had been set up. I was firm with Paul, who I knew was in trouble with the city for not paying back taxes on his restaurant. Either he was out to stick to me to help pay for the back taxes or the committee member who I didn't trust to begin with had lied to me. That restaurant eventually closed its doors a few weeks later. Talk about karma.

We had a heated exchange over the bill, but we settled for eighteen dollars per head. I paid with the Hall of Fame account, but that put the committee in the red. I needed to make up the difference, which added to my stress. I ran some fundraisers, which the committee didn't want to get involved in, but I was able to get everyone paid, except for the trophy business. I was $800 short for that. I had a meeting with the committee members, but of course the two that started the problems—the retired judge and retired business man—didn't show. Imagine that, they had caused this collateral damage and then didn't have the guts to show up at the meeting. I did bring it up with the rest of the committee, but some of them, you know the politically connected, didn't believe me. Unfortunately, as of today, I don't know if the bill was ever paid.

Even though I was still looking for answers as to why I was being demoted, my full concentration was on my job interview on Thursday. I figured the end of the school year was coming up fast, and I knew that there was an underlying problem for me having an administrator's position anywhere in the system. I needed this job. I was prepared for the interview. I had brought a folder with all of my accomplishments and my future plans. I found the school administration building in Seatown without any problem. I was early, so I thought I would take a quick trip through Seatown. I loved it.

When I got back to the administration building, I was prepared. I understood the culture of the school and its demographics, which I studied online. I also was able to get a feel of the athletics program when I went to the sports facilities in the town. I knew I was one of fifteen being interviewed for the position, and I thought that was excellent since twenty-three had applied for the job. I checked in and waited patiently for my interview. I wasn't nervous, which I thought I would be. I believed it was because I was prepared, and of course, how many interviewees had managed the number of schools and programs that I had managed? I thought I had a good shot.

When I was called in, I was sitting in front of ten to twelve interviewers, including the former athletic director, parents, principals, and other staff personnel. They introduced themselves to me. I knew I would never remember who was who. I passed around a "bidder," which I explained would give them a feel of who I am as an administrator. My only regret was that I should have printed more bidders to go around. They were very fascinated by my work and asked me plenty of technical questions about my job. I left the interview feeling great. Now I had to wait to see if I got a call back.

It didn't take long. On Monday, I received a call from the human resources director from Seatown, and he informed me that I was one of two that was going to meet with the superintendent for a second interview. I was excited. *This is awesome*, I thought. Then my thoughts ran wild. Was I about to leave the Urbanville School Department? I couldn't hold in my emotions for long. I quickly told my wife and the children, but I told them to be optimistically cautious.

I was the last of the two being interviewed. The superintendent started asking me how to jump start a football program, as well as how to run a successful homecoming. He was intrigued by my answers and wanted me to explain how I accomplished so much with all of the programs and schools for which I was responsible with no help. I believed that I was going to get the job, no doubt. The next day, I received a phone call from the human resources department that they want to offer me the position, but they had to do a criminal record check and call my place of employment. That concerned me.

Weeks went by, and no phone call. I decided to call Seatown myself. The secretary answered and told me the human resources director was busy. She then told me I didn't get the job. I was dumbfounded.

"Why?" I asked.

"You have to talk to the director," she replied. I waited for the return call, but it never came. I found out months later that Aisha had told them that I was under investigation. She had bad mouthed me to another school system. I knew this was illegal but try to prove it. Furthermore, why was I under investigation? The school department never mentioned a thing. My concerns started to grow.

I was so devastated, and the more I dug my heels in, the more I received resistance from the school department. I was getting no representation from the union, the politicians didn't want to know me, and

I didn't receive the position I was excited about. The only result I was getting was declining health. I needed some answers, but nobody within the school department would give me the time of day. It was almost like I had a contagious disease.

As Memorial Day weekend approached, I exhausted all of my choices, and I was getting more and more frustrated knowing that I had paid all of this money toward union dues and never used the union for help. The one time I had needed them, they failed me. I understood that Antonio was part of the abuse, but what about the others that worked in the union office? The president, secretaries, and even the one who had replaced Antonio all failed me and my family. Why pay union dues? All I was looking for was the TRUTH.

Time was running out, and I did very little for the department except for setting up the schedules for next year. As I talked to each athletic director, I told them I had been replaced and would not be in this position the following year. I knew that I was still going to do the schedules through the next year because I was not going to stick it to the children. As I was working on my schedules, my phone rang. It was Mary. She was very angry and in a stern voice told me that I had no business telling anyone about the move. "KEEP YOUR MOUTH SHUT," she said. Something just wasn't right. She then proceeded to tell me on Friday before Memorial Day weekend that she was coming over to have me show my replacement, Marsha, how to do my job. *REALLY? WHY DO I HAVE TO KEEP MY MOUTH SHUT? WHAT ARE THEY HIDING?* I wondered.

This meeting angered me. I knew she didn't even understand the position at all. I picked up on this right away when she was quoted in the paper that her getting the job "made sense because she would go to her grandchildren's games." Now that's a qualifier. It was evident when the two of them showed up at the meeting in my office. What really hurt is when they brought the former athletic director that I replaced, Hal. He couldn't handle the job then, but now he was going to provide moral support. What a joke. The worse part was he was coming in to help me in my job. Was he a friend or a foe? Was he spying on me, or not? It didn't pass the smell test because it stunk.

One thing I didn't want to do was to be a sore sport even though I hated every minute of this meeting. My pride and my self-worth dwindled. I was like the leftover scraps that the restaurant was throwing out. Here I was at the top of my game just three years ago, and now I was giving up the farm. As I showed her around and explained the position, I could see the confused look on her face. It was just like making a high-pitched noise to a dog and seeing the dog's head move side to side. I could have told her the Earth was flat, and she would have believed me. The worse part was, my supervisor and the former athletic director had the same confused look. The only subject that those three had on their minds was whether to fire the head football coach at Sage High School. Why? Then I realized that the person who Marv had assigned to the football stadium project also wanted to be the first Sage coach to play on the new turf field. I knew what they were trying to do so I called in the current coach and warned him by helping organize his coaching staff. Right after that, he had a winning season and in a few short years, he won the state tournament at Gillette Stadium, the home of the New England Patriots. I spoiled their party.

After the magical tour concluded, it was just my supervisor and I left so that she could give me my evaluation. *Here we go*, I thought. *I know what's coming*. As she gave me my evaluation, she told me to read it first and then we would discuss its contents. It was the worst evaluation I had ever received in my life. I couldn't believe it. I looked at her.

"What garbage is this?" I asked. "I ran a great department, except you and the others at central office never supported me."

At that point, one of my assigners interrupted the meeting to say, "Sorry, John, but it's starting to rain. Do I postpone the softball games today?"

"Yes, thank you," I replied.

"See!" My supervisor jumped in, "This is why you received this evaluation. You are confusing everyone with their job." I jumped right back at her and told her he was my assigner. This was normal, no matter who the athletic director was. If it rained, spring sports are postponed.

This was coming from a person who didn't know the difference between a tennis ball and a baseball. She would try to look like she knew what she was talking about, but she had no clue. The funny partwas that she told me when I was first hired, "I don't know anything about sports. That is up to your discretion." I never went to her about a scheduling need or any other problem with my department because of the lack of knowledge on her part.

After receiving the terrible evaluation, I knew they were serious and there was no turning back. I was done. When I showed my wife and my children my "destroy my career" evaluation, the look on their faces said it all. I turned to my wife and asked if she would go with me the next day, a Saturday, to clean my office. I was worried that they would set me up, so I wanted to save emails and other documents that would protect me. This would be the perfect time because it was Memorial Day weekend, and no one would be around. I also took the next week off to clear my head and use up some vacation time.

As I took items out of my office, such as documents (I made copies, the originals stayed) and the refrigerator and the microwave that I bought with my money. Fortunately, I had the receipts for all of these items. My office was also a mess because I would be working with schedules before uploading them to the software, so I organized that. All other equipment I placed in a locked closet that I only had the key, so nothing would be stolen. I didn't trust anyone.

We left after about two hours later, but it seemed like ten hours. I really loved this job, and it was about to come to a crashing halt. My wife felt my pain and would tell me that they were just jealous of me. She also encouraged me to hold my head up high. I still struggled with that. The real character assassination hadn't even hit yet, and what was next felt like tons of cement blocks coming down on me.

I tried to relax over the weekend, but the mere thought of how they were getting rid of me made me break down in tears. Here I was, a person who was into sports all of my life, but now I was crawling into my shell crying the night away. I exhausted all of my options: politicians, administration, and the union, and nothing came from these resources. The politicians told me they would get back to me, NOTHING! I spoke to multiple administrators, NOTHING! I had asked for two grievances to be filed by the union, NOTHING! I just had to wait and hope that maybe something might happen that would provide a way forward.

After the weekend, on Wednesday, I received a strange phone call from Mary.

"Where are the football uniforms stored?" she asked.

"The schools keep the uniforms in their locked closets. Besides, football is four months away," I told her. She said okay and hung up the phone. I didn't think anything of it, so I just tried to keep my mind off work for the rest of the week.

Monday, June 4, 2007, was when the hammer started to come down. The bullying intensified, and they were all working together to come after me. (I know now that it's called MOBBING. This is when a group of people team up with a bully to target a person to help destroy their reputation.) This is the date I would always remember as the first day traveling down the road of destruction.

When I walked into my office, I knew that I needed to finish my schedules. As I was sitting at my desk, the school department carpenter walked in and started to take down the partitions in my office. I asked him what he was doing. He told me he needed to prepare for when Marsha started in the job. I asked him, "Can it wait? I am still on the job until the end of August." He responded, "No."

Two hours later, the electrician showed up and started to dismantle the light fixtures. I sat there in the dark trying to do my schedules. They took all of my furniture and all was left was a small desk, a computer, and my chair. I was in the middle of the room by myself trying to do scheduling, but the distractions got worse. The former athletic director, Hal, came in and started laughing at me. I became a laughing stock in the office, as one by one they came in to mock me. The secretary, the grounds crew, and I did everything not to break down in front of them. I had one thing left, my pride.

Some people would ask me, "Why did you stay? You should have gone home." But again, I was doing this for the children, and I knew that these political hacks were not qualified to finish the schedules. I was not going to stick it to the children, but the next day presented more of a challenge. Raul, the former athletic director before Hal, who retired in 2004, came in to see me. He wanted the schedules to check them with the other athletic directors from other schools to ensure that I was not sticking it to the children. I told him, "How dare you? How much are you getting paid for this?" He told me fifty dollars an hour. Three hours later, he came back to tell me the schedules were good. IMAGINE THAT!

When Wednesday came around, I was feeling the stress. I knew that my blood pressure was high, and I was not sleeping well because I had severe acid reflux. I felt at that point I would take sick days for the rest of the week. I needed a break from the torture, and my wife was worried that I was going to have a heart attack. I decided that on Thursday I would go to my primary care doctor for a checkup.

When I came home from the doctor, I received a phone call from Hal. He asked me what was going on because they just changed the locks at my office. I knew that he was giving me a line. He knew what was going on, and he was baiting me. I wouldn't go for the bait, and I acted dumb by saying, "I don't know, do you?" He wouldn't answer, and I was not going to volunteer any information, but I knew that it wasn't good.

Friday, June 8, 2007, I wanted to just relax and not think about what they were doing to me, but it was hard. The stress of the job was bad enough, but the bullies I had to deal with made it even worse. I couldn't figure out what their hidden agenda was, but I realized that it wasn't caused by good intentions. One thing that I was able to lean on was my family and my yellow labrador, Sandy. She seemed to put a smile on my face when she knew I was down. It was warm out that day, and I decided to go into my pool to cool off. It was Friday, and I knew that Saturday and Sunday would give me some peace. I also knew that I could stop looking over my shoulder, but it was that dreaded Sunday night around 7 p.m. when it started. That sick feeling that I had to go back to work. It never was that way before. I would pop right out of bed and couldn't wait to get to work. Not now. It was like I was carrying cinder blocks out of bed and into the shower.

I just dried off from the pool and I got dressed in shorts and a T-shirt when the doorbell rang around 4:15 p.m. My wife answered the door before me. Sandy started to bark as though I was being robbed, and when I did get to the door, my dog wasn't too far off; I was being robbed of my integrity. I saw Walter from human resources at my door. He was the assistant director under Aisha, who came into the position after his last term as president of the teacher's union (conflict of interest?). He had already handed my wife a letter, and I abruptly took it from her and yelled, "What is this, Walter?"

He responded, "Got to go, John, got to go."

I looked down my long driveway that needed paving and there was Sam, the other assistant human resources director, driving the getaway car. They sped off like out of a scene of *Fast and Furious*, spinning their tires as they left my driveway. The two of them acted like Bonnie and Clyde after a bank robbery. I have never expected this type of treatment. PROFESSIONALS?

Confused and taken back, my mind started to race. "What is this?" I said. As I opened the unsealed letter, my wife and my family waited patiently to learn of its contents. These words hit me, and I never fully read the letter because my whole life came to a screeching halt. "EMBEZZLEMENT, LARCENY, AND/OR FRAUD." I fell to the floor in front of my couch. My head was in my hands, and I went into a zombie stupor. I couldn't speak, and in my eyes, I feared that they were going to plant something on me. The next thought was, *Are the police, FBI, or any other law enforcement coming to my door to arrest me?* Fear and anxiety fell over me. I could hear the stress in my wife and my children's voices. Was I going to jail?

My wife decided to call my friend Robert and my oldest sister, who was like my second mother growing up. Her husband was excellent. Unfortunately, both lived an hour away. I believed her husband should have been a lawyer, but one of their two daughters was a lawyer and is married to a lawyer. My other niece was also my rock and was very supportive in my time of need. I had a good base of supporters who believed in me, and I thanked God for that.

As I sat there, I was only interrupted when my wife said Robert was there, and my sister wanted me to fax that letter to them. Robert said, "Let me read the letter." I handed it to him and it read as follows:

*Dear Mr. Pepi:*

*It has come to my attention that various items under your control, in your role as the Urbanville Public Schools Athletic Director, are missing, and/or presently unavailable to this Administration.*

*Specifically, this is a formal demand for you to return all property purchased by the Urbanville Public Schools and/or funded from the proceeds of any events and/or activities associated with the Urbanville Public Schools, including, but not limited to the following:*

1. *All documents, statements, paid and unpaid checks, cash, members lists, bills, invoices, receipts associated with the "Urbanville Public Schools Hall of Fame";*
2. *All documents, statements, paid and unpaid checks, cash, members lists, bills, invoices, receipts, associated with "Urbanville Athletic Association";*
3. *All documents, statements, paid and unpaid checks, cash, members lists, bills, invoices, receipts associated with your "Spring 2006 Raffle";*
4. *All documents, statements, paid and unpaid checks, cash, members lists, bills, invoices, receipts associated with any fundraisers, events or activities which you have organized during your tenure in the Urbanville Public Schools;*
5. *A report of all checks issued out of the Big Bank account for the Urbanville Public Schools Hall of Fame, including explanation of each expenditure;*

6. *Any and all files, binders, contents of notebooks/three-ring binders or other items utilized in your role as the Athletic Director in the Urbanville Public Schools;*
7. *Any and all office equipment, athletic supplies and equipment including, but not limited to the following:*
    - *Air conditioners(s)*
    - *Answering machine(s)*
    - *Portable telephone(s)*
    - *Safe(s) (with combination(s)*
    - *Tape dispenser(s)*
    - *Stapler(s)*
    - *Sanitary napkins*
    - *Trash bags*
8. *All 2007 Entertainment Books and a report of monies received expended as a result of their sale*

*Effective immediately, while we investigate the possibility of misappropriation of funds, embezzlement, larceny and/or fraud, you are placed on paid administrative leave for the remainder of the school year and until further notice.*

*You are hereby directed to refrain from conducting any business and/or engaging in any communication, in which represents yourself as an employee, agent or authorized representative of the Urbanville Public Schools.*

*Please provide me with your responses relating to Nos. 1-8 above as soon as possible, but no later than June 22, 2007.*

*Sincerely,*
*Aisha*
*Human Resources Director*

After Robert read it thoroughly to me, it made me sick to my stomach. I secluded myself from that weekend onward. I didn't want to see anyone and going to the store gave me anxiety. I was in a greatly depressed mood. I could not imagine what my future was going to hold. This was the first time my children saw me break down and cry. I was always there for my family, but now I felt useless. What was happening to me? I was looking to become an administrator to make a bigger difference in a child's life, but now I felt hopeless and couldn't even help myself. The biggest question that rang in my ear was, *WHERE DO I GO FROM HERE?*

When Monday morning came, I called the union, which claimed they knew nothing about the letter (*yeah, okay*). I sent them a copy and they called me back stating that they hired an attorney to represent me. Still being furious about the union not filing any grievances on my behalf, I questioned them. "Are you sure?" They said by Wednesday I would have an attorney. In my mind I thought, *Okay, we will see, but I won't hold my breath.* Sure enough, they finally did what they said they would do, and Attorney Stuart contacted me. I set up an appointment with him at the union building for Friday, June 15, 2007.

I was in constant communication with my sister and her husband to inform them about the lawyer. Antonio, who just so happen to leave the Urbanville union to go another office outside of the city , was also in touch with my sister to see what she knew. My sister knew he was a snake especially when he said to her, "You don't know your brother. Let me tell you what John Pepi is really like." At this point my sister and her husband distanced themselves from him, knowing that he was nothing but a bully who worked with the other side.

It was later that I found out that Antonio came into the union building (he didn't work there anymore), stole the letter dated June 8, 2007, off the secretary's desk, read it, and called my oldest sister. He told her that her brother would be in big trouble, and if he resigns now, they would not press charges. My sister told Antonio that he was a "conduit of rumors and lies." It was at this point she knew Antonio was the enemy. His tactics were evil, and she knew then that he was out to destroy me. Antonio had no problem spreading these rumors and fabrications from the letter to anyone who would listen. He started the defamation of my name and thought this was his opportunity to gain back the family house that I bought from my family. That was his hidden agenda from day one.

On Friday, I traveled to the union building at 5 p.m. to meet the new attorney and gave him all of the copies that I had (not the originals). As I discussed the situation with him, he was more interested in getting through the June 22 meeting that was in the letter, and he felt it might be a good idea to resign. I said in a loud and harsh voice, "Under no circumstance am I going to resign. I didn't do anything wrong." Right then and there, I didn't trust this attorney, and obviously, I didn't trust the union. They were not there for my best interests, which led me to believe that Antonio had something to do with forcing me to resign.

That weekend, I talked to my brother-in-law and sister. I didn't like what was going on between the union and the school department because I could smell a rat. They wanted me to resign, and for what? I didn't do anything wrong, and I had the documentation that cleared me. I knew that the city was trying their hardest to set me up, and they used their minions to do their dirty work. Like I told my sister, I was happy that I took out my evidence that Saturday morning, or else I would be sitting in jail at this point—not to say they weren't going to try it anyway.

Every day of my paid administrative leave, I very rarely left the house and I was looking over my shoulder constantly. It seemed like eternity until June 22 arrived, and I had no idea what to expect. Do you think the attorney should have prepared me for that day? My union dues, $750 at the time, went toward political campaigns, not toward my protection as an education professional. I couldn't even talk to this union attorney because I would have to leave a message and received no response from him. In fact, after that meeting on the June 15, I would not see or talk with him until the June 22 meeting in Aisha's office. Wonderful, what a scam.

The day of June 22, I met both Pete, my union rep, and Stuart, the union lawyer who was supposed to be defending me. In the room was Aisha, Claire, who was the union president, Brendon, who was a city attorney, the two Petes, and me. I also brought a wildcard that I hoped would prove their foolishness. Aisha started the meeting and asked me if I knew why I was there. Of course I knew, but it was a good time to act dumb. She ended up explaining that she was going through the letter step by step to see if I had everything with me to prove each claim. She did, and I had every receipt, bank statement, and document that she asked for. I explained where the air conditioner was as well as the safe and all of the other important items that she asked for, which were locked in my closet. I gave her the key so they could look. What I found out that day was disturbing. I was guilty and had to prove my innocence instead of being innocent until proven guilty. Why were they asking for information to prove my innocence? What kind of investigation was this? It was obvious that my due process rights were violated.

Aisha was dumbfounded and didn't know what to say because she had never come down to my office at all. She was asked many times, and she said that she didn't have the time to look. My question was, HOW CAN YOU CONDUCT AN INVESTIGATION WITHOUT LOOKING? I guess that was the million-dollar question. Also, there was no mention of the sanitary napkins, so I mentioned it. "I don't know where the sanitary napkins are because I don't use them." Everyone started to chuckle. Then I laid down the bombshell. My wildcard.

At the beginning of each school year, the school department gave the athletic director $600 so that he could break the money down into small bills for change during football games when selling tickets. This was one of the changes I pushed for, because in the past, the money had to come out of the athletic director's own pocket, and he would take it out of the first football game receipts. I felt that was dangerous. I also pushed for the ticket sellers and ticket managers to be bonded in case they were robbed. It was protection for both the person working and for the school department. If they did get robbed, both the employee and the employer would not become liable. I used this as my bombshell to dumbfound Aisha and prove she didn't know my job. I brought the $600 to the meeting and I waited for the right time. This money was never recorded in the June 8, 2007 letter, and if they were trying to say I was a crook, right back at you.

At the end of the meeting, Aisha said she would take this under advisement and asked if there were any questions. That's when I spoke up and said, "Are you missing anything?"

"No, I don't think so," she replied with a blank look on her face.

"How about the $600?"

She looked at me and then to Brendon, "What $600?" she asked.

I then had to explain it to her, and I took the money out of my bag. With an embarrassed look on her face, she was about to take it and thank me, but I pulled it back. I took out a form and told her to sign and date it as proof that she was going to have the money, and it was her responsibility to return it to the city's treasury office. She did, and I gave one more dig. "Are you going to count it?" She looked at me with a foolish smile and stated back, "Oh yes, maybe I should." She counted it, we both agreed, and we left.

On the way out to the car, I turned to the union representatives, "Thanks for the effort." Obviously, I was being sarcastic because I did all of the work. As I was driving home, I thought the meeting went well, but it still didn't give me any hope that they would reassess whether the letter should have been sent at all. Furthermore, I knew they were not finished with me. This was just the beginning of more abuse and lies. It was evident that they were out to destroy me. The bullying escalated further.

I tried to contact the union attorney to keep me up to date, but it would be days before he responded—not verbally but through letters sent to my house. There were still no developments. My family knew that my mind wasn't present half of the time—it was millions of miles away. Physically, yes, I was present, but not mentally. I was trying to stay positive for them, which meant I did most of my crying at night, those sleepless nights. I still isolated myself by staying home. If I did go out shopping, it was to another town. When I would take a trip, in my mind, I would wonder, *Where does so and so live?* The follow up question would be, *Would they shop or go to this restaurant?* If I saw one of them at the grocery store, for example, I would leave even though I had groceries in the cart.

It wasn't until July 6, 2007, when I knew that their plan to destroy John Pepi was at its apex. I was finally at my financial end. I knew that if they drained me, I could not recover to fight back. I received my paycheck but noticed it was not a full check. I called human resources, and they told me that was my vacation and sick time cashed out. I would not receive another check during July, August, and part of September. After hanging up the phone, I consulted my contract because in this school system, assistant principals and directors were still on the teachers' contract under administration. As I knew, the contract ran from September 1 until August 31, and they should not have ended my pay before then. In other words, I went from paid administrative leave to paid administrative leave WITH NO PAY.

It really hurt since I had a mortgage to protect and other bills to pay. How was I going to do this? Fortunately, my wife went back to work at the hospital, and I was getting money from sports camp, which called after the word got out that I was finished as the athletic director. That was still not even close to what I needed to make to support my family. My daughter had just graduated from elementary school, and my family still needed my financial support. Then I broke out in a cold sweat. WHAT ABOUT COLLEGE? My oldest was in school, and my second son wanted to go to Berklee College of Music. The stress started to build.

I went to the union the next Monday after finding out about my check to fill a third grievance. Why did I think it was going to be easy? Again, they said no to me.

"Is it really against the contract?" asked Pete, the union rep. Even when I showed him, he still wouldn't budge. I had to leave the union because I was ready to explode and that would play right into their hands. I just can picture it now after punching one of them in the face. "See, I told you he was crazy, and that's why we got rid of him." I did the right thing. What I realized from my experience was that bullies do not follow laws or contracts. They make them up and follow their own agenda. They believe they are above the law.

It didn't help that after one month of missing my mortgage payment, I started getting messages from them. I should not have remortgaged my house, but I needed major home repairs and who knew that this was going to happen. I remortgaged when I received my new director position, and now I was fighting to save my house.

Everyone that I had approached would not even give me the time of day. I even went to the new mayor's office after Jim McMurray went on to become lieutenant governor of the Commonwealth of Massachusetts, but even that didn't stop the bleeding. It wasn't until the fall when I finally figured out what their plot was and their conspiracy scheme.

I was still worried about my employment status and couldn't help but wonder what was next on their agenda. It became the ultimate witch hunt that I never thought would end. Then on September 21, 2007, I received a certified letter from the superintendent, Dr. Hal. My heart was in my mouth as I read the letter to myself in my backyard. It read:

*September 17, 2007*

*Dear Mr. Pepi:*

*This is a formal letter of reprimand for conduct and/or deficiencies which amount to insubordination; and/or unauthorized purchasing; and/or violations of established policies, rules and regulations governing purchasing and/or poor professional judgment.*

**So far, I didn't like what this letter said because it painted me as a crook and insubordinate and other garbage. It continued:**

*When you were placed on paid administrative leave* **(with no pay)**, *purchasing irregularities were confirmed within the Athletics Division. Specifically, the vendors listed below are demanding payments from the Urbanville Public Schools for the following invoices for goods for which there were no required Urbanville Public Schools' requisitions and/or purchase orders:*

**They listed the football uniforms that I mentioned earlier in the book that were not purchased. I had numerous emails from**

**the purchasing department that confirmed I did not make these purchases. Also note that all of these so-called illegal purchases were dated 2005, which meant they had to dig REAL DEEP. They came up with a total of $22,572.82, but the real question was why these companies were acting in this way since they had been doing business with the city for years. Could this have been planned? Was this a set-up, or did they see that I was conducting business on the up and up, so they had to come up with something? I mentioned earlier that my secretary had my signature stamp. That didn't count according to the swamp. Continuing along:**

*You intentionally and deliberately misrepresented the facts by act and/or omission when you denied ordering and/or receipt of Riddell football equipment. While you were in the role of the Urbanville Public Schools Athletic Director, said football equipment was distributed to the schools and some was recently discovered at Urbanville Stadium. As the Athletic Director, it was your responsibility to assure the return of any such equipment which was not purchased in accordance with Urbanville Public Schools procedures and/or Massachusetts General Laws, Chapter 30B. Your failures to follow proper procedures have created financial liability for the Urbanville Public Schools.*

*You intentionally and deliberately misrepresented the facts by act and/or omission when you denied ordering and/or receipt of xxxxxxxxxxx xxxxxxxx from xxxxxxxxx xxxxxxxx. As the Athletic Director, it was your responsibility to assure the return of any such books which were not purchased in accordance with Urbanville Public Schools procedures. Your failures to follow proper procedures have created financial liability for the Urbanville Public Schools.*

**Wow, he kept on piling it on. What books? Furthermore, I lied? To whom did I lie? I misrepresented the facts? Talk about a complete destruction of my character, which I have protected since childhood, and in one letter, it's gone. Clearly the facts, which were in documents and emails to prove this, are false and don't count. Oh yes, like I said before, laws and contracts don't count. Let me add that facts don't either. These people are master manipulators.**

*You intentionally and deliberately misrepresented the facts by act and/or omission when you denied ordering and/or receipt of towels or posters, printed with Urbanville Public Schools schedules.* **(Denied ordering them? It's because I never did.)** *These towels and/or posters were thrown out, with your consent, when athletic schedules were changed and the printed towels and posters were no longer accurate. As the Athletic Director, it was your responsibility to assure the return of any such towels and/or posters which were not purchased in accordance with Urbanville Public Schools procedures. Your failures to follow proper procedures have created financial liability for the Urbanville Public Schools.*

**Dig deeper, Dr. Hal, all of these accusations were not even included in the June 8 letter, but they zeroed in on towels, books, and posters this time. Interesting.**

*The conduct and/or deficiencies noted above amount to insubordination; and/or unauthorized purchasing; and/or violations of established policies, rules and regulations governing purchasing and/or poor professional judgement.*

*You are hereby ordered to cease and desist any activities which require you to purchase goods and services, fundraise or handle any monies on behalf of the Urbanville Public Schools or as its agent. Additionally, you are ordered to cease any involvement with the Urbanville Public Schools Hall of Fame Committee. Failure to comply with these directives will result in further disciplinary action up to and including termination.*

**At this point, I thought I was fired. My blood rushed to my head, and I felt like vomiting. What a bunch of lies and fabrication, but what did I expect from these career bullies? The letter ended like this:**

*Effective Wednesday, September 19, 2007, you may resume your position as a system-wide physical education teacher. Please contact Marsha xxxxxxx regarding your specific assignment.*

*Sincerely,*
*Dr. Hal*
*Superintendent of Schools*

Wait, he said Wednesday, September 19, and I received the letter September 21? Is this a trick to terminate me? Since my mail came so late on Friday, I had to wait until Monday to call. The secretary who answered told me to come in for my assignment. Wonderful, now I had to face them all over again. Plus, the real kicker was I had to report to the same person who took my position knowing that I had more credentials then she did. Talk about an awkward situation.

When I arrived the next day, I got the look-over, and I didn't know what they were thinking. I disappeared after June 8 and never heard from them again until this day. Did they think I was a crook? They had to feel something because at this point rumors were going around stating that I was fired as the director because of stealing. What were people thinking? I knew what Marsha was thinking because she would express it to me and started in on my lesson plans as well as passing forms that were supposed to be passed in the beginning of September. I told her right up front not to go there because at this point I was fuming.

Two major problems were coming up fast on me: the mortgage situation and getting the union to do their job. I held off the mortgage with letters to Senator John Kerry and Attorney General in Massachusetts Martha Coakley. I found that the mortgage company was caught for fraud and there was a class-action suit filed against them. That kept them quiet for the next nine years. The union finally filed grievances about my demotion, the poor evaluation, the money I never received over the summer (breach-of-contract violation), and the September 17 letter. I knew it was too late, but at this point, I had to see what would happen.

So my question still stands from the beginning of this chapter, was it conspiracy theory or conspiracy reality? Let's think about it:

- I was offered a bribe, which I felt was designed to set me up. If I took the bribe, I would have been fired and placed in jail. **I refused the bribe.**
- They used budget cuts as the reason I was demoted to cover-up an incompetent, unqualified, and unlicensed political

person. **I caught on because five people were hired to take my place.**

- I received an extremely poor evaluation stating that I was the worst athletic director. **I rebutted that claim and had proof that all other evaluations were excellent.**
- The June 8, 2007 letter stated I was under investigation of misappropriations of funds, embezzlement, larceny and/or fraud. Basically, they called me a crook. **I rebutted that claim, and through the so-called investigation, they came up empty.**
- They stopped my pay from July 6 until September 21. They tried to hurt me financially.
- Finally, the September 17, 2007 letter basically said that they decided to accuse me of insubordination since they couldn't find any stealing. Funny thing about that is they used items that I never heard of, and uniforms, which were already taken care of.

All this time and energy wasted trying to ruin me because I questioned their motivations, and they now want to destroy me. So what do you think? Conspiracy theory or reality?

# 9

# THE UNION SCAM

The month of September was very trying because I was not getting answers I needed from the union, and I was looking to recover three months of unpaid wages. I wrote a strongly worded letter to the mortgage company, as well as letters to politicians, and I didn't hear from the mortgage company again, not even for a payment (I fell behind three months, and they would not help me to catch up). I also started officiating football again, which brought extra money into the house, but it was still hard to catch up on my bills with the missing money. Even with three years of being an athletic director under my belt, I wasn't betting on the salary being okay because I even had to fight for the appropriate money in my previous situation, as the district didn't pay me the correct amount. I realize now that the school system was using me as a temporary replacement so that they could get the person (who was politically connected) they wanted in and bully me right out the door. The school system couldn't even tell me the truth. I call that gutless.

Finally, the union called me and said that they filed grievances on my demotion, my evaluation, the salary cut, and the September 17 letter. I was still cautious because I told them the grievances were months late, and you cannot grieve a letter of reprimand according to the contract.

Pete the union rep insisted that the grievances were unimpeachable, and everything was all set. I didn't believe him, but what else can I do? The grievances had to go through a rigorous process, starting with Marsha. What a joke.

The grievance process would last until December. While I waited for the outcome, I still had to teach under severe circumstances. I was placed in an elementary school where Congressmen Tim Jones' two sisters were teachers and a few alternative schools where the students were either emotionally disturbed or had been removed from other schools for weapons violations. They thought they were punishing me by assigning me to these schools, but I got along with the students. It was the administration that gave me a hard time. It was almost as if they were told to ride me hard. The biggest challenge I had was getting to the schools. I couldn't afford a car because my credit had been damaged from the mortgage situation. I was given a car from my sister and brother-in-law, which my wife and I had to share (my car that we previously owned needed a new engine, which we couldn't afford).

The first step of the grievance process was denied before we showed up (this first step went to Marsha, and she denied the grievance before the meeting). I believe that Marsha didn't want me to see her, which personally, I was happy we went to the second step. The next step involved Aisha, who said the most profoundly angering statements that I started to realize the corruptness of the school system. She told me, "Don't take it personal, it's just business," "I would never do anything that would hurt you," and finally, when she knew I wasn't going away, "Sue me." This is when I realized that they didn't care because it wasn't their money, it was the taxpayer's money. That meant they had bottomless resources to handle any lawsuit.

After Aisha, the grievance went to Marv, who offered me $7,000 out of his budget to have me go away. It wasn't clear if he was going to have me borrow it or keep it, but I told him no because the city owed me $15,164 that I had already earned. It was money that was owed according to my contract, but no one budged on making it right. The final step was to meet with the superintendent, Dr. Hal, but that was not until December 8, 2007. However, the incident that happened on December 4, 2007 would put me over the edge.

My first year back as an official of high school football earned me a chance at officiating a playoff game. I was assigned to Urbanville Stadium as a neutral site for two teams from outside the city. I hesitated to accept, especially after what happened to me as the athletic director. I was not looking forward to confronting the trauma that I experienced and seeing the same people who tormented me. I said no at first, but after a little convincing by the assigner, who was a friend at the time, I decided to go.

The day of the game, I waited in the parking lot across the street from the stadium to see if any other official doing the game was walking in. *I shouldn't have taken the game,* I thought to myself. *I don't feel right.* I was on suspension for 107 days with no pay, which had ended three months earlier. I had to be there at 3 p.m. for the 4 p.m. game, and it was already 2:55 p.m. Finally, one of the officials I knew was getting out of his car, so I went up to him and he assured me that everything would be okay. I was not so confident.

As I crossed the street, I started to say hi to all of the police officers and the ticket sellers as well as the ticket takers, who were all people that I hired. What a great welcome I received. They came up to me to let me know that I had been "screwed," and they stated that they supported me. It made me feel good. One police officer mentioned that this place ran better with me. I was thrilled that at least these workers had not been let go since the new administration took over. It was still sad to know that I had put my heart and soul into this position. I was still grieving the loss of the job. The administration had ripped my heart out of my chest and watched me bleed out. The school system had no conscience.

Once I got to the locker room, I started to change for the game while talking to the other officials. We started to talk football and the rules as well as our positioning for that day's game. This took my mind off the stadium for just a brief time. As we sat there waiting to go onto the field, the door swung open and Joe, the athletic liaison, walked in. Joe was a physical education teacher and close friend of Marsha's. Also, his father was a state representative, so he was another political hack. He wanted to hand over the game ball to be used in the game, but he was distracted by me as he stared in my direction. It looked as if he saw a ghost.

"What are you doing here?" he said in an accusatory manner. As I looked down at my striped uniform, I thought to myself, *What a stupid statement, is he for real?* Staying calm, I said, "Hi, Joe." He just handed me the game ball and without saying anything else, he left the room. I then turned to my other four officials and said, "Well now, let's have fun and officiate a good game." We all got up and left the locker room for the field.

This was the first playoff game at the stadium since it had been refurbished with the new turf. It looked beautiful, and on a crisp late afternoon in December, it was a great day to play football. As I walked onto the field, I looked around and said to myself, *You did well, John, no matter what those administrators said about you*. I was blessed, and I fought for this field and for the student/athletes of Urbanville. No matter what was going to happen in the future, I knew in my heart that it was me who pushed for this field and not the self-loathing, egotistical, narcissistic administrators who attacked me over the years. As I walked to the middle of the field, I thought of a painter I spoke to earlier in the week at one of my schools. He had said to me, "They screwed up the field, it's five yards off." At that point, I was not going to take full credit. It was typical municipality who would try to do a project and still screw it up. Again, karma.

I stood at midfield and the referee said, "Let's go to the fifty and get ready for the coin toss." I then corrected him and said we were on the forty-five-yard line. He looked up at the press box and turned to me.

"The field is five yards off?" he asked.

I laughed, but my laughter turned to concern when I looked across the field to see the two grounds crew members looking in my direction. Jay and Bill, I knew, were talking about me as they pointed in my direction. Jay went on the two-way radio, and sure enough, Marsha came out of the athletic office and went up to them. As I stood there observing what was happening, she started to briskly walk over to the assigner. It looked like she was yelling at him while pointing to me. I didn't have time to observe the whole incident because the game was about to begin.

The game went well with no problems, but I wanted to take a shower and get dressed so I could head home as quickly as possible. Fortunately, everyone was distracted by the second game scheduled for the evening, and I was able to make my escape. I wouldn't know what Marsha said to the assigner until the next day.

The next morning, I received a phone call from the assigner. He told me that Joe called and said that Marsha didn't want me at any more games at Urbanville Stadium.

I corrected him by saying, "I saw the whole thing, and Marsha approached you and yelled at you because of me. I am your friend, are you going to defend me?"

It was silent over the phone for one small minute, but it seemed like forever. "I have to keep everyone at Urbanville Stadium happy because I need their field." It was at that point I knew where our friendship was going. More than thirty years of friendship was erased over a football game. I hung up the phone depressed, and I felt violated as a human. I trusted him, I defended him from other officials when he was under attack, and for what?

The football officiating board never stuck up for me, like they believed the lies of the school department. It was upsetting, plus I was the only two-time president of the board, for Pete's sake, but it didn't matter. It wasn't until the next season that I found out their true colors. I had to travel for an hour and a half to do a playoff game. That was it; I retired after that. As I left the last board meeting after handing my retirement letter, I received not one thank you or acknowledgment. I realized then that they were not my friends. As I drove away, I grew angry knowing that this chapter of my life was over forever.

I still had to deal with more important issues with the union and the grievances that were finally filed, but it didn't change the fact that this situation with the school department was now affecting me outside of my place of employment. I realized that I had started to internalize what they were doing to me during a visit to my doctor, who said my health was being affected by this abuse. He suggested I see a psychologist, but at that time, I was so wrapped up in the fight, I felt that seeing a psychologist would take away from my time going after the truth. Boy, was I wrong. I needed professional help.

I finally made an appointment the next week to see a psychologist that my primary doctor had suggested. But I was focused on the last step of the grievance procedure, Dr. Hal, the superintendent. As I sat with my union rep, Pete, I started to ask him what the attorney or the union was doing to restore my reputation. I was very aggressive at this time because I was sick and tired of the way I was treated by the school department and the union.

"You need to calm down," Pete advised.

I started to snap and raise my voice out of frustration. I told him that he needed to do his job. We argued all the way to the superintendent's office. I was angry that the union president, Claire, and the executive secretary, Pete, had not done a thing to help me out. In my eyes, I knew the fix was in.

As we walked into the superintendent's office, Aisha, my supervisor Mary, Brendon, the city attorney, and Dr. Hal were sitting at a large table just in front of the superintendent's desk. Their greeting was cold, and as I looked at all of them, I knew that they loved the power. Great use of taxpayer money. As I sat there, Pete made his argument, and after it was done, Aisha said, "Thank you, and good luck." As she said this, the superintendent didn't once look at me or pick his head up from his notes. What a bag job.

I responded, "That's it?"

Then I started to think of all of the comments she stated to me, "Don't take it personal, it's just business," "I would never stick it to you," and the famous one, "Sue me."

We then got up, and I left with many things running through my mind. It seemed hopeless, but Pete told me that we would apply for arbitration if I lost. I reluctantly agreed, but in the back of my mind I wondered how I was going to win if the grievances were not filed on time. The only thing I could do was wait.

During my lunch break at school, a teacher came up to me and said that she heard I was going after the system. Hesitant to reveal too much, I nodded my head in agreement. She handed me a piece of paper and told me to call a particular lawyer. Once I saw the person's name, I asked her if he was once a city council member. She told me yes, but she convinced me he had a problem with the city. I thought to myself, *I will give it a shot.*

I made an appointment for the next week. When I showed up at his office, I gave him the third degree. Even though he told me everything I wanted to hear, I was very skeptical. He ended up writing two letters on my behalf to push the union to represent me. He charged me $400, and even though the grievances were filed late, he assured me that it would be taken care of. Only time would tell, but I was not betting the farm.

On January 2, 2008, my appointment with the union board was set. I showed up and the room was filled with union reps from every school in the district. I knew most of them from my years of service within the school system. Pete greeted me and told me to wait in the hallway so they could conduct some other business. I thought I was about to see Congress or the President by the way I was being treated. All I was thinking was, *Are we going to arbitration or not?*

As I came into the room, I was wondering what Pete was going to say to the board since he knew the grievances were late. Of course, why think differently? He told them this was a slam dunk and that I had a great case. Even though the board asked some specific questions about the grievances, Pete stood tough and convinced the board we would win. *He lied through his teeth.* The board voted and allowed me to go to arbitration, but I was not confident.

The next several months we met at Irving Street, where central office was located. We had arbitration on the fourth floor in a conference room. The whole building knew why I was there (embarrassing). The first two meetings were on enemy grounds, but the last one was held at the union hall, which brought back bad memories of dealing with my corrupt and bullying cousin, Antonio. What did I expect? The city officials had Aisha and Mary as their main witnesses. Of, course the school department's attorney, Brendon, was also there representing the city side, but it didn't matter. They were going to lie, forget dates, and bully me all over again by making me out to be the worst administrator ever.

My evidence was very strong, except the school department had one thing in their favor, the fact that the union didn't file the grievances on time. It's easy to win if the deck is stacked in your favor. The union didn't hide the fact that they did not act in my best interest. Even when I went back to school the day after that first meeting, I was being pushed to take a settlement of $15,164 that I worked for and I would have to sign a paper to say that I would not sue the school department. The union thought it was great. Would that give me my reputation back? How about my character and integrity? How about my family's struggles? Would the $15,164 take care of all this?

I decided to call that attorney who was recommended to me for a second opinion. I thought he was neutral. When I questioned him, he snapped at me as I stood in an empty school yard during my lunch. After I hung up the phone with him, my question in my head was, *Why is he so interested in me settling?* When I got home from school I found the answer after googling his name. He was still on the parks commission for the city. He lied to me, and this seemed like a common occurrence within this corrupt city.

When I attended the second arbitration hearing, the union lawyer started on me harder. He told me I was a fool not to take the settlement. The other part of the settlement I didn't agree with, because if I took the money that I had already worked for, I would have to sign a paper to wave my right to sue. *What?* That was not going to happen, and as far as I knew, that was extortion.

During the third and final day of arbitration at the union hall, the union pulled no punches and told me that I was in danger of losing everything because I would not take the money. Even the president of the union, Claire, who was very close to Antonio, finally showed up to a hearing and showed her true colors. It wasn't good, and I started to really feel the heat of mobbing from both the union and the city. The union, during lunch break, surrounded me in one of the offices, and I was getting it from all sides. I had nowhere to turn, and they were treating me with hostility for not taking the settlement. Why? What was so important for them? They were not hiding the fact that they were for the school district and not for me. I started thinking that I needed a lawyer, and fast, before the statute of limitations runs out. The problem was, who, how, and with what money? I was a mess.

I left the union hall with my head down in defeat, and it felt like a train had just run me over. As I left the parking lot, I drove to the nearest supermarket parking lot and pulled into the furthest parking space away from the store. I sat there, and I felt more anxious than ever before. I believed I was headed toward a nervous breakdown. Emotions came over me. I couldn't believe that they were not only trying to ruin my position in the Urbanville Public Schools, but my life. I wondered, *What do I tell my family? Do I give up? What about my reputation?* I was lost, and I didn't know what else to do or who could I turn to for guidance.

Two weeks later, it became official: I lost arbitration because the grievances were not filed on time (what a shock). The city and the union succeeded, and they did what they intended to do. I was right all along, and in the process, they made me look like a fool. To rub salt into the wound, after confronting the union, they told me that it was my fault and that I should have filed the grievances instead of them. HOW? They made it even worse for me and lied again. I could not file, and why did I even pay union dues? As I left Pete and Claire in the union office, I told them I should have taken my union dues and bet them on a race horse. I would have had better odds. I was very angry with them, and I knew that collusion among my cousin, the city, and the union was very evident.

# 10

# STRESS-RELATED INJURY

Going through this ordeal with the City of Urbanville not only consumed my life, it also took a toll on my health. Trying to find the truth and wanting to know the answers, I exhausted every avenue, except instigating a lawsuit. There was one other outlet I thought might help: the media.

I was standing in the school yard of one of the schools watching the children during recess. Every day was a reminder of the torment I was going through. I would see administrators who abused me and falsely accused me of horrible crimes that I never committed, even though I knew I was innocent. If I wasn't innocent, I would be in jail right now. My pent-up anger would rise whenever I saw the bullying grounds crew show up at the school and take out equipment. *Were they giving me a wise smirk, or was it my imagination?* This went through my mind day in and day out. *What about my career? Did I go back to school for administration for nothing? How about the assistant principal's job at my old middle school?* The more I thought about this, the more I became angry and upset.

Another week went by, and then a sense of urgency came over me. I was at the gym with one of my classes, and who should walk in but Dr. Hal. *What does he want?* I thought, *Maybe he wants to stick that knife in my back a little deeper.* I didn't realize it, but he was retiring, and he was passing through on his going-away tour. He called out to me, "Take care, John," with some sarcasm in his tone. I could feel the hair stand up on the back of my neck. Instead of saying something I was going to regret later, I said nothing. I felt at the time that it was for the best.

I thought to myself, *I have to go to the newspaper, they can't get away with this.* After Dr. Hal left the gym, I became more anxious. *How am I going to pull this off,* I wondered, *and whom should I see at the newspaper?* It didn't come to me until after Dr. Hal's last day. The school district had hired a former administrator to take over the superintendent's position until they found a suitable replacement. Just when the new superintendent arrived, the skeletons started to come out of the closet, and the human resources department started to show its true colors. Unfortunately, it affected the children, which seemed to be the norm in this system.

One of the lowest-income schools in the district needed a special education teacher, and for this school, it was extremely important to hire the right one. Around the time that Dr. Hal was retiring, the interim superintendent was trying to cut corners in the superintendent's office. The first cut she made was the head secretary. I often wondered what a secretary would make in central office. Well, now it was in the open. Aisha decided to make her the special education teacher. *Wait, what? All right,* I thought, *maybe this woman had a degree in special education and just wanted to be a secretary instead.* I didn't want to prejudge.

Then it hit the newspaper. The story was on the front page and also in the Sunday edition. Wow. As I read the article, I found out that she was making $70,000 as a secretary. Teachers didn't even make that. Are you kidding? Then she wanted to be a special education teacher at a school where the children needed an experienced teacher. It looked like someone reported this, because the next thing I know, it became newsworthy. TV stations from Boston were coming to Urbanville to report this fiasco.

Then you had the central office, especially Aisha, who was trying to walk it back by saying that she didn't know that this woman was not licensed. The former secretary even stated that she taught CCD in a Catholic Church. Oh, like that will get you a teaching job. Then, of course, they were looking for a scapegoat and targeted the acting superintendent, but she fully denied it by saying, "I am only acting on what was given to me, and that was from human resources." Okay, then I started to wonder, *Who is going to get fired since this became a huge news story?* The answer was NO ONE.

Instead of a firing, the school committee decided to HOLD AN INVESTIGATION. This was almost laughable because I knew it was going to be a "dog and pony show." I still thought it was worth watching the school committee meeting that Thursday night. I didn't usually watch these meetings unless I had a hard time going to sleep. Anyway, I grabbed some popcorn and sat and watched.

Not one school committee person said anything negative toward the human resources department, but they asked questions about how they recruited teachers. Aisha presented an hour-and-a-half long PowerPoint presentation. If I ever saw BS, it was then. Instead of being reprimanded, the human resources department was praised. Besides, it was the fault of the secretary for wanting to become a teacher, according to the school committee. How dare she do such a thing! Even though I was angry with the result, I figured I should go to the newspaper and tell my story, which would back the human resources department into a corner. Boy, what an awakening I would receive. I decided to go anyway, so I went to the T&G building and asked for Brendon, who was an investigative reporter.

I met Brendon with boxes of evidence to back up my story. He stopped me in mid-sentence and told me to wait. He called in other reporters, including sports reporters I had dealt with when I was the director. They told me that they were happy to see me because they had gotten phone calls from someone telling them that I was stealing. The person never left a name, but I bet anyone from the district could have been the culprit. I completed my presentation, Brendon said thanks, and I went home. Once in a while, he would call me with some loose-end questions. Then, in April 2009, I did not hear a thing from the paper for at least three weeks.

After the third week, I decided to call Brendon at the newspaper's office. I left a message. No return call. He did leave me a cell phone number. *Let me call him on this number*, I thought. He did answer the phone, but his tone was different, and what he said left me in shock. "We cannot print this article unless you sue the school system," he said. "My editor will not allow me to continue." I couldn't believe my ears. Sue? Go through a lawsuit? I couldn't even find a lawyer. I went through multiple lawyers, who all said I didn't have a case! Now what?

I started to spend more time at the doctor. I would have panic attacks and wake up in a cold sweat. The doctor gave me sleep aids to take the edge off, but nothing seemed to work. I was suffering. My children and my wife knew it, but they felt helpless watching me go through my living hell. My doctor told me I should go to a therapist, and I knew I needed professional help, but I refused thinking that it would take me away from my goal of clearing my name. My ultimate goal was to find a lawyer.

Just after Easter, my sister said that my brother-in-law's brother had a friend who was a private investigator. They decided to organize a meeting with the private investigator at my sister's house. When I arrived, I thanked them for taking the time, and I began my story. I started to tear up when I told them of the toll this case had on my family, both financially and emotionally. The private investigator told us that this story hit home, as he had been bullied as a police officer. *This was the first time I heard the word bullying from someone else.* He then proceeded to tell me that the only attorney who would take such a case was a prominent attorney out of Newtown.

After getting the attorney's name and thanking the private investigator for taking out the time, my brother-in-law and I called the next day to make an appointment. When we reached the attorney's office, the secretary told us we had an appointment with a different attorney.

We stopped her, and I said, "With all due respect, we were told to see the head attorney."

"No problem," she said. "Sit here and I will let him know." My brother-in-law and I sat down with him and organized my case. The attorney sat there quietly and finally stated he would take the case if we could come up with a funding source.

I didn't realize how much this would cost, plus there was no guarantee of winning. All week I had been thinking about how this was going to happen. I was thinking of a GoFundMe, but I didn't want the city to believe that I was weak. I had to show a strong front, but how was I to pull it off? I had until August 1, 2009, to file a lawsuit or the statute of limitation would run out, and I would not be able to sue. Even though I had three years according to Massachusetts labor laws, I only had two years for labor relations, and I wanted to include the union as well. I wanted to go through both a civil lawsuit and labor relations suit to hit every avenue. Now the pressure started to build as I was heading toward my fiftieth birthday. I was ready to blow, but the worst news was just a week away.

I went to my doctor for my yearly physical, and part of the exam was a blood test. I scheduled the blood test a week before the physical so that I could see the results when I came in for the office visit. Right away the doctor told me that my liver function numbers were too high and said that the results were too alarming to ignore. He suggested an ultrasound test in his office.

I called my wife to let her know that I would be home a little late and that I had some more tests to be done. As I sat waiting for the ultrasound technician to come into the room, I could not help looking out the window from the sixth floor of the old hospital where my doctor's office was located. It just so happens to overlook Urbanville Stadium where my old office once was. I had to look away because I felt my blood pressure rising.

A few minutes, which seemed like a few hours, went by. I heard the cart that held the ultrasound machine come down the hallway. The nurse came into the room. She was very pleasant and asked me to take off my shirt and lie on my back on the table. She started with the gel and she warned me it was going to be cold. I didn't care. I want to know the results. After about fifteen minutes, she stopped and told me she would be back. She returned with someone else to look at the screen. She turned to me and said, "Wait right here. I have to get the doctor."

*What could this be?* I thought, *I hope it's not bad.*

Within ten minutes, the doctor appeared. "It seems like you have a mass in your liver, and it's about the size of a softball," he said. "I don't know what it is, but it looks like you have a nonalcoholic cirrhosis of the liver and may have developed a cancerous tumor."

"Are you sure, Doc?" I asked.

"I can't be certain, but it doesn't look good," he replied. "The numbers from your blood work and the ultrasound led to this. I will order a CT-scan just to be sure, and I will sit down with you to discuss the results."

He left, and I put my shirt on to go to the front desk for the time and date of the CT-scan. As I left the office, it felt like someone just punched me in the stomach. I thought, *Why? I have to fight for my reputation, support my family, and find an attorney. What am I going to say to my family?* I wondered. As the elevator opened, it descended six floors to the main lobby.

As I was walking to my car, I was fighting back tears and walking like a zombie. If anyone I knew walked by me then, I wouldn't have recognized them. I sat in my car for a least an hour balling my eyes out. My nerves were shot. I started to pray and asked why I was going through this. How could I be victimized by bullies multiple times in my life only to end my life dying from cancer? I couldn't tell my family until I found out the truth.

The next week came, and I had the CT-scan done. As I entered the room, I saw this huge machine that looked like a doughnut, and I was going to be in the middle of it. As I was lying there, I could not help thinking back to my situation with the city, yet here I was hoping and praying that my life would not end abruptly. After the test, I thanked the nurses and went home. After this, my wife was wondering why the extra tests. I only told her that given my age, they wanted to check some numbers that are off.

I made an appointment for the end of the week to see my doctor, and he told me that he received the results. In a straightforward tone that almost knocked me off my chair, he said, "I don't know how to say it, but I believe that you have a tumor in your liver that may be cancerous. I am sending you to a GI-liver specialist. I am also going to set up an MRI to make sure that it is a correct reading." I was in shock. I didn't want to cry, but I was thinking of my family and my children. How were they going to take it? It was time to turn to God for the answers. At that moment, I turned my life over to Jesus. I needed a miracle.

Before I went to have an MRI done, which would give me the final verdict, it was my fiftieth birthday, and my children wanted to celebrate by going out for dinner. The only two who were working at the time were my sons John and Anthony. I was in a bad position financially, medically, and emotionally, and I was worried about how we would afford the attorney who was going to clear my name. I flat-out told my family that I was not going to dinner and we had to cancel. My family was devastated because this was a family tradition. My son John took a stand and said he would help pay going out. He was the only one with a full-time job.

I reluctantly decided to go. We went to my favorite restaurant, Applebee's, and I figured the prices would not be that bad. As we sat there waiting for the waitress, my children who were young at the time started to ask questions about what I was going to do. They didn't know about my medical condition and the overwhelming financial stress. I snapped, which made everyone uncomfortable. I told everyone, "I AM DONE WITH FIGHTING, AND I DON'T CARE WHAT HAPPENS." My daughter, who was eleven at the time, ran out of the restaurant crying, followed by my son John. I was certain he went after her to comfort her.

My wife turned to me and said, "Why? Why do you have to act this way?" I didn't say a word the rest of the time. I didn't want to tell her about the tumor because it would have made her upset. My job was still to protect my family and wait for the results of the MRI. My daughter came back in and saw that I was still upset. Everyone ate except me. It wasn't until we got home from the restaurant to have birthday cake that I told the family about the likely cancer diagnosis. The family started to cry. They were confused and uncertain about their future. I told them to have faith. "I have an MRI on Monday," I said. "We will see where we will go from there." I hugged my children and my wife, but I didn't want to let them know that I was scared. I had to be strong. This was up to God, not me.

Monday came quick, and I drove to the MRI office to report in. As I sat in the waiting room, I started to pray to Jesus to give me some resurrection power, and I asked for forgiveness. I prayed all the way to the room where the test was going to be done. As I lay down on the hard bed and started to roll into the MRI machine, I continued to pray. *Please Lord, heal me of this cancer, and I will do your work to help others that are being tormented.* This was my simple prayer. I firmly believed my work on this earth was only beginning, but I needed strength. It couldn't just end here. I started to pray more. *What the enemy meant for evil, God will turn for your good.* I also prayed, *No weapon formed against you shall prosper, and every tongue which rises against you in judgment you shall condemn…* (Isaiah 54:17). It was now in God's hands.

As I entered the MRI machine, the technician asked if I was comfortable. I nodded in agreement, the test began. Lying on the table, I was listening to my favorite music, country, and thinking over the past three years. I had to forgive all of the people who tried to hurt my family and the bullies who made my life a living hell so that I could move forward. Not for them, but for me. I was not the judge, and it wasn't for me to say their fate. For me, I had to pray hard for my wellness and for the opportunity to have the strength to keep moving forward. I needed that second chance to hold my tormentors accountable and to help others to strive for theirs.

As the machine was ending its work, I continued to pray. At this time, I felt a warm feeling, like an inner peace. I thought nothing of it but when I got home, but when I checked the mail, my heart stopped.

It was a letter from my attorney. My hands started to shake as I opened the envelope. As I read the letter, tears started to roll down my face. My family looked at me in confusion. I looked up with a smile on my face. "He is going to take my case," I told them in a low but confident voice. My celebration was short because I still had to meet with my doctor the next day to see about my results. Before I went, I figured it was a good time to sit the family down and explain my health condition. I already received my first miracle, and I was praying for a second one.

I told them about the mass in my liver, which the doctor believed to be cancerous. Everyone in my family started to tear up. I told them everything was going to be okay and that God had this. I reminded them that I just received good news that the attorney was going to take my case.

"Let me find out the results of the MRI," I told them. "It will be okay. I feel good about it."

As I entered the doctor's office, this time with my wife, the secretary told me that the doctor was running behind schedule. We sat in the waiting room for what seemed like hours when the nurse called my name. We went into one of the rooms, and it seemed like another hour went by. Suddenly the doctor came into the room and greeted my wife and myself before he gave the results of the test. He began by saying, "I had to have the other doctors see the results because they really confused me."

I was puzzled and asked, "What do you mean, Doc?"

"I don't know because I've never seen anything like it," he said. "The mass is gone. You don't have anything showing." At that point I looked over to my wife, who started to tear up. Her tears were contagious because I started. *I can explain it*, I thought. *It was a miracle from God. Two tests and blood work said yes, I may have cancer, but* after *prayers to God, one test said I* was *cured. That's a miracle.*

The doctor still sent me to another specialist who dealt with livers and upper GIs. More tests were taken, which proved that I had three ulcers in my esophagus, but medicine helped with my acid reflux. I also had a liver biopsy, which showed no damage to the liver. Both doctors said that my condition was definitely a result of stress. I told them what was going on, which angered them. My primary care doctor told me if I didn't get out of the situation, it would kill me. I told him I understood but I didn't know where to go. The miracle, in my mind, gave me a second chance, and I wasn't going to miss this opportunity that God gave me.

Anyway, the lawsuit was filed on July 31, 2009, my article of the lawsuit was printed on August 16, 2009, and now I had to go back to school in September knowing that I sued the Urbanville Public School System. Finally, I could look for my name-clearing and put the city on its heels.

The stress and the harassment intensified, and different administrators would come to observe what I was doing. Sarcastic remarks from my boss, Marsha, and other physical education teachers isolated me. I felt alone. I did have two friends in the school system and one outside the school system who stuck by me every day, but everyone else that I had respect for treated me like I had an incurable disease.

This lasted until January 10, 2010, when the principal of the school I was assigned to called me to her office. She stated that she had to observe me, but at that time, I knew I wasn't going to get a fair evaluation. The stress had to be showing on my face because the principal looked at me and asked if I was okay. She sent me to the nurse, and I went home. I stayed out of work for the next three years due to stress-related illnesses. This was only the beginning. I had a lawsuit to prepare for, and I knew it wasn't going to be easy.

# 11

# THE LAWSUIT

There were many different avenues I had to take before the lawsuit ever materialized because I was suing the union as well. The first stop we had to go to was the federal courthouse in downtown Urbanville. We were hoping that this suit would keep us away from the superior court, which I believed was connected to the city. It didn't take too long for the federal judge to remand the case out of federal court and into superior court. I wasn't too thrilled with that decision, but at least the case was still active.

The next step was labor relations, as my attorney was told by superior court that the union case could either be argued at labor relations or superior court, but not both. We dropped the union in the lawsuit and decided to go after them with labor relations. The union never fulfilled its fiduciary duties, and we were looking for a settlement. We thought this would be over in a day, but the judge ruled against us and we lost in labor relations. I felt I didn't have a chance because when I sat in the courtroom of labor relations, I was face-to-face with a picture of Lt. Governor Jim McMurray. I knew this decision would be political, and I was right. The union got off, and they got away with bullying me. Now I had to concentrate on the big lawsuit.

I could go through the details of every little deposition, discovery, and interrogatories that go into a lawsuit, but it would be another 200 pages of work. The idea is to show the stress bullying can do to a professional, and whoever reads this book will understand that lawsuits are expensive, time consuming, and leads one to be victimized over and over again. For example, the attorney for the city was not my friend, and he would take a word or a sentence and manipulate it into something the city could use against me. I also learned that the establishment's job is to make you look like the worst educator, and they made it seem like it was all your fault you were in this situation. The city will also drag out a lawsuit as long as they can because it's not their money, it's the taxpayer's. Last point, they will harass you until you break, and they always give you an out by signing YOUR RIGHTS away, which I suggest you never do.

With that said, I was in a position where I had no clue what was happening. I was looking to help out my attorney with documents and other supporting materials. My attorney was impressed that I was so organized, and it made the city's attorney nervous because I saved and documented everything. This is what made it easier for my attorney to prepare, but it was a threat to the city, which forced the school department to look for any angle to destroy me. While preparation was taking place, I was regularly going to my therapist and collecting my sick time. This led to numerous attacks on my family as well as myself.

The first attack from the city was after my pay. They thought to drain me from all my funds and assumed I would beg for them to stop. I was out for more than three days, so I had to get a doctor's note. But because of the stress, I was seeing my doctor once a month and my therapist once a week. Getting the note from the doctor was easy, but when I gave the doctor's note to Aisha, she wouldn't approve my absence. She wanted the details of my condition, but when she contacted my doctor, he told her of the privacy act called HIPAA. Even though it stressed me that she was not going to approve my sick time, I had a lawyer and a doctor looking out for my best interests. Imagine that—she had the nerve to call my doctor to see what my condition was. This echoed what Aisha said to my lawyer: "We do things differently here in Urbanville." The scary part of all this was she is a lawyer, which means she knows better.

After that was straightened out, I knew that I would run out of my paid time off, so I applied to the school system's sick bank at the end of the 2010 school year. How this works is that all teachers take one of their sick days every year and donate it to the sick bank in case a teacher is sick and doesn't have enough sick time. At first Walter, the assistant human resources director, told me I didn't qualify. I just so happened to have a copy of the rules and regulations to prove him wrong, but he countered with, "You're too late to apply. You would have to wait until September." Another summer without pay! More stress!

In September, I did reapply and received 138 additional days from the sick bank. The rate the lawsuit was going, I knew these days were numbered as well. I was concerned about money and worried about what I should do. I couldn't go back to school because they would definitely target me again, but if I ran out of sick days, I didn't know how I was going to pay my bills. Fortunately, I had a truly close friend and my oldest sister to fall back on, but I just needed the attorney to keep on going. Then it came to me that I was truly sick from the stress the school system put me through. I had trouble with my liver, my ulcers, and my high anxiety, as well as a diagnosis of PTSD, which made me feel that I should be collecting workers' compensation. All I needed now was an attorney.

The second attack centered around workers' comp, which gave the city another opportunity to stick it to me again. My lawyer from my lawsuit suggested I use an attorney from Rising River. I went to meet him at the industrial accident department in downtown Urbanville. After looking at my medical records and my case, he told me it would be a hard case to win. Usually the judges like to see physical injury and they hardly ever rule with emotional damage. I did mention to him that they targeted me and that I was sick because of them. He just said, "Let's see what we can do."

This was worse because now my financial situation was in the hands of a judge, but even worse than that was the timeline, which just dragged out. There were meetings between the city's workers' comp attorney and my own attorney. Then there were conciliations in which each party tries to come up with a settlement. My attorney was careful with any settlements not to jeopardize my lawsuit, but the process still went on forever. Since this process was long, I was out of pay when my sick bank ended. I was relying now on my wife, my children's part-time work, my friend, and my sister for survival. Without pay, I started to go into a deep depression. Fortunately, my therapist helped me through, but that ended as well when another blow hit me hard: my therapist passed away. It was devastating.

Dr. Patrick was a great, compassionate man who truly cared about me. My wife and I both started to use him, and his method was remarkable. I am sad, even today, that he never got to see the end of my case because he knew how evil and brutal the city was toward me. Every time I see a candle at Christmas time, I think of him and pray for him. He made the most beautiful scented candles, and I cherished them when he would give us one as a gift. I believe he is looking down on me and is very proud that I kept on pushing forward even in the face of hard adversity. God bless your soul, Dr. Patrick.

With all of this going on, I finally received a hearing in front of the judge. It was the one meeting where I would just sit there and listen to my attorney (who told the truth), and then the city's attorney (who would lie) without saying anything or reacting. I showed up a half an hour early as my lawyer suggested, and we went into one of the conference rooms to discuss the case. He told me up front that he felt I didn't have a prayer in getting workers' comp. I looked at him and said, "Let's find out." With confidence, I walked out of the room and into the courtroom.

My lawyer came to my defense with his opening argument, and when he was finished the city's attorney tried to erase what my attorney said. She basically told the judge that I was faking and that there was nothing wrong with me. The judge looked over at me like he was trying to figure out how credible I was. He then turned to the two attorneys and said, "I will take it under advisement."

As we left the courtroom, my attorney asked to speak with me in the conference room before I left. We sat down opposite each other and my attorney told me that the case did not go well, and he believed I wouldn't get workers' comp. I thanked him without saying another word and walked out of the building to my car with my tail between my legs. It had already been twelve months without any pay. How could I afford to move forward in my lawsuit? I would have gone back to my therapist to try to get it off my chest, but I couldn't. I couldn't go to any other therapist because I didn't have established trust with anyone else. This was the time when I really needed Dr. Patrick. When I walked into my house, I couldn't tell my wife and the family about what had happened because they were worried about me as it was. I just stayed within my own misery.

Three days passed before I received a letter from the industrial accident department. I read the letter that the judge put me on a temporary income of $865 a week. I know that wasn't close of what I was making, but it was something to get me through the lawsuit for now. The only problem was that I had to pay for my own health insurance at $500 a month, and I wouldn't get back money until later on. My attorney kept my case open for the time being. I could live with that for now.

The third attack involved my family. Since I started to receive workers' comp, personal attacks on my family and myself made me wonder if these were all connected. I have lived in Urbanville all of my life, and nobody had ever threatened my family until the City of Urbanville had to pay me workers' comp. I just want to make it clear that I do not believe in coincidence, and every action has a reaction. I had to put up my guard and protect my family.

One day my wife and I were home and our children were at school when the doorbell rang. My wife went to the door as I lagged behind (still traumatized from when I received the letter falsely accusing me of embezzlement, larceny, and fraud). A police officer was at the door and told my wife that he was here to pick up our dog, Sandy. I was watching this occur from the front window. I was in disbelief. My wife asked why, and he said there had been complaints about her barking.

I couldn't listen to this anymore, so I intervened. "Excuse me, sir, what did you say?"

"There have been complaints of your dog barking," he piped up with a cocky attitude and a smirk.

"Where were the complaints? Let me see the forms that have the complaints." I stared at him until he couldn't look at me anymore. He then started to look through blank pages, and I knew his purpose.

"Orient Street," he said in a low tone.

"Orient Street? Well, first of all, you're lying to me because that street is over the hill and through thick woods. Also, my dog is an inside dog and only goes outside when I walk her or if we are outside with her." I was now getting upset. "Please remove yourself from my property. I respect the badge, but not the person in the badge. Go tell whoever sent you that it didn't work." I shut the door without any reaction from the police officer. I watched as he walked back to his animal control van and he drove off. I never heard anything else from the city on that issue.

A few weeks later, I had to go to Home Depot in a town just outside of Urbanville. As I took a left out of my driveway, I noticed a man in about his early forties sitting in a car on the opposite side of my street. Not thinking anything of it, I saw through my rearview mirror that he was following me. I thought about being on workers' comp as a reason why he might be following me, but then again, my injury was psychological and not physical. I could do anything because the injury was on the inside. Now the question was, why was he following me?

As I got to the end of my street, I had to take a right turn onto Route 9, which becomes a three-lane road until I get to the bridge and travel over Lake Profondo. It then becomes a two-lane road. I looked in my mirror and saw he was still following me. I started to get nervous. *What is his objective here*, I thought, *and why would anyone put in the time?* As I got to the town line and the road became two lanes, I moved into the left lane and he passed me on the right. I looked at him as he passed, and he drove parallel to me holding up his cell phone. He looked like he was trying to intimidate me. He then took the next right and he left. I went to the next parking lot, pulled over, and tried to stop my heart from pounding against the walls of my chest. Once I got my composure back, I went home and never made it to the store.

These three attacks were not only devastating to me, but also to my family. I would go to the supermarket and other stores looking over my shoulder. My daughter played volleyball for Urbanville Tech High School, and we would go to the games as a family. Some of these games I would miss because I feared something happening. My daughter would look at me and say, "Don't give in to them, Dad. I want you at my games." With a tear running down my cheek, I knew she was right, but it hurt. Then one day something happened at my daughter's home playoff game.

My whole family went to the playoff game. As we walked into the gym at Urbanville Tech High School, I saw my daughter warming up with a smile on her face. This was a great moment until I turned and saw Marsha. My heart jumped into my mouth. She was sitting in the front row, glaring at me. I ignored her because my family didn't even know what she looked like. We walked passed her and sat in the bleachers about five rows above her. Five minutes later, her assistant, Joe, came into the gym and started to talk to Marsha. At the same time, they both looked up. Obviously, they were talking about me.

It wasn't until I went to her deposition when I found out that she used this situation against me and said, "A gang of people walked in with John Pepi, and I was fearful for my safety." Even my lawyer was stunned and asked her, "Did Mr. Pepi look violent?"

"No," she said. "Just scary." What? Scary? That's when I realized I wasn't dealing with normal people, and they would turn the situation around and blame the target. Isn't that what bullies do? Take the onus off themselves and apply it to the target, like it wasn't their fault.

This is what I was dealing with going from one deposition to another. Listening to lie after lie. I did see a bright spot when my attorney questioned Barb, the purchasing director for the Urbanville Public Schools, during her deposition. He asked, "Did John Pepi steal anything?" She answered, "No." The second question was, "Did he fail to follow protocol on ordering equipment?" Her answer again was, "No." This was a big deal and proved that what I was saying all along was right. Finally, someone who told the truth.

The saddest interview was with the former athletic director, Hal, for whom I took over the position when he became ill. His deposition should have proved that the school department was wrong in getting rid of me and prove that they were all lying. When he showed up in Newtown for his deposition, I figured that was a good sign. *He drove an hour and a half to get here*, I thought, *he will be great for me*. I was excited because he worked with me, just for an hour or two in an unofficial compacity, after he came back from being ill. The city didn't want to hire anyone to assist me, so I asked him as a favor, and he did help. We would go out for lunch together and enjoy each other's company. This is why I thought he would be great in a deposition. I was looking for the truth.

We introduced ourselves to everyone in the room. I sat on the side of my attorney. The city attorney sat on the opposite side of us, and Hal sat next to him. At the end of the table sat the stenographer who recorded all of the depositions (it was a different stenographer each time, but they all worked for the same company). The process lasted for over a year. This deposition started off well for the first ten minutes. The city attorney turned to my attorney and asked for a recess. I looked at my attorney with a puzzled look.

"Recess?" I asked. "We just got started."

My attorney kept on saying, "Don't worry, we have to be cordial." *Forget cordial*, I thought, *I want the jugular. These people don't have the right for cordial. They are trying to ruin me for life.*

I didn't have a choice but to follow my attorney's lead. We went back into the room and started again. This time, the city attorney spoke up before the first question was asked. "He can't remember too much because of an injury he received." *Are you kidding?* Then Hal apologized, "Sorry, John, I can't remember a thing." I looked at him with a glare and thought, *I hope you make it home okay since you have memory lapses.* After an hour, my attorney stated that is it, and I spent money on a stenographer as well as gas getting there for nothing. What a farce.

After they left, I asked my attorney, "Why is the city attorney representing him? He is not being sued, and all we are doing is questioning him." The only answer I received was that he worked for the city and was allowed his representation. Even to this day, I disagree with the city attorney representing someone who was not involved in the case but was acting as just a participating witness. *What a bag job!*

The other depositions included the former superintendent Hal, Aisha, the Chief Financial Officer, Bobby, who were all arrogant and acted as if they didn't know why they were there. *I knew by the end of the depositions* that they were all elitist and believed they were above the law.

Every single one of them blamed one another. The superintendent placed the blame on Aisha, that it was her decision to demote me. *What bothered me was how they handled themselves and lied under oath, with a straight face. What a scam. They ran the school department? That was scary in itself.*

During Aisha's deposition, she blamed Hal and stated that it was the superintendent's job to hire and fire. The CFO came in and showed how hiring Marsha saved money. The only problem was it was typed on a piece of paper that could have been done by a second grader. No hard evidence was shown on that paper. The hardest deposition was Mary because she was the person who, no matter what, stuck up for her friend Marsha, which she admitted.

They saved the best deposition for last, which was Antonio's. I didn't attend his deposition because I get upset when even his name is mentioned. He is my lifelong tormentor and gifted at twisting stories. He is the master manipulator, and his whole goal in this case was to make sure I lost the house so that he could save the day.

I knew then, that this was not good. The depositions were showing me that the school system was all a great conspiracy. In the meantime, I was becoming a victim over and over again, including when my wife and I went to our own deposition. This was held at the central office building of the school department. I had no idea what was at stake.

Going back to the scene of the crime was nerve-wracking. As I walked through the main door with my attorney and my wife, I started to break out in a cold sweat. The school system treated me like a criminal, destroyed my character, and questioned my integrity. What was I to expect next? The first floor was actually on the second, and we had the deposition in the school department's library. The city attorney, Brendon, greeted us and we went into the library. My attorney, my wife, and I waited in the library for Brendon to return, which seemed like forever. While we waited, many school department workers, including the people participating in the lawsuit, walked by and looked in at us. I felt like I was in a fish bowl and everyone was gawking at me like I was some kind of freak.

Finally, Brendon walked in with a stack of papers. It looked like he took it from the ream of paper out of the copy machine. We decided that my wife would go first. Her questioning was more about her loss of consortium, which was very awkward for not only the city attorney but also to the rest of us in the room. Then when the topic came to me, my wife started crying, but he continued with the questioning. Finally, Brendon said, "Take a tissue and take your time." If I didn't lose it then, I don't think I would ever lose it. *This is what they wanted me to do, lose it, start swearing, and threaten people. Then they can tell everyone I was* crazy, *and they would win. I WOULD NOT GIVE THEM THAT SATISFACTION.*

I could see why the city attorney wanted my wife to go first, because it lasted only an hour. I started mine, and it lasted three days. The school department didn't even offer us water, while my attorney had made sure they were well taken care of during their depositions at my attorney's office in Newtown. I was happy my wife brought water with her (she always thinks that way). After eighteen hours of deposition testimony,

I was drained, especially when they asked the same questions over and over again. This was not a deposition but more of an interrogation. It was easy for me because I told the truth, and I am sure that the city officials during their depositions had to keep reminding themselves of what they said. *IT'S HARDER TO REMEMBER A LIE, BECAUSE IT USUALLY ENDS UP BECOMING ANOTHER LIE.*

The next week, I finally got word from my attorney that we had a court date for summary judgement. Both sides would present their case, and the judge will take it under advisement. The judge would then rule on the evidence to see if the case would go to trial. After the court appearance, it would be about one or two months before a decision was rendered. Instead, it lasted eleven months. At that point, I finally called my attorney to ask about the delay. He told me that it was very unusual to have such a delay, and he promised that he would look into it. What happened to the paperwork? Was it the court? Was it politics? I would love to know these answers.

A few days went by, and my attorney called me back. He told me that the judge called his office personally and said he was sorry it took so long. He told my attorney that he didn't understand what happened because he approved us going to trial and then the paperwork disappeared. They found the paperwork, and the judge said he was going to process it. Our court date would be in October. I was excited, but my antennas went up. Why was the paperwork missing? Was anyone tampering with my case? As I said before: IT IS NOT CONSPIRACY THEORY BUT CONSPIRACY REALITY. I felt that I was going to court with both hands tied behind my back. The only option I had was to go to court and see what happened.

# 12

# THE TRIAL

The pressure mounted as my court date approached. Even though I was receiving workers' comp, it wasn't enough to pay off my long overdue bills. Before the summary judgement paperwork was found, I knew that I needed a distraction from my anxiety, so I decided to go for my doctoral degree in educational leadership. My son was graduating from the University of Phoenix in May 2013, so I decided to apply to the same school. With me going back to school online (which meant plenty of writing assignments), my oldest son graduating in May, his wedding in August, and my court date in October, my plate was filled to the brim. I still had to live my life amid the craziness. But in the end, I expected someone to be held accountable for what my family went through.

Once the date arrived, we had to appear in court. I didn't sleep much the night before. I didn't seem tired, but as I looked at my children and my wife, I could see the weariness on their faces. None of us felt up to eating breakfast. The moment of justice has arrived (at least that was what I was hoping and praying for) after what had seemed to be an eternity. Even though I had been told by my attorney that there are no guarantees in litigation, I was determined that the verdict was going to be in my favor because of the overwhelming evidence we had.

We arrived at court at 8:30 a.m. for the 9 a.m. trial, and we made sure that we had plenty of time. After paying fifteen dollars a day for parking (every day, which in itself was a struggle to pay), we proceeded to enter the front door of the new courthouse. The building looked more like a mall than a courthouse. After going through the security check, which included taking off your belt and depositing your cell phone, we started to head up to courtroom 19. While we were waiting for my attorney, I discussed with my children the trial procedure. My wife and I felt awful that our children had to go through this. We didn't belong here. On top of our money struggles, my wife had to miss three weeks of work for these court appearances, for which she had to forego paychecks. The city tried to bury us with lies and false accusations, and it was obvious that they didn't care about our financial struggles.

As we sat outside of the courtroom with our support group waiting for our attorneys for what seemed like an eternity, the city officials showed up. As we sat there, Aisha, Mary, Dr. Hal, and Brendon walked by us and went to the other courtroom door. They kept looking in our direction before our attorneys showed up. It was awkward. Before we went into the courtroom, my legal team went over our game plan, which included a settlement. I felt reluctance to take a settlement because of the pain my wife and I went through.

Maybe we might have been unrealistic believing our case would award us in the millions, but in all, we believed it was worth $500,000 at least. In reality, if this case had involved a death, a severe life-altering injury, or a false incarceration, that would have warranted a bigger price tag. All my family wanted was to hold the members of the school system accountable for their actions, clear my name, and of course, repay the people I borrowed money from. As 9 a.m. approached, we all went into the courtroom. We sat on the left toward the jury box, and the city officials sat on the right. Right off the bat, we felt uneasy. Maybe it was because the original article had gone to print in 2009, and here it was in the year 2013, and there was not a reporter in sight. This was even after friends and relatives called the newspaper. But still, no one showed up.

After a couple of quiet moments, the court officer appeared. "All rise, the honorable Judge — presides." (It was a different judge than the one who passed us through summary judgement. What's up with that?) After the judge sat at the bench, he called for a side bar for both attorneys before the jury was chosen. Even though I had served on a jury before, this felt different and I didn't like it. We were not supposed to be here. How did we get here? This was when I started to pray. I was hoping that all this would disappear, but obviously, I had to go through the valley to get to the mountain. That mountain seemed miles away, but the real question was, Would I ever get to the mountain? Only time would tell. But one thing was for certain, I never in my wildest dreams thought that this trial would last three weeks, and the jury would have to deliberate for seven hours before rendering a decision. I felt victimized all over again.

I trusted my attorney would use his ability to choose the right jurors because I was not an expert in this field. All I saw were bodies going up to the stand to either be confirmed by both attorneys or rejected. The only thing I remember was that one jury pool member got up from his seat and started heading toward the judge and attorneys. The reason why I remember this is because he looked like he just rolled out of bed with the same clothes he had worn for a week. In fact, it took him ten minutes just to walk over. It wasn't because he was older. He was in his twenties, and his demeanor was "I don't want to be here, why am I here?" He never made it to the judge because both attorneys rejected him.

After the jury was selected, we had a recess. But before the jury was dismissed to the jury room, I looked at the jurors to see if I could read their body language. They all had stone faces like they were in a poker game, but the one person with a distinct characteristic was the one who ended up being the foreman. She looked at me like she was trying to figure me out. At the same time, I was trying to figure her out as well as the rest of the jury.

As we left the courtroom, my family, friends, and I left the area to talk, as the city officials were in a powwow on the other side of the hallway. As we were talking about what we had witnessed so far, my attorney came to us to see if we would consider a settlement or mediation. At that time, I should have said yes, but I was convinced that we could win this case, so I refused and said, "Let the case go on for a little while before I decide." As we entered the courtroom, I was still confident that I had the evidence and my case was strong. The only problem was the city's attorney. His job was to destroy me and destroy my family. It was evident from his opening statement.

My attorney went first with his opening statement, in which he laid out the case against the city by showing that I was falsely accused of embezzlement, larceny, and fraud. He also showed that because of these false allegations, my reputation had been destroyed, I was diagnosed having symptoms of PTSD along with other stress-related ailments, and I lost enough income to place me in financial ruin. He mentioned that I was looking for relief due to these careless allegations, which had been reckless and damaging. "Somehow these false accusations got out and defamed Mr. Pepi's name, which placed him in a position that affected his professional career," he said. It wasn't until the city attorney began his opening statement that I found out what the city was made of.

As Brendon approached the jury, I never expected to hear what he was about to say. I didn't realize that a human could stoop so low to win a case, and he would continue the abuse throughout the trial. He stood there and pointed to my family and told the jury, "DON'T LISTEN TO THEM, THEY ARE NO GOOD." *What?* I wondered. *How dare he make such a statement?* It wasn't the only demeaning statement he said to the jury, but before he continued, I heard, "I OBJECT" from my attorney. I then looked at the judge, who said, "OVERRULED." Then Brendon continued, "YOU WILL SEE THAT MR. PEPI IS A MALINGERER, AND ALL HE WANTS IS TO SIT HOME SO HE CAN COLLECT MONEY." *Are you kidding?* Again, my attorney objected, and again it was overruled.

I looked at the judge, but he would not make eye contact with me. I didn't understand the court proceedings, and I couldn't believe that the city attorney could say these false accusations to the jury at the beginning of the trial. I believed this set the tone for the whole trial. I felt it was unprofessional, and again I was victimized by another bully, the city attorney. I didn't understand what was going on at the time, but as I worked toward my doctoral degree at the University of Phoenix, things started to make sense to me. My dissertation was on workplace bullying, and as I prepared, I read a lot of research on the topic. What was happening was a severe level of mobbing and gaslighting. Mobbing, as I've defined previously, is when a group of abusers attack a victim, both verbally and in action. Gaslighting occurs when facts are manipulated and twisted around to make it look like the victim is the problem. These tactics are both used to gain power over the target. In this case, the city attorney was in on it, and the judge allowed it to happen.

Now from here, what could I expect? I had already been abused and tormented for six years from the city, and now I had to relive their lies and manipulation all over again. At this point, I wanted to crawl under the bench, but I couldn't. It was fortunate that I had my family and friends in the courtroom supporting me. I didn't have much time to think because I was called to the stand. For the next day and a half, I presented my testimony. I wasn't nervous when my attorney questioned me (I was happy to tell my story), but the city attorney was like a vampire and tried to suck the life out of me. After saying those lies to the jury, what else did he have up his sleeves?

After swearing in under oath, I sat down, and the judge gave me instruction about speaking into the microphone. After I acknowledged him, I raised my right hand, and I was now sworn in under the pain of perjury (the same oath everyone else took). I turned to the jury, my attorney, and all of the city officials who were listed on the compliant, and I was prepared to give my testimony. To make it easier on myself and to avoid getting overly stressed, I primarily looked toward the jury and my attorney when he questioned me. After stating my name and answering the first simple question, I felt comfortable.

My attorney made sure that I faced the jury when I answered questions, and I did, looking each of them in the eye as I surveyed the jury box. I told them how this bullying had affected my family, how my reputation was ruined, and how the stress had controlled my life. As I continued to explain my situation, my attorney also asked if I liked to be home and what had I accomplished in the past. I told the jury how this was unusual to stay home, and I wanted to go back to work, but the abuse I received at work had led to my stress-related illnesses. I finished that day by telling the jury how I loved my job, and I was effective doing the work because my evaluations had said so. I even mentioned that I had never received a bad evaluation in my whole teaching career.

During my testimony, the jury was handed the June 8 letter (falsely accusing me of embezzlement, larceny, and fraud), and the September 18 letter (which told me to go back to work after suspension but keep my mouth shut) along with my evaluations that I received high marks on. They were all put forth as evidence. The judge called it a day, and we were to resume the next day. As I got off the stand, I was drained, but I asked my attorney, family, and friends how I sounded. They all confirmed that I did a great job. It was only the first day, and I was already sick of the courthouse. We had a long way to go.

The next day came, and I continued on the stand with my testimony. This continued for many more hours, and I had to explain to the jury how the events that occurred within the school system affected my health, my professional life, and my personal life. It was very difficult to talk about myself in this matter because I was always a giving person, but I was now in a position where I was hurting professionally and personally. I was made to feel like I did something wrong. When my attorney stated that he was done with the questioning, I felt sick and helpless knowing it was now the city's turn.

Once I started to understand that the city attorney would do anything to make me look bad, I realized that this would be as stressful as the bullying that had occurred at school. He asked me some simple preliminary questions, and then he started bringing up information that I couldn't believe. He knew I went to California to help my son settle into his new apartment, and he also knew that I went with my son to the Jimmy Kimmel show. I was thinking to myself, How in the world did he know this? It wasn't until break that I found out the answer.

As we stepped outside of the courtroom, I asked my attorney where he got this information from. My attorney responded by stating that my psychologist (this was a new psychologist after my other one passed away) gave him all the information from my therapy sessions. I said that I thought that my therapy sessions were confidential. My attorney made me aware that I had signed a release for my medical records to be sent to my attorney and the city attorney. Even today, I feel that this was wrong. If I knew this was going to be used against me, I would not have said as much. My sessions were supposed to be my healing.

I disagreed with him, and I still believe that using someone's therapy session against them is disingenuous as well as unprofessional. I could not believe that I was continuously being targeted by the city attorney. I felt helpless and angry during the rest of the proceedings in my case. This was totally wrong and made me not trust the judicial system. I knew I had to be strong for my family, and I had to fight back against mobbing going on in that courtroom. My question was, How is the jury perceiving my family and myself? I was sick to my stomach.

When I went back on the stand after lunch, I did everything I could not to cry because I had to show strength as I watched my family fall apart. I believed that my family, who all knew about my past health issues, was worried about me. When I looked at the members of my family when I was on the stand, I felt bad for them. No one should ever go through this, and it was especially unfair to my family to drag them into this situation. After glancing at the jury and my family, I looked directly back at the city attorney for more questioning. During the rest of my time on the stand, I would be questioned on my finances, my health, and my professional career. They dragged my character and integrity through the mud.

Yes, there were times when the city attorney, my attorney, and the judge would sidebar and discuss what could be used as evidence as well as the questioning. I had no idea what was being discussed, but as I sat there waiting quietly, multiple thoughts came to my mind. I wanted this to end. I didn't have any friends on that stand. For that moment in time, I was alone, and I couldn't turn to anybody to give me a boost of confidence. The city attorney took no mercy on me. His job was to smear my good name.

The next day, my tax returns were put up on the courtroom's TV screen for everybody to see (the city attorney wanted the jury to see that I couldn't handle money and not the lack of money from the absence of pay from the city). The prosecution's line of questioning implied that I was not a good teacher, let alone a good administrator. The attorney showed me my past evaluations that I felt were not negative but constructive criticism to make me a better administrator. He outlined points of contention about the evaluation and say to me, "This was a bad evaluation." I strongly disagreed with him.

What happened next on the stand made me upset the most. The attorney continued with his false accusations. He told me that I never started the Hall of Fame (he knew that accusation would hurt me the most) and had me look like an ineffective administrator prone to mistakes. This made me extremely upset because I could not believe that an attorney could be so ruthless and unprofessional to make me look like I was the worst person who has ever held that job. Of course, he made Marsha seem like the best thing to happen to that department. He read from her evaluations dating back to the 1980s and asked, "Wouldn't you think she is the person who should have this job?" Before I was able to answer, my attorney objected, stating that this was irrelevant to the case at hand. The judge overruled him, and they had a sidebar. The results of the sidebar were that they would put her evaluations dating back to the '80s as evidence.

What a shame. At this point the case didn't feel right, and it seemed that the judge himself was in on the mobbing. My attorney was working hard, but I felt like I was at a football game and they kept on changing the rules and moving the goal posts. I continued on the stand longer than I should have, and it seemed like the whole time it wasn't about looking for the truth, it was all about destroying me. It was at this point, after days of testimony, I wanted to get off the stand.

When my testimony ended, I stepped down from the stand and my wife was next to be called. I knew based on how I was treated that the city attorney was not going to be lenient on my wife. Before she took the stand, it was time for lunch. Like always, we could not leave the courthouse because we had no money for lunch. Our struggles were real between my wife not getting paid and my limited workers' comp, we had no money.

My oldest sister and her husband helped us throughout the case, and they were very good to my family. Between the two of them and my niece, they paid for our lunch every day. We would sit on the first floor of the courthouse to eat, and I would see former students of mine walk by to say hi. It was at this point I was really embarrassed that I was an educator in their lives, and here I was fighting for my life in a courthouse. As they walked away I would tear up, but my family would encourage me to continue. It was an awful feeling to know that I was in court with my family, and I had been abandoned by many friends as well as other family members. My closest friends would call me after each day of the trial to see how I was doing. It's funny, you do learn who your friends and family are when you are in time of need. Many of them would show up at my office when I was athletic director, but once I lost that position, they abandoned me. I call these people social climbers.

My wife and my children were big supporters of me. If I hadn't had them on my side, I knew I would not have been able to make it. I can now understand how a bully's mistreatment can harm not only the target but the target's family. I was blessed to have a supportive wife and children to pick me up when I was down. Now it was time to go back to the courtroom and hear my wife's testimony. This broke my heart.

Watching my wife sit on the stand and give her testimony, I could see that she was very uptight and nervous. She did everything she could hold back tears because deep down she did not want the city to see weakness. She was calm and explained thoroughly how it affected our family, from the financial cost to the emotional cost of losing a father. When the city attorney cross-examined my wife about the unfounded, false accusations against me, she stood up to those ludicrous accusations and remained firm when dealing with this abusive attorney. My wife was not going to have my name dragged through the mud. She stood strong against what I call secondary abusive behavior.

Here's where I'll explain what I call primary and secondary abuse, which any victim of workplace bullying will be able to identify. Primary abuse is what happens in the workplace, including mobbing, gaslighting, and bullying. When the target decides to fight back, either by suing or trying to recoup workers' comp, the target becomes affected by secondary abuse, in which they experience the trauma afflicted by the bully all over again. In my situation, a municipality had multiple bullies to fight a lawsuit, the expense of which they don't care about because it is on the backs of taxpayers. The media protects these municipalities so that the taxpayers don't know that their money is going toward lawsuits instead of educating students.

After my wife gave her testimony, the worst possible abuse came right after she stepped down from the stand. My children, from my oldest son to my youngest, were called to the stand one at a time, starting with John. John had just married two months prior to this trial and was looking to start a new job. He knew that he needed to support his father, but he also needed to work to support his own household. My third son had to leave college because he missed three weeks, and my second son left California and lost income at the start of his career. My daughter was supposed to start college that fall but could not complete the first semester, plus she had been promoted to groomer at a pet salon but had to hold off because of this trial. They all wanted to support their father and see justice delivered.

As my son sat on the stand, my attorney asked him how the demotion had affected the family after seeing what his father went through. He was very thorough and was very strong in his testimony. I was convinced that anybody with a soul would hear his testimony and understand how it hurt to see his father dragged through the mud. I would think the jury would understand if they had a heart, especially if they were from a family that always believed in righteousness. I did nothing wrong, and my family knew it, but it was brutal to see my son up on a stand trying to protect his father's good name. When the city attorney cross-examined him, he began to taunt my son. One of the most agonizing parts of the testimony was when the city attorney said to my son, "Enough about the life lessons from your father." That killed me, and at that point I knew the city attorney was no good. I was a malingerer, my family's no good, and now he taunted my children about life lessons.

As I watched the final testimony of my son, I became angry and hurt to see my family that I raised to be honest and trustworthy destroyed by my friends-turned-lynch-mob. No one should have to go through this torment, and no one should be treated in this way. After thirty-four years in education, I was respected by students and parents, and I always placed the children first. Now my thirty-four-year career was being destroyed by a pack of cowards hiding behind a corrupt municipality. I started to realize that everything that had been done to me was premeditated and calculated. As my son stepped down from the stand, my daughter was next. I cringed as she was called to the stand, knowing my young daughter, who was eighteen, would be exposed to the same hate my son had experienced. She had been in the sixth grade when this started, and she remembered the torment her father went through. Every night she would give me a hug and would tell me, "Everything will be okay, Dad."

As my daughter got up from the bench she was sitting on, it was hard to watch. I turned to my wife, and I could see that she was also visibly upset. As difficult as it was, I was proud of my daughter that day. She held herself well until the attorney asked how this had affected her and her dad. She could not hold it in any longer, and she began to cry. She told them that her dad was a proud man and to see him this way broke her heart. She talked about the days we had no money and needed food for the house because of the city was holding back checks. "I would find change in the car and gave it to my dad, so we could eat that night," she said. "My dad is a proud person who was embarrassed that we could not even go to the store near our house." As we scrambled to find money, she would say, "Dad, it will get better. Don't worry."

She told the jury how I would comfort her by cracking a joke or two, just so it didn't upset her, but she knew that the situation was eating me alive. As she continued, she started to tell the story of my fiftieth birthday, but she stopped because she couldn't go on any further. My attorney told her to take her time and get herself together. She continued to say how stressful the birthday was, and she wanted to see her "old dad back." She concluded by saying, "My dad is a good man, and he worked hard at his job, which he was very proud of." Despite her tears, I looked over at the jury and saw they showed no emotion. That bothered me. How cold could they be? Then I looked over at the city officials as they sat there stone-faced, like they had no compassion or remorse for what they had done to me. Not even an eighteen-year-old daughter bleeding her heart out on the stand could not even phase them. What kind of people were they?

As my attorney said to the judge, "No more questioning, Your Honor." I looked to the city attorney who had his head down, and he said, "I don't have any questions, Your Honor." *WOW*, I thought, *And why's that?* Could it be that he didn't want the city to look worse than it already did, or did he really have a heart? Whatever the motive was, I was happy that Gina was able to get off the stand. After her testimony, the judge had us break. When we returned, the circus started up again with the lies and manipulation from the city officials.

As we stepped outside of the courtroom, I gave my daughter a hug to let her know that I was proud of her. Then I turned to my son and hugged him as well. Something came over me, and I thought of raising my children with my wife and how special that was. I felt that I let down the family. Even though I knew they all supported me, I was overwhelmed with emotion. My attorney went up to my children and told them they did a great job. He turned to me and told me that I have a wonderful family, which I believe gave him a reason to fight for us.

My family and friends who had been there for the entire trial decided to go downstairs to grab a bite to eat, like we did for the full three weeks. My stomach was in knots, and I could barely eat half a sandwich because I knew that once we returned to the courtroom, it would upset me more. Just before the hour lunch was up, my attorney came up to me and said, "We have to wait for the human resources director, Aisha, because she is in Chicago on business. We will have others on the stand and call her when she comes in tomorrow." I thought to myself, *Business? When did she leave? Is she looking for teachers? This is why education is expensive, because of wasteful spending. The money should be going directly into the classroom. The administrators have no shame.*

As we went back into the courtroom, I was worked up, even more so when I came face-to-face with Dr. Hal, who opened the courtroom door for my family and me. Awkward. We sat down, and I kept on thinking to myself, *The jury has to see it our way. They have to know that I am a good person who is being hurt by a mob of bullies.* Then my attorney came over to me and said, "Even if they lie, don't react to it." I nodded in agreement as the court officer called for us to rise for the judge. Then the two attorneys and the judge did a sidebar to discuss how the rest of the trial would proceed.

As different city officials were called to the stand, I was amazed how they could lie under oath and twist facts to benefit themselves. The chief financial officer started by saying he suspected I stole from the Hall of Fame, but when it was time to show evidence, he couldn't. A bank statement from the Hall of Fame committee was produced as evidence, and he questioned particular purchases at a supermarket.

My attorney quickly jumped on this. "How did you get that bank statement?" he asked.

"From the bank manager," the CFO replied.

"Do you have authorization to have that bank statement?" asked my attorney.

The CFO stated in an arrogant way, "The bank manager is a friend of mine." That infuriated me because I gave those bank statements to the human resources director, but he would not admit it. Furthermore, my attorney showed him a receipt from that supermarket that these purchases were for floral arrangements for the tables at the Hall of Fame dinner. All the CFO did was give a wise smirk.

The CFO also tried to say that I misappropriated money to buy football uniforms, which again was followed up by emails from the purchasing department in the school system. The purchasing agent had cleared me of all wrongdoing. I knew that this was done behind my back by a revengeful secretary who was friends with Marsha. This was all proven in court.

Whenever the CFO was asked a question about how a move by him saved money for the city, he would type it up on a scrap piece of paper without showing the figures to back up his claim. This person was making more than $150,000, and he'd been at this for many years. How could nobody get a straight answer from him? I was reminded of a meeting from when I started as athletic director, where we were told that the system had to pay back a $5 million grant. We were told it was paid back at a rate of $1 million a year for five years. Digging deeper, I found out that the money was going toward other items instead of helping children pursue career pathways. What were those other items? Higher salaries at the central office? Talk about misappropriated funds. I wondered, *Why doesn't this make the paper?*

At the end of the CFO's testimony, after questioning by my attorney and the city attorney, I knew that this was not going to be an easy trial. The problem was, these people seemed like they didn't care about lying under oath. To me it seemed like an orchestrated attempt to confuse the jury and make it appear that I was the problem. I knew we still had other witnesses, but as we went further into the trial, I could see the pattern clearly.

The next day, Aisha was called to the stand after she returned from Chicago. During her testimony, she could not show any evidence or prove her claim that I embezzled and was involved in larceny or any fraudulent activity. She couldn't even produce any evidence to prove that I misappropriated any funds from the city. When my attorney asked her about the licensure of Marsha, Aisha responded foolishly, saying her "license is only valid when she uses it." *That doesn't even make sense,* I thought. *In fact, that is illegal, and you are required to have licenses to obtain any position in a public school district within the Commonwealth of Massachusetts.*

The Educational Reform Act of 1993 eliminated lifetime licenses in education within the Commonwealth of Massachusetts. Every five years, educators, whether they are administrators or teachers, have to renew their licenses or else they are not allowed to practice within the Commonwealth. In order for them to renew their licenses, they have to either take classes or workshops that equal 150 professional development points (PDP). I remember after finishing my master's and going for my practicum to become an administrator, I was told by my successor that she did not have time to do what I was doing. The problem with the city is that they didn't realize I have an excellent memory.

When I was replaced, that exchange with Marsha was the first thing I thought of. I was able to retrieve her data from the Department of Education's website and found out that she was not licensed. I also used the same database to discover why she was licensed in one day, only a month after I filed a complaint with Superior Court (normally it takes six months to obtain an educational license). I found out through this source that Aisha was on the committee of the Department of Education that deals with licensors. I didn't believe this was a coincidence. How could she get a license on September 11, 2009, when she applied for a license on September 11, 2009? Besides, she was not licensed in 2007 when she took over my position.

The problem with Aisha was she denied everything that was black and white and proven on documents presented to her. It was amazing to me how anyone could lie under oath to make me look like I was crazy, incompetent, insubordinate, dishonest, and that my family benefited from the money I supposedly stole. If this was supposedly true, then why was my house broken down beyond repair, why was I extremely late on mortgage payments, and why were we in financial ruin? Listening to her testimony made my blood boil and angered me because she knew exactly what she was doing to my family. When I questioned her after she accused me of these heinous crimes, she told me that I was a racist and acting against the children. What does race have to do with her accusations, and how could she possibly say I was hurting children?

The most disturbing part of Aisha's testimony was that she was asked if she ever made a trip to my office, since she had accused me of stealing and misappropriating funds. When she said no, even though my office was a ten-minute drive away, my attorney was really shocked.

"How could you accuse somebody of stealing if you never went to the scene of the crime?" he asked.

She couldn't answer the question, and all she could do was smile and shrug her shoulders. This was very compelling—why would she list things as missing in her June 8 letter but not have the decency to do her own personal investigation? If that didn't raise questions among the jury, I didn't know what would. Even though she never had evidence to prove her point, she had plenty of options to try to ruin me. Another disturbing fact that emerged from her testimony was that she didn't even know the simple phrases that any school system uses, such as "petty cash."

She used her position to degrade, manipulate, and fabricate because she had political ties and a hidden agenda to attempt to dismiss me from my position. Since I was onto the school system's game and had outsmarted them to foil their plot, the only thing they could do was destroy my reputation, character, and integrity. As Aisha was finishing up her testimony with the city lawyer, they looked like they were in step with her excuses about her decision making. There were more documents presented as evidence, but it didn't matter. She was a great deceiver. After both attorneys said they had no further questions, she stepped down from the stand. This was the last we would see of her for the rest of the trial. She had a trip scheduled to go to China. I didn't know if it was school related or vacation.

As we began the second week of the trial, Mary was called to the stand. She twisted and turned stories to highlight my incompetence and claimed I made a lot of mistakes. Of course, my attorney asked her, "How can you make these claims when you gave Mr. Pepi excellent evaluations, except for the last one, when it was clear that you were trying to terminate him?" As she looked toward my attorney, she answered in a cold, calculating way to say she had been firm in her assessment. She was asked about her relationships with Marsha and my secretary. There was no hesitation on her part to say that they were friends. She even stated under oath that she was helping her friend take over the new position before she retired.

Listening to this testimony made me realize that the whole time I was working as athletic director, she had protected the principals who attacked me and was in a rush to complete forms for the next year. Mary and Marsha shared an office, and she knew exactly what needed to be done so that her friend would not fail. It all started to make sense to me, and I started to connect the dots to see that this was a deep-state type of organization. They had organized with the central office staff to destroy me, and together, they formed a "mob." The abuse did not come from just one person, but a group of people all working with the same goal of taking me down so that I would quit.

Fortunately for me, I outsmarted them, and I was strong. My strength came from God, and I would never give in to this hypocritical, narcissistic behavior. I needed to continue the fight, which I knew would endure after the trial. I could not show my wife and my children that I was weak, but I did know it wouldn't be easy. It wasn't until Marsha took the stand that I had all the proof I needed that this was all political.

As Marsha was called to the stand, I was remembering all the research and information I had about her past and her connections. As I stated before, she was not licensed until 2009, which happened to be a little more than two years after she took my position. Even though she received her license in one day, she hadn't obtained a master's degree to go along with her administrative position, and there was no record of taking the MTEL, which is the test one takes to become licensed. The master's degree had to be in educational leadership, and she should have been licensed as a supervisor/director. That was not the only red flag I had seen; her father-in-law used to be a former mayor of the city. Her brother-in-law used to be on the Governor's Council until he was forced to resign, an event which was written about in the Boston Herald. He was also very close friends with Jim McMurray (a former mayor and disgraced lieutenant governor) and as an attorney, he worked within the courthouse.

I also learned that her sister-in-law was married to a city counselor who Jim McMurray had campaigned for. It just so happened that this city counselor dropped out of the race back in the 1990s to allow Jim McMurray to take his place. The other sister-in-law was a principal for a middle school in the city, and her husband worked for the lottery along with Jim McMurray's brother. Her father was a popular track coach, and the track at Urbanville Stadium was named in his honor. I guess you could call this a deep state, but I will discuss this corruption further in the book.

As she sat there and took the oath, she used a voice that was typical of somebody playing the victim. That infuriated me, knowing that my family was in living hell having watched their father and husband dragged through the mud. The attitude of my former colleagues throughout this whole ordeal, dating back to 2007, was along the lines of "how DARE YOU question me?" I tried to focus on Marsha's testimony, but her voice sounded like an adolescent who was looking to play the victim and insisting that someone else was at fault. Isn't that what a bully does? Here she is making a six-figure income, taking all the credit from my hard work, and she did not care what she did to my family. People may say that she was forced to take my position, but she had the power to say NO. She even received the Contribution to Sports award from the same Hall of Fame committee that I started. *How did that happen?* I thought. *She received an award for her contribution? Isn't it her job? She received an award for doing her job?* That award was intended for someone from outside the school system who helped contribute to athletics in Urbanville. Ironically, Jay, the groundskeeper, also received this award a year later. He also received a promotion and became a boss. I guess they received their reward for bullying me.

I knew her testimony would be a farce. She was not only playing the victim, but the city lawyer also provided her evaluations dating back to 1988 as evidence. Really? I assumed that the city attorney wanted to show the jury how nice of a person she was, but there was no relevant reason why those evaluations were evidence. My attorney objected, but again it was overruled. All I could do with my family was to watch her throw me under the bus during her testimony.

She claimed that I had come with a "gang of people" to a volleyball game and walked right by her, which made her feel that she was in danger. The reason why I was at that volleyball game was my daughter was playing, and the "gang of people" I was with was my family. My attorney looked at her and asked, "Have you found Mr. Pepi to show signs of violence?"

"No," she answered almost immediately.

*Wow*, I thought, *and I suppose that's the reason I'm not able to officiate anymore football games at the city's stadium?* I was the one who had been bullied and slapped around. My family was struggling financially. Marsha made a six-figure income, and I WAS THE THREAT? Of course, the city made me look like the bully and made her look like a gentle flower. This is when I learned that whenever a bully blames the other person of something, it is usually because they are guilty of that same action.

As both my attorney and the city attorney finished questioning Marsha, it was time for them to question the superintendent, who had retired from the school system in 2008. It was late in the day on Friday at the conclusion of the second week, so everybody advised that we extend to Monday. This would bring the trial into November, which elevated my stress level even more. My son John and my daughter Gina started new jobs. I understood, but it was heart-wrenching that they had to miss any work just to be with me. My family was frustrated that we had to return for week three, and I didn't blame them.

My attorney gave me something to think about as we left the courtroom on Friday. He told me to think of what sort of settlement I could live with between myself and the city. Deep down, I wanted to tell my attorney, "No way, after what they put us through." Realistically, I was fearful that this case would not go in my favor. It was at least something I could think about, and maybe I could have some closure after six years of trying to clear my name. At least I had some time to watch the Red Sox win their third World Series, but I couldn't concentrate. I knew when Monday came around that I should ask for a $500,000 settlement because I was fearful that the fix was in.

When Monday came around, I let my attorney know my intentions, and he approached the city attorney. The city attorney said that he had a make a phone call and would get back to us. Before the superintendent went on the stand, just shy of 9:20 a.m., the city attorney returned and said no. The city was going to continue with the case. We made two more offers, lowering the price with each offer, but both times the city attorney came back with a no. Before this week was over, I had a bad feeling about this case. I believed that the city lawyer knew something we didn't.

While on the stand, the superintendent gave us worthless information because all he did was reiterate what was said by the other defendants. It almost seemed like he had been coached and prepped for his testimony so that he would not contradict the other defendants. My attorney continuously asked the superintendent how was he not aware of what had been going on, because by law in Massachusetts, it was the superintendent who hires and fires within the school district. I knew that he was playing the game because when he retired in 2008 he went on his farewell tour to all the schools. When he got to my school, he popped into the gym and said "Goodbye, John," in a way that sounded more mocking than sincere.

His testimony had taken a good portion of the day. With just a short time left, the court was able to fit in a vocational evaluation professional. I had never seen the woman who took the stand, yet she was talking about my ability to go back to work like she had known me for years. She stated that there was nothing wrong with me, completely ignoring my diagnosis of PTSD and other stress-related illnesses. My attorney asked her if she had ever met me or sat down with me, and she responded, "No." My attorney then asked how she could come up with these conclusions without first meeting me. This was evidence that bullying continues even during court proceedings. My family and I were targeted over and over again, and the only one who was sticking up for me was my attorney. *Where was the media?* I wondered. I knew they were in on it, as well as the courthouse. There was no doubt in my mind.

As the next day approached, we still had two more witnesses. Dr. Compass, who was hired by the city to evaluate me, and a mystery guest. As the judge and the attorneys did some preliminary work before the doctor took the stand, I started to notice a change among the city officials on the other side. The city attorney who dealt with workers' comp came in, as well as a few people I'd never seen before. The delay was longer than usual, and I believed it was because the doctor was late showing up. By the time he got on the stand, it was closer to 11 o'clock in the morning, and he only testified for two hours before lunch. My lawyer really grilled him about how long he had sat down with me to evaluate my medical conditions. The doctor told my attorney that he had only met with me for fifteen minutes, but he reviewed the 600 pages of my medical records.

As the doctor sat on the stand, he seemed meek and like he had been intimidated into testifying. The best question my attorney asked him was how much he was getting paid by the city. The doctor said $5,000, and it had only taken him two hours to review the 600 pages of medical records. My attorney couldn't believe that he read all 600 pages within two hours and asked him, "Are you a speed reader?"

"No," the doctor said in response.

My attorney continued to grill him because the doctor kept asserting that my diagnoses were false and basically that my doctor and psychologists didn't know what they were talking about. As I sat there listening to him, I couldn't believe that he believed I was faking illnesses after having only met me for no more than fifteen minutes. Knowing what I went through medically and what my family went through, how could Dr. Compass lie on the stand about my medical condition? It was evident that this doctor was a quack and an ambulance chaser who was looking for money no matter who he hurt.

When the city lawyer started to ask the doctor questions, he was trying to prove that I never had PTSD or any other stress-related illnesses. He was trying to prove that all I was trying to do was stay home and collect money. That is why he had called me a malingerer to the jury at the beginning of the trial. The doctor and the city attorney had absolutely no shame. The city attorney as well as all the witnesses called on behalf of the city had a singular purpose and that was to tear me down. There was one more witness to be called, which my attorney didn't tell me until the day of.

The surprise witness was Anna Marie, the former principal of the Catholic school where I once taught. I don't know how they found her, and why she would testify for the city was beyond me. I got flashbacks of how she treated me and the sexual abuse from her, and I felt old psychological injuries begin to flare up. My wife turned to me and asked if I was okay. She knew that this bothered me. I turned to my attorney and asked him, "Where is the relevance to this case?" He assured me that there was a limit to what she could be asked.

Even still, I couldn't witness anymore attacks on me. My eyes filled up with tears once I saw her walk past me and approach the stand. All I could think of was this person had taken time away from her school to stick the knife deeper into my back. All I could think of was how evil she was. The scowl on her face showed me that she was not a happy person, and the only thing I could do was to pray as she started to tell the jury that I was no good. It amazed me that my track record over the years between the Catholic schools and the public schools could be great, but all it takes is one person to fabricate stories about you and ruin your reputation.

I tuned her out and started to reminisce about my father and mother. My father and mother, with their eighth-grade education, were focused on raising their children to be honest and college graduates. I was very close with my parents, and I had felt like an only child. I had a great childhood, and I had no regrets about taking care of my parents even after I moved out of the house. Growing up in my neighborhood on Plantation Street, the friendships that I developed there were very important to me, and I cherish them.

As I continued to let my focus drift away from the stand, I remembered how my father once told me that when you are in a tough situation, you will know who your family and friends are. Boy, he was 100 percent right, and now I do know who my family is: my wife and my four children. My friends were the ones who would call me to see how I was doing. I knew this trial was close to ending, but for the first time in my life, I felt lonely. I don't know how others deal with the trauma of being bullied in the workplace, because if I didn't have my family and a few close friends, I don't know where I would be. As I was reminiscing, I started to tear up. Then all of a sudden, I stopped thinking of the past when my wife shook my shoulder. It was almost like she knew what I was thinking of.

Anna Marie left the stand to sit with the city officials. She sat looking at me the whole time with evil in her eyes. I looked right back at her and thought, *How Christian is she, this woman who was a former principal of a Catholic school?* Then I started thinking, *With the Catholic Church's covering up the problem of priest being pedophiles, just moving offending priests to other parishes, do they truly care about their followers?* I know I am a Christian, and that was why I left the Catholic Church. Now my question was, *What about public school administrators? Do they care about the children who are in their care? Do they care about their teachers?* I realized then, if you disrupt the "cash cow," you'd be attacked. Now it made sense.

There was a brief pause after the last testimony, in which attorneys and the judge reviewed the evidence that would be sent to the jury. There were 170 pieces of evidence, which I thought should have been halved. The judge and the attorneys worked out jury instruction, which included defamation of character, interfering with contractual relationships, and loss of consortium. Once they got that straightened out, the judge would have the jury go out for deliberations. There were only two hours in the day left, so I figured we would go into the next day, which was Friday.

The judge gave the jury instructions on how to proceed. If there were any questions, they could give it to the court officer to relay to the judge. The judge would answer in the courtroom to clarify any questions that the jury had in front of both the plaintiff and the defendants. After the judge finished giving instructions, he was ready to dismiss the jury for deliberations, and we all had to stand for when they left the room. Strangely enough, I saw Dr. Hal reach across our bench to try to get the attention of one of the jury members to hand him a piece of paper. We all stopped him and looked toward the judge, who either didn't see what was going on or allowed it. The good thing was Dr. Hal wasn't able to give the paper to the juror, but something was definitely going on here.

After the jury left, the judge said that he would let the court officer announce when the jury reached a verdict. After the judge left the courtroom, we walked out into the hallway to start the waiting game. My supporters stayed with me, and we all moved to the other side of the hallway to be away from the city officials. The city officials only stayed for about fifteen minutes and then they all left. It was just my supporters, my attorney, and I left waiting for the verdict. It wasn't a long wait because two hours went fast. Before anyone realized, 4 o'clock came upon us, and we were called back into the courtroom. The judge reentered the room, and the jury entered shortly after that. The judge told all of us that we would pick up with the jury deliberation at 9 a.m. tomorrow. So we left for the day with more questions than answers, such as, WHAT IS TAKING THE JURY SO LONG?

After we left the courthouse, I went to see my sister, brother-in-law, and niece who were staying at the hotel behind the courthouse. We discussed what would happen if I didn't win the case (which I had no clue at the time), as well as the pieces of my life I had to reconstruct whether I won or loss. Whatever the outcome was, I knew I had big decisions to make. I did know for sure that I was going to write this book. The city attorney had said to the jury, "Mr. Pepi is loaded with conspiracy theories." These weren't theories, but reality. I knew this whole courtroom case was a sham, and every one of the city officials was a part of it. After my discussion with my sister and her family, I said goodnight and told them I'd see them in the morning.

It was November, and the air had turned crisp yet refreshing. We made it back to the courtroom, hopefully for the last time. We all met in the hallway and worked our way to the judge, who gave more instructions to the jury. The jury went back to deliberate. We made the last settlement offer in the hallway after the judge left the bench. This offer was very low, but at this point, I would have taken anything. I really wanted to see if they would take it. They didn't, which made me believe that something was wrong here, from the court losing my paperwork for summary judgement, to the newspaper that wouldn't announce the trial, to the note the superintendent tried to hand the juror, to the relationship ties to the courthouse by the city. It didn't feel right, and I was very suspicious of this whole case.

My attorney and I spoke to each other during the wait, and he told me that he would try to give me a recommendation when I applied for jobs. He said that I should not go back to that school system, and he felt they wouldn't even accept me anyway. As we headed for lunch, we decided to eat at Uno's, which was attached to the hotel where my sister and her family were staying. My attorney came with me and my supporters. We sat there and tried to talk about anything except the trial. The Red Sox winning the World Series was a good start. Just after we placed our order, the city officials and the city lawyer entered the restaurant. My heart was in my mouth, but I tried not to look at them as they entered the room.

I could hear them laughing and carrying on like they were out on a Saturday night with a bunch of friends. It aggravated me a bit, but I tried not to give them the time of day. It did seem to me that this was planned, and it looked like it didn't bother them at all. Did they know something we didn't? *No*, I thought, *it's my mind playing tricks, or is it?* I couldn't eat because all I cared about was finishing this trial and trying to put these three weeks of hell behind me. All I did was pray for God to give me strength whether I won or not.

After lunch, I dismissed myself and started to walk back to the courthouse. I told everyone that I would meet up with them, but I just wanted to be alone. The walk back in the crisp air felt good, and it gave me time to think. I was way behind on my bills, and my electricity had been turned off multiple times. With my wife missing three weeks of pay, I didn't know what we would do. If I won, the case still might be appealed, and I would have more money tied up in the courts. If I lost, well, I didn't want to think that because when I did, my heart went into palpitations. I finally reached the courthouse and went through the metal detector for hopefully the last time.

I entered the elevator and went up to the third floor. I was the only one there, so I went down to the end of the hallway and sat there deep in thought. My worries about my reputation, my character, and my profession were starting to become reality. I started to become anxious, the feeling I had endured for the past six years. The Pepi name has been in the city since 1919, and I was a third-generation Pepi. I said to myself, *How dare they treat me this way?* My father and grandfather had made the Pepi name synonymous with integrity, and all of a sudden, this reputation was destroyed.

I started to break into a cold sweat, but before it got too bad, my wife and my family came up to me to see if I was okay. I didn't want to worry them, so I got up to join the rest of my supporters. It was now 2:30 p.m., and the court officer came out of the courtroom and said the jury had come up with a verdict. Life stopped for a minute and I thought, *Everything I have been fighting for is coming down to a jury decision.* As we walked in, I noticed right away that the city officials were missing. The city attorney was the only person on their side. Everyone who had supported me throughout the trial was with me. The moment seemed to last hours and waiting for the judge was excruciating.

The court officer entered the room and told everyone to rise as the judge came in and placed himself at the bench. Then the court officer went into the jury chambers to walk the jury into the courtroom. As they filed in, I observed that the jury was different. Every juror had an indescribable look on their face. They did not make eye contact with me, and this started to worry me. I didn't like it, and I didn't feel confident about the outcome before the verdict was even read. We all sat down, then the judge asked, "Did the jury come up with a verdict?"

The jury foreman answered back, "Yes, Your Honor." The jury foreman handed the verdict slip to the court clerk, who turned and handed it to the judge. The judge read the slip then handed it back to the clerk to read the verdict out loud. We all had to rise again as the clerk read the verdict. It was now the time to see my whole life within a verdict. The continuous bullying by the school district and the treatment I received that made my life hell all came down to this verdict. *Please God*, I thought. *Get me through this*.

The clerk started reading through the five counts listed against the city and its officials. From defamation to loss of consortium, he read "not guilty" for each. Each of the city officials got away with the torment, torture, and destruction of my name. As I listened to each verdict, I was in shock. I don't even know what happened in that courtroom afterwards, since I was not listening. I looked at both my attorney and the city attorney for their reaction. My attorney had his back to me, but as clear as day, I saw the city attorney's expressionless face. After the judge dismissed the jury, he left the courtroom. My supporters left for the hallway, but I stayed behind.

I sat there and felt like I had lost in double overtime, a one-point loss that knocked us out of the playoffs. I looked at my attorney, who put his arms up and said, "What happened?" to the clerk, who gave no response. My attorney got up and started to walk toward the door to leave the courtroom, but before he did he went up to the city lawyer, who was doing paperwork, to shake hands. My attorney said, "Good job," and without looking up or standing up, the city attorney raised his hand sheepishly and said, "Thanks." That was strange. More questions entered my mind. Why were the city officials not there for the verdict? Why did the city attorney act that way? Why didn't the clerk say anything when my attorney asked him what happened? Was it a conspiracy? Was I dealing with corruption? I thought my attorney did an excellent job. Where was the newspaper? It didn't add up.

As we walked out of the courtroom and into the hallway, the news media was finally there. A reporter stopped my lawyer and me for a comment. My lawyer gave his comments first, and before I gave my comment, I told to the reporter, "Make sure you're good to me." After I gave my comments, my attorney told me I shouldn't have said that to the reporter. I told him that I knew this newspaper and that they were biased toward the city. It didn't matter anyway because the headline the next day read, "Court Clears the Urbanville School Department of Defaming Ex-Athletic Director." With this article, plus the two previous articles about my lawsuit against the school system, who would hire me, especially being fifty-four and at the top of the pay scale?

My wife and my support team relayed some strange comments after my interview, which supported my suspicion of conspiracy. Two jury members apparently walked past them while the other jury members walked away from my supporters. One jury member said loud enough for everyone to hear, "They were not going to bully us." Now, what did they mean by that? What happened in the jury room? The longer we were, there the stranger it got.

My friend Robert came to the courtroom after he got out of work to see what the verdict was, and as soon as he found out, everyone was crying and very upset. We all talked in the hallway for a while and said goodbye to my attorney. We all thanked him for his service. After another ten minutes, we started to walk to the elevator and leave the courtroom. Before we went out of the revolving door at the main entrance of the court, another strange incident happened. Stan Rush, a city council member, was about to walk through the entrance. But when he saw that we were leaving, he turned around and walked out. I later found out that he was the brother-in-law of the district attorney, Bob Lately. As we headed toward the car, this event left a bad taste in my mouth. I felt that I had been taken to the cleaners with a corrupt organization. There were too many coincidences. Again, I do not believe in coincidences. The only question I had was, *Where do I go from here?*

# 13

# THE AFTERMATH, ROUND 2

This whole court case put me in a financial mess. Even though my attorney submitted a motion to reconsider, I still had to find a way to catch up on my bills, and without my wife receiving pay for at least another week, it had become a daily struggle. It was even more stressful now that we were coming up on the holidays. We didn't know how we would pay for food, let alone other items you needed for the holidays. You can only borrow so much, and if I did, how was I going to pay the money back? I would eventually have to think about what I was going to do for my future. My attorney said that the city would never take me back since I sued them. My life was on the edge, and even though I was completing my doctoral degree, I still needed an income. I couldn't stay on workers' comp forever.

It was ironic that I had been thinking about workers' comp when my workers' comp attorney called me. He let me know that my benefits would end by December 31, and he wanted to know if I wanted him to reapply. I told my attorney that I was fifty-four years old, but I wanted to go back to work. He warned me that because of the lawsuit, the city would not take me back. I thought about what he said, and then I thought, *What do I have to lose?* My name was already ruined, and I would not be able to work anywhere else. I decided to email Aisha to ask if I could return.

Surprisingly, she emailed me back almost immediately to say that I could start in the New Year. I couldn't believe it. Why did she accept me back? As much as I was happy to go back, my antennas shot up, almost to the point where I started to second guess myself. My wife and my children, especially my new daughter-in-law, didn't want me to go back. As I told them, what else could I do? I was too young to retire, and there was no future collecting workers' compensation. Besides, I was looking to finish my doctoral degree, and they would not bully me going back to work. At least, that's what I thought.

On the first day of school, I was greeted at the central office by one of the liaisons, Sandy, who was helping Marsha. (Again, I was never afforded the same help. Budget cut? Wow!) It seemed that Marsha wouldn't want to see me, since she was the one who took my position. Sandy was considered the physical education/health liaison, but she was only licensed in health. Again, that seemed to be the norm in this school system. I just wanted a paycheck every other week and to take care of the children who were in my care. Whatever they did in the school system, I was not going to worry about it. I knew what the system stood for, and I wanted nothing to do with them. I didn't know what I was getting into, but I know it placed a strain on my wife when I left for work every day. She warned me, "Watch your back." It wasn't easy, but I knew she was right.

Having to go to the central office, or "the Evil Empire" as I called it, was very stressful because of their bullying attitudes, fabricated stories, and attempts to destroy anyone who disagreed with them. I found that everyone in the building looked at me like I had worn the same clothes for months. I just wanted to grab my schedule not heed to the same talking points and listen to their spiel as if they really cared about me. I needed to leave the building before I threw up. As I was leaving, I did notice I was taking the schedule of a good physical education teacher who was out sick for the rest of the year. All I knew was that I was going to do my best without dealing with the bureaucracy of the system.

I taught at one school on Mondays, Tuesdays, and Wednesdays for half the day. This was a school that had a good reputation for academic excellence. I knew quite a few students' parents from previous years, and I felt comfortable with the staff. The principal was definitely a company girl who never wanted to rock the boat with the school system, but she was effective in pushing the educational objectives to the students. She did hold students, teachers, and staff accountable, and eventually she was granted the deputy superintendent position. The positive part of being at the school was the fact the gym was away from the flow of the school. I also had my own office with a private bathroom.

One Wednesday morning, I was waiting for my last class to show up before I had to travel to my second school. My cell phone rang, and I answered a call from my workers' comp attorney. He asked me how my job search was going, and I told him that I was back to work for the city. He was shocked, and he warned me that this was unusual. He echoed exactly what my wife said, "Watch your back." I agreed and told him I would stay in touch in the future if needed. I thanked him and said I had to go because I heard the children walking into the gym with their teacher.

I arrived in my second school that Wednesday afternoon, and I had to see the principal to get my schedule. I was at this school on Wednesday afternoons, Thursdays, and Fridays. This school was also run very well, but it was smaller, and the school culture was different than the other school. This school was a true neighborhood school, whereas the other school bused in a lot of their students. This principal had a unique way of disciplining students, a system he wanted the whole staff to participate in. I knew this principal because we had developed relationship when I was an administrator and we had a circle of friends in common.

I was waiting to see which administrator was assigned to evaluate me. The principal was chosen. When I was an administrator, I did all of the evaluations of the physical education staff as well as my other duties. When Marsha took over, she told the principals to evaluate the physical education teachers. Amazing, since she had more help than I ever had. When the principal and I greeted each other, it was like he didn't even know me, and in an abrupt tone he said, "I am busy, wait for me downstairs." I felt like he treated me as a hostile employee.

I went down to the basement and I noticed tables with multiple computers on them against the wall. I found a little space on one of the tables, took out my plan book, and started to do lesson plans for my other school. It had to have been at least an hour before he came downstairs looking for me. He saw me and right away accused me of being on the computer. "First thing you did wrong!" he said. "You never go on a computer unless you have permission from me!"

Right away I defended myself. "I was not on the computer!" I said, "I was doing my lesson plans!" He looked at me and said, "Oh, okay," and we both went upstairs to his office. As soon as we entered his office, he closed the door. He started in on me about the dos and don'ts in "his school." He mentioned that he would be evaluating me, and he would submit the evaluation to the school department. It seemed that he thought to treat me as trouble, and it was his responsibility to handle it. Before he continued any further, I told him that I wasn't just anybody working here and that I knew everything about the operation of this district. I knew he had a past of bullying teachers, and after what I had been through, I was not going to let him intimidate me.

He stopped in his tracks, looked at me, and started to laugh. I proceeded to tell him that I was on the verge of receiving my doctorate degree, and I made sure that he understood that what the school district did to me was not going to happen again. After that, for the six months that I was there, we got along just fine. I even enjoyed teaching there. The teachers as well as the children respected me, which made me feel at home. The beginning of the week may have been stressful at one school, but I ended the week on a positive note.

The rest of the school year went by pretty fast. I was scheduled to be there until June. The highlight of the school year was having the opportunity to organize students for the Mini-Olympics. The Mini-Olympics has been run by the city for many years. The physical education teachers chose the twelve best athletes to compete out of the forty-plus elementary schools in the system. Six girls and six boys would participate in running races and jumping events. Since there were numerous schools competing, it was very difficult to win the event. Going to this event, I had to face many of the politicians who never helped me, as well as Marsha, who ran the event, and the other physical education teachers who were wondering what had happened to me. For me, it still was very awkward to have gone from running the event back in 2007 to having to step back, knowing that the person who was now in charge was far less qualified than me.

To make it easier on me and to reduce my stress, I hung around with two physical education teachers who were close to me and who believed in me. One of those teachers was my son's former football coach at Westly High School, Tim. He and I always had a good relationship and did a lot of joking around. He would bust my chops, and I would bust his, but it was all in good fun. During the Mini Olympics he joked that he shouldn't stand next to me, in case a sniper tried to shoot and missed. He told me that I was the legend of the city, and that forty years later people would still hear about John Pepi. I laughed and so did he, but we knew that the city did not like me because I stuck up for myself.

As it was getting toward the end of the day, Tim came up to me and said, "I think your school is going to win the whole thing." He was right! During the last race, one of my students lost by inches. We ended up in second place out of the whole city, which was the first time the school placed so high. I went back to the school just before dismissal to tell the principal, and he was excited. He announced it to the school. At the end of the week, when I went back to the school for classes. We had a team picture with the children who participated, along with the principal and me. I didn't lead on what I was about to do, but I went out and purchased, with my money, frames for the pictures so that each child received one. I also gave one to the school, so it could be hung in the trophy case. And, of course, I kept one for myself.

Again, I wanted the children to have a positive experience and feel like they had accomplished something. I wasn't out to show anybody "look what I have done," because I took a step back and let the children share the limelight among their peers. I don't know what the future held for these children, but I did know that I cared for them, showed them respect, and became a positive mentor so that they could move forward in their lives. Even though I had a very negative experience with the city, I NEVER took it out on the children. In my profession I believed that it was all about the children. This was the only saving grace and kept my sanity, but it was short-lived. Remember, the administrators at the central office still had their hidden agenda, and even though I was invited back to teach, I never trusted them.

In summer 2014, I received a notice that I would be going to three schools for the new school year, which was unheard of for a veteran teacher like myself. That was usually reserved for younger teachers. But it didn't matter, I was collecting a paycheck and teaching children, which was my passion. On Monday and Tuesday, I was teaching in a small neighborhood school, which I thought was pretty good until I met the principal. She used to work for the central office and had plenty of political clout. She used that power to fire or harass any teacher that she personally didn't care for. For example, she found out two the teachers on the principal hiring committee didn't vote for her. Obviously, this information was leaked by central office, and she bullied those two teachers until one left from the stress and the other she fired. She replaced them with friends of hers, so she could develop a stranglehold over the school. When I first met her, she showed no personality. Right away, I had my guard up.

The school was so small that in the wintertime I had to use an all-purpose room, which was also used for a cafeteria and school concerts, for physical education classes. The problem was that this room was right near the main office. I became very friendly with the custodian of the school and the cafeteria workers. No matter what school I was in, I respected the custodian, cafeteria workers, and the secretary. I believed if you wanted to know everything about the school, you should ask them and not the principal. I was warned about Judy, the principal, by multiple sources.

I was not afraid of her, and I always gave suggestions to teachers that she bullied. Since I went through the ordeal of being bullied out of my position and into the courtroom, teachers started to encourage me to run for president of the union. I did not think anything of it. All I wanted to do was to keep a low profile, teach, and finish my dissertation so I could graduate with my doctorate degree. What bothered me was this principal was a micromanager with my class, almost to the point that it seemed she did not trust me with children. I knew she couldn't think of anything on her own; she was motivated by the central office. Bullies use *groupthink* when it comes to harassing their targets. Judy fell in line with that ideology in the central office.

On Wednesdays I taught at a school that helped immigrants arriving to this country transition into the public school system. This school didn't bother me because the principal was a good person, and other than the language barrier, the children were eager to learn. The only drawback was there were no facilities at this school. It was tough to teach during inclement weather. The principal of the school did everything he could to make my job easier. I also had a close relationship with the teachers, who were very professional. One of the teachers I had in the kindergarten at Urbanville Central Catholic. I was surprised she remembered me.

On Thursday and Fridays, I ended the week at an underperforming school that had recently installed a new staff and a new principal to improve the school's test scores to prevent the state from taking over. The staff was excellent and really cared for the children. The students were a challenge, but it was rewarding because these children were needy and appreciated what we did. I loved going to this school where the staff and students seem to be working together. The next year, that they achieved their goal of improving test scores. The school made the newspaper, and they had a huge celebration.

At the end of the 2014–15 school year, I had to select a student who excelled in physical education for the year. This student would be awarded during a ceremony outside in the schoolyard. The child they gave the award to had challenges with me at the beginning of the year.

He had come from a severely tough home, but I was not about to give up on him. I gained his trust gradually and gave him plenty of compliments, and I saw his angry look soften over time. Within a couple of months, he even started to smile. I decided that he was going the get the Physical Education Award. When the principal announced his name to receive the award, he was so proud of himself that I even had a lump in my throat. Isn't this what education should be about? We weren't just educating, we were also building children up.

Even though I enjoyed going to my one school on Thursdays and Fridays, I felt unmotivated going to the other school on Mondays and Tuesdays. It wasn't the fault of the children or even the staff, it was the principal, Judy, who I did not trust. She was not a leader but a bully. I believed she lived off making people's lives miserable. Every time I set foot in that building and crossed her path, she didn't even have the audacity to acknowledge me or say hi. I was just getting comfortable, and I was beginning to love teaching again, especially after a tough trial and having my name dragged through the mud. I did not feel right with this principal. I always felt I was good judge of character. Unfortunately, I was right, and on December 7, 2015, my life and my career changed forever. This was the beginning of the deep corruption and bullying that would place me out of the education field.

December 7 started off as any other Monday, but on the bright side, there was no snow on the ground, and I was still able to take the children outside for physical education class. The morning went by fast, and I had my normal recess duty before I finished my last three classes of the day. Things seemed a little bit different when I went out to recess that day. I was in charge of the fourth-, fifth-, and sixth-grade children, but as I scanned the area, I knew there weren't enough teachers to chaperone the 132 children in the schoolyard. Since I was always a stickler for safety in the school, I approached the assistant principal and mentioned it to her. She turned to me and said, "Don't worry, we'll get through it." It still bothered me, but since I was not an administrator, I had no control over the situation.

In this school they had recess first and lunch after, and I was responsible for being at both. After lunch I had a first-grade class, followed by kindergarten class, and I finished the day with third grade. The kindergarten class was always a challenge because there were two children who never followed directions. Fortunately, I had an instructional assistant (IA) who would come with me in case a child took off on me. This was a problem all year long. I even approached the principal about it on numerous occasions, but she would never address the issue. The IA and I would have to watch over twenty-six children. Luckily, class was held in an enclosed area behind the school.

It was a chilly December afternoon, which meant the children had to wear their winter coats. That day we were teaching the class how to catch and kick a ball. I set them up into rows facing each other, and I had enough balls so each child could partner up. As I instructed the children, it was up to the IA to watch over all the children to make sure they were engaged in the activity. I was ten minutes into the forty-minute class when one of the female students turned to me and told me that her partner, a male student, had showed her his privates. I gazed at her with a puzzled look. The children were right in front of me. Nobody had left, and they all had their winter coats on. "Are you sure?" I asked the five-year-old girl. She nodded at me and said, "Yes."

Immediately, I went into mandated-reporter mode. I used my training from the school system and what I'd learned from the many hours of courses for my master's in educational leadership. I sat the students down and asked my IA to collect the equipment. She looked at me and whispered, "What's wrong?" I quickly responded, "I will tell you later." I then lined up the students with the little girl next to me and the boy next to the IA, who was at the back of the line.

We started to walk to the doorway of the school, which had an outdoor entrance into the classroom. I knocked at the door hoping the teacher was in the classroom. The kindergarten teacher did come to the door, and with a perplexed look on her face she asked, "Is everything okay?"

"No," I quickly responded as I ushered the children into the classroom and told them to have a seat. I explained to the teacher what happened, and we both agreed that it had to be reported to the school as well as the district. We instructed the IA to watch over the children while we left to fill out reports. The IA still was baffled as to what happened, but we didn't have much time to discuss the situation because we felt it was important to take care of the situation immediately. I knew from reading plenty of materials on five- and six-year-old children that this sort of action isn't sexual but more motivated by curiosity. Even still, it was important to report the event.

The kindergarten teacher and I went down to the main office. I wasn't aware at the time that Judy was out of school all day long. There were so many speculations about where she was, but it was none of my business. The secretary told me she would get a hold of the assistant principal after I told her what was going on. The assistant principal came right away. She was young and inexperienced in her position. This school was very small, so she was a teacher/assistant principal, but she was clueless about filling out paperwork. Since I had been an administrator before, I was able to help her fill out the forms. I also told her that the parents had to be notified so that the school could cover all its bases.

I had to involve the school adjustment counselor because her job was to take care of children and their families during crisis situations. The problem was that she was close friends with the principal, who I didn't trust. The school adjustment counselor was also arrogant in dealing with the assistant principal, but I knew she had to be brought in on this situation. I showed the assistant principal how to fill out the paperwork, and between the school adjustment counselor and the assistant principal, they decided to call the parents themselves. I took a step back and let them do what they needed to do.

I was still standing in the office. The school adjustment counselor told me that they spoke with the little boy's grandfather but could not get a hold of the little girl's mother. The assistant principal said she would see the mother when she picked up the girl from her usual afterschool program. I volunteered to stay, but the school adjustment counselor and the assistant principal told me that I was all set. I repeated myself because I wanted to make sure the parent knew what had happened, but they told me that I did a great job and I was all set. So I left for my last class of the day.

When my class ended, and after I did my duty of dismissing children to their proper bus line, I went to the office to ensure that they didn't need me. I asked one more time, but again, they told me I was all set. At this point, I thought everything was handled. I didn't realize until later that I was being set up. As I walked out of the building and headed to my car to go home, I had an uneasy feeling. *Was it in my head,* I thought, *or was I being too critical of this simple situation? Well, I followed protocol, so why should I worry?* The problem was, I wasn't dealing with honest people or an honest school system. I had let my guard down, and I was about to get a huge bite from the snake called the Urbanville Public Schools.

On December 8, I went to school like any other day. I said hi to the secretary, signed in, and went outside to fulfill my duty in the schoolyard. When I walked outside the door, the assistant principal was crying. I asked her what was wrong, and she proceeded to tell me that the principal yelled at her because we did not follow proper protocol with the children yesterday. I assured her that we followed the proper protocol and not to worry. I didn't think anything of it until after my first class was completed.

During the second period of the day, I had a planned prep and decided to relax in the teachers' lounge. I knew there would be nobody in there and it would be a nice, quiet place for me to relax. I normally do preparation work but with two and a half weeks left before Christmas break, I thought taking a rest for my mental health would be best. I wasn't there more than two minutes when the music teacher joined me. We talked about what we were going to do during the two-week break. My plans were to drive my son Anthony back to California with a car he purchased in Massachusetts. She thought it was exciting, but our conversation was cut short when the door to the teachers' room swung open abruptly and so forcefully that it sounded like a football team breaking out of the locker room before the big game. It was the principal, and she looked like she was going to bite someone's head off.

"YOU! GET INTO MY OFFICE NOW!" she shouted. The whole room shook, and the music teacher put her head down as if frightened that she would be next. I knew what this was about, and I wasn't going to be intimidated by this bully. I had seen how she treated other staff members, and to be perfectly honest, I didn't know how she still had a job. Especially as a principal of a school. Anyway, I went to her office.

I waited until she returned with the IA, and the both of us sat in front of her desk. We sat in low seats while she placed herself in the higher chair behind her desk. She was psychologically trying to gain advantage over us, so we would cave to her antics. As soon as she sat down, her rant began. I had a small idea what about was going on, which had to be from the incident report I filled out, but what she did next broke every human right. Her mannerisms were demeaning, and her tone was accusatory. After what the city put my family through over the years, I was ready.

"WHAT THE HELL HAPPENED IN YOUR PHYSICAL EDUCATION CLASS?" She said in a loud, accusatory voice.

"What are you talking about?" I responded as the IA sat quietly, fearful to speak.

"YOUR CLASS WAS OUT OF CONTROL. CHILDREN WERE RUNNING AROUND NAKED, AND THEY WERE INAPPROPIATELY TOUCHING ONE ANOTHER!" As I listened to her rant, I was thinking, *What is her angle?* I knew the children were right in front of me. What was she talking about? *Wait,* I thought, *is this an attempt at revenge by the city after I sued them?* At this point my blood was boiling, but I had to keep cool. If I didn't, they had me.

"Obviously, this is a disciplinary meeting," I said firmly. "As far as I am concerned, this meeting is over because you're violating my Weingarten Rights." I knew from studying educational law that I had to have legal or union representation at any disciplinary meeting, and I had a right to stop the meeting. I could even walk out after telling her that she was in violation without being insubordinate.

She didn't even stop to take a breath. At this time, she was trying to bully me into admitting that this unrealistic, false situation occurred under my watch. *Does she think I'm stupid?* I got up from my seat and told her that I wasn't being insubordinate, but that I was leaving her office. Again, she violated my rights and kept talking. I walked out with the IA and didn't look back. I felt she was playing "gotcha," and I was not having it. I only had a few hours left in the day, and then I wouldn't be back to the school until next Monday. I informed the IA not to talk about it, and we would see what happens.

The next week came up quick. When I entered the school on Monday, I saw a woman sitting in the main office. She didn't look familiar to me, and I knew she was not a parent. She was young, like she was just out of college. After I signed in, I walked to the all-purpose room and saw the custodian, who told me the woman was from the Department of Children and Family (DCF). *That's strange,* I thought, *I wonder what's going on.* The custodian was always good to me, and he was my eyes and ears when it came to this principal.

I, for one, was not a fan of her antics I saw through my observation of the school. The former assistant principal at the school was demoted because this principal didn't want any competition. The way she was demoted was humiliating because she was the sixth-grade teacher, and the staff as well as the students knew that she was not the assistant principal anymore. She probably hired the young assistant principal thinking she could be easily manipulated. It was all about the power.

Then there was the third-grade teacher who clearly had control over a very tough group of children, at least that's what I saw every time I went into her classroom. This teacher was on the selection committee to pick a new principal at the school, and the principal later found out that this teacher didn't vote for her. After a year, the principal decided to bring one of her friends to teach third grade and move this teacher to second, even though she didn't have the license to teach second grade. After she made the move, she was placed on a resource team, which is the last step before being fired. She had seventeen years behind her and all of a sudden, she couldn't teach. This went on for two years, after which time she left because of the stress. When the money ran out, she came back to a flurry of evaluations. The superintendent, Sara, told her she was not babysitting for her and the assistant superintendent observed her thirteen times. Yes, you heard it. THIRTEEN TIMES. After that, she was fired.

This wasn't unusual for this principal, and I never trusted her. She used to work at the central office (the "Evil Empire"), and she had a hidden agenda like the others I had dealt with before. Then the hammer came down, and I was called to the principal's office like I was in elementary school myself, as if I was waiting for my parents because I was a bad boy. As I walked in, she informed me that they filed a 51A (the form that needs to be filed if there is a suspicion that someone either neglected or abused a child) against me. "First of all," I asked, "Who is 'they'?" She would not give me an answer to that question, but I knew I needed a lawyer. I proceeded to tell the principal that I was not going to discuss this any further until the union obtained an attorney to represent me. I turned around and went back to class. The next couple of weeks were awkward and stressful.

Every time I was in that school, she would try to talk to me and set up a meeting with DCF. Every time, I told her I would once the union hired an attorney. I did notice one thing, which was reinforced by the IA, that the principal was conducting interviews with the child who she claimed was involved. It wasn't just two children involved, but now five. I didn't care if it was twenty children, because I knew what went on in the class, and no one had taken off their clothes. Besides, did she have the credentials to interview children without parental consent, or did she have the proper license as a social worker? Given the way she handled the situation, I would say the answer was NO to both questions.

It was now December 17, 2015, ten days after the incident, and still no lawyer. I was driving home from my Thursday school when my phone rang. It was Judy. She wanted me to go in to meet with her, someone from the central office, and my new supervisor, Karen, to discuss how to teach kindergarten students. It was bad enough that she had an administrator stay with me when I taught classes until this point, but now, she had the audacity to teach me how to teach after thirty-four years in the field. My answer was to-the-point, but I did stay as professional as possible, even though she didn't deserve it. After I told her how I felt and I would not meet with them, I called Larry, the union president, and said I was going down to the union building to make sure I had a lawyer. This was when the president started to back step. No sooner I hung up than the attorney who was representing the IA and myself called.

He assured me that everything would be fine, and on December 22 I had an interview with DCF. *That was quick,* I thought. Again, how did I trust the union? I didn't. He told me to show up thirty minutes before the interview to go over my case. *THIRTY MINUTES?* I thought, *THIRTY MINUTES? WOW, AGAIN A CON JOB.* I guess I didn't have any choice at this time, so I agreed. We met at the union hall at 3:30, or at least that was what I expected from the attorney. Instead, the attorney called me to say he was stuck in traffic and would be late. Why not? He showed up at 3:55 p.m., and the DCF investigator was ready to go. The attorney turned to me and said, "I will learn about your case as we go." *Really?* He didn't know anything about my case. The interview didn't go well. I went first, then the IA. Once I entered the room, I felt this cold feeling from the investigator, and she was very upset. I found out in the first five seconds who she was upset with.

The attorney showing up late didn't help, especially when he didn't even know my case or the details behind it. The investigator, who was right out of college, was trying to save the world on her first case and didn't even want to hear what I had to say. I was getting aggravated and knew no matter what I said, she would tell me that was not the way it went. She would tell me that five children were touching one another in my class, and I let them get away with it. She even suggested that I encouraged the behavior. *Are you kidding me?* This was worse than I expected, and I needed protection. If I was going to protect my interest, the union was not the way to go. It all came to a head when the investigator left.

We met with the union lawyer and the IA. I was very upset to begin with, but then the attorney turned to us and stated, "You are dead out of the water." I piped up right away. "Wait, you showed up late, and you didn't even have the courtesy to hear our side of the story. How can you sit there and say that?" He got up from his chair and said, "Time will tell. I have to go." I was so beside myself that I told the IA I would call her, and I left the building.

I rode out the rest of the week because we were now going into the Christmas holiday, and I was out of school until the beginning of January. I tried not to think of this situation and looked to enjoy my family during the holiday season. I told the IA to do the same and we would see what came out of the investigation. To pass the time, I drove cross-country to bring my son's car to his home in Los Angeles. I found it to be the best trip I ever had. It was good bonding time with my son who I only see twice a year, and it felt great to get away from the corrupt Urbanville area.

It took me three days to drive there. People thought I was nuts, but I am in my own little world when I drive, especially seeing the sights and sounds of our beautiful country. When we arrived in LA, I stayed for a day, and on New Year's Eve, I flew back. My oldest son, John, met me at Logan Airport the next morning. It was time to go back to school again, but this time I did it with a pit in my stomach.

That Monday, I went to school expecting the worst, and the school district didn't disappoint me. After signing in, I went to meet the custodian and the cafeteria staff to tell them about my drive to California. I wasn't there for five minutes when the secretary came in to look for me. She handed me a letter to give me a heads up. She stated to me, "This is from DCF and I thought it might be important. Judy received the same letter." Nervous about opening the letter, I didn't want to wait and find out any bad news from the principal. Sure enough, it was bad news. The investigator from DCF sided with the five children, and I had been charged with NEGLECT. *Are you kidding me?* DCF fell under scrutiny multiple times for child abuse and neglect that resulted in children being found dead. Now here I was, a teacher of thirty-four years, charged with neglect. Worse than that, the school district never defended me. Was this their revenge on me?

As soon as I finished reading the letter, I was called to the office. Judy was sitting at her desk and told me about the charges. "You cannot work here with these charges against you." I snapped, "YOU COMPROMISED THE WHOLE INVESTIGATION. YOU AND YOU ALONE ARE RESPONSIBLE TO WHAT HAPPENED TO ME!" I started to walk out of her office, and then I turned to her and continued, "I AM GOING HOME SICK. I AM STRESSED OUT. YOU'VE STRESSED ME OUT, AND YOU HAVE CREATED A HOSTILE WORKING ENVIRONMENT. YOU AND YOU ALONE! I ALSO WILL NOT BE IN TOMORROW AS WELL!"

I started to walk out, and she called my name, "John, I told Walter, and he knows all about this." I yelled out, "GOOD!" I turned around and walked out of the school and to my car. I was shaking, but I knew I had to drive home and let my family know the result. The further I drove, more thoughts poured into my head. *Why did I come back? My children told me not to come back. Why didn't I listen to them? They first falsely accused me of embezzlement, larceny, and fraud. Now, neglect of a child? What is next, abuse, inappropriate touching? They are capable of accusing me of anything. Anything to ruin me. They don't believe in due process. They don't believe in the presumption of innocence until proven guilty. I need another lawyer. More money, more money. When will this end?*

By the time I got home, I was a wreck and couldn't even speak to my wife. I just let her read the letter as steam came out of my ears. I was thinking that my career and my life were over. How could I recover from this? After my wife read the letter and I saw the pain in her eyes,

I took it from her and read the whole letter again. It did say I could appeal the charge, but I was not going to hire the union lawyer. It wasn't even twenty-four hours that I had fired him, but I had to search for an attorney who dealt with DCF. The first thing I thought of was my last attorney who took on my case against the city in 2009. Sure enough, he gave me a name from Newtown, where he was also from. I was able to make an appointment for Wednesday.

In the meantime, I had to do something about the corruption in the City of Urbanville. The politicians from the city routinely looked the other way, so I decided to go to the top. I had helped campaign for the governor, and I figured Governor Stan Parker would look into the DCF debacle. I decided to take my wife with me for support, but she couldn't make it because she had to work and was worried I wouldn't be home on time. So I went alone. I believed this was the right thing to do, but boy, I was wrong. I learned quickly that politicians want you to vote for them, but don't ask them to fix a wrong. That's below their pay grade.

I went to Governor Parker's office at the statehouse three times, and all three times he wasn't available. I decided twice to write a letter, and both times I never received any response. This made me realize that the promises he made to the residents of Massachusetts meant nothing to him, and I will remember this when I go to the polls. My feeling is, if politicians don't look into your situation, it's time to vote them out. All it indicates is that they are full of hot air and just want your vote. This was very disheartening.

After I returned from Boston and the statehouse, my wife asked me how it went. No sooner I was ready to answer than the doorbell rang. I looked at the clock and then back at my wife. It was 1 p.m., and right away I said, "A school system representative is at the door." This was déjà vu. I knew the city's game plan.

Sure enough, Walter was at the door with a letter in hand. Unlike the previous time, the getaway driver was Claire, another former union president who now worked for the human resources department. I knew what the letter said, and I didn't want to hear anymore foolishness from

Walter, so I took the letter and closed the door while he was still talking. I would not give him the time of day. The letter read as follows:

*Dear Mr. Pepi:*

*Effective immediately, you are hereby placed on paid administrative leave for allegations of failure to supervise your physical education kindergarten students, while in your care, at __________ Road School on or about December 17, 2015* **(it actually was December 7, 2015, they didn't even get that right)** *and/or other conduct unbecoming a teacher. The allegation of failure to supervise students while in your care, resulted in a finding of neglect of 5 students by the Department of Children and Families effective December 29, 2015.*

*You are prohibited from discussing these allegations with any Urbanville Public School staff, parent or student, or taking any action that could be considered retaliation. Any violations of these directives will subject you to further disciplinary action up to and including termination.*

*A copy of the allegations is enclosed for your reference. An investigatory meeting will be scheduled once the investigation has been completed.*

*Sincerely,*
*Walter*

After I closed the door, I looked outside, and Walter was standing there wondering what just happened. I opened the letter in the kitchen and read it to my wife, who I thought I would be upset, but it was par for the course. I knew I was dealing with a corrupt organization and after I sued them, they were out for revenge. Walter was always part of the problem and never part of the solution. He liked showing his authority, which included deceptive practices, manipulation, and narcissistic behavior. I knew again that I had a fight on my hands, and this time it wasn't going to be me spending a ton of money and losing the case. It was going to be me fighting fire with fire.

Their assertion that they were going to perform their own investigation raised red flags for me. It was not an investigation to find the truth, but rather an investigation to destroy me. It only took me a week to find out that the IA was not on paid administrative leave, only I was. Right away I needed to put the city back on its heels. After I met with my new attorney, I knew I needed time so I could have my appeal heard through the state. I decided to go to the Massachusetts Commission Against Discrimination (MCAD) to file a discrimination complaint because I was the only one placed on paid administrative leave, and I was the only male teacher on staff.

I didn't need an attorney for this complaint I filed. I decided to represent myself and force the city in a position where they could not fire me. Again, as I stated before, I do not believe in coincidence, but as soon as I filed this complaint, the city placed the IA on paid administrative leave. In the meantime, the custodian of the school called me to make me aware that Judy and Walter approached him. They wanted him to lie to say that he saw the whole thing when he took out the trash. He refused to do so because he was honest and also pointed out that the dumpster wasn't even near where my class had been. When I found this out, I called my attorney.

My attorney, Sara—the new DCF attorney I hired—told me that I should take pictures of the school grounds, so I could use them during the hearing. I was fearful to do so, and I made her aware of it. I knew I could not go on school grounds or they would have me arrested. My children came up with an idea to check Google Earth, which gave a clear picture of the grounds at the school. In the meantime, I was being harassed by human resources to come into the central office for an investigatory meeting. I knew the game plan, and I definitely did not want to be involved in such a matter. I told them repeatedly that I was waiting for my appeal hearing with the state. I made it clear that the investigation that was done by DCF was biased and subjective. Then, on March 11, 2016, I received a letter from Jan, the new director of human resources.

*Dear Mr. Pepi:*

*Please be advised that we have scheduled an investigatory meeting for 1 p.m. on March 17, 2016, in my office to discuss of* (sic) *failure to supervise your physical education kindergarten students, while in your care at __________ Road School on or about December 17, 2015, and/or other conduct unbecoming a teacher. The allegation of failure to supervise students while in your care, resulted in a finding of neglect for 5 students, by the Department of Children and Families effective December 29, 2015.*

*You are prohibited from discussing these allegations with any Urbanville Public School staff, parent or student, or taking any action that could be considered retaliation. Any violations of these directives will subject you to further disciplinary action up to and including termination.*

*Sincerely,*
*Jan*
*Chief Human Resources Officer*

Let me start by saying this particular letter was received on March 18, 2016, a day after we were supposed to meet. This was not the first time they had sent out a letter that I had no chance of responding to. Let's look at the lines within the letter. For example, "discuss your failure to supervise your physical education kindergarten students," which means that I was guilty of not supervising. My understanding was that they believed I neglected children and what Judy said to DCF was true. By stating I performed "other conduct unbecoming a teacher," it was clear they considered me a sick person who committed inappropriate acts as a teacher. What did that mean?

This bothered me as I read the letter, but what really got to me was the fact they wrote, "the allegation of failure to supervise students while in your care, resulted in a finding of neglect." They were not allowing me to go through the hearing process, which is considered by DCF to be a "fair hearing." Where was my due process? Where was my presumption of innocence, which is protected by the Constitution? Furthermore, they infringed upon my First Amendment right of discussing these allegations, and they threatened to fire me if I violated this directive.

This was where I really noticed how the city operated and learned from other victims of bullying in the workplace in different areas of the country. One thing I have learned, which was difficult to swallow, is that the city doesn't care about me, my health, my family, and my financial situation. They were well funded by the city's taxpayers, and they could wait out court cases and financially drain anyone who tries to go against them. They were protected by the municipality, just like the Catholic schools were protected by the cloak.

Knowing this, I was not going to give them the satisfaction of draining me financially again as well as making a mockery of me in the courthouse. My strategy changed, and I believed the best method was to expose them. The problem with exposing these people was I couldn't go to the local news source because they were picky about what they printed, and they always protected the municipality. I had to win in the "fair hearing" because if I didn't, I would have to pay more money to go to court to clear my name or face termination as well as losing my retirement. The stakes were high, but I was ready for them this time.

After sitting down with my attorney, I felt confident and positive about my battle to clear my name. I presented evidence to my attorney, who pointed out that the incident in question never actually occurred in my class—it happened at recess, two periods before my class. The student decided to tell someone, so she told me. No one ever asked the children if this happened in their physical education class, but the five year old was subjected to leading and biased questioning like, "What happened in gym class with all of the touching?" Judy also had a reward system called "White Wallies," so students could buy something at the school store. In other words, she bribed the students to get the answers she was looking for.

At this point, I wanted to get the hearing over with, but my attorney warned me that the hearing was on April 21, 2016, at 9 a.m., and the results would take a long time to come in. Sometimes six months to a year. In the back of my head, I thought, *Who cares, as long as my name is cleared. This means I have to battle the school system, so they don't fire me before I received the results.* The only sad part was that I had to cancel our trip to California to visit our son, but the hearing was more important. I needed this nightmare to go away.

The day of the hearing, I walked into the DCF facility in Urbanville, which was next to the lottery office. Too bad I wasn't going to the lottery office instead of DCF. My wife and I showed up early, and we met the IA in the lobby. She was noticeably upset, but she felt a little better in our presence. Ten minutes later, our attorney showed up, and then it became a waiting game. We sat there and listened to babies cry, which made us feel terrible. We watched fathers having visitation with their children and the ugly scene of boyfriend and girlfriend fighting over custody of their child. Sitting there and watching this, I started to ask myself, *Why am I here? I spent thirty-four years of my life protecting children. Why am I here?* This made my skin crawl, and the city was to blame for us being here. *HOW DARE THEY? THEY HAVE NO SHAME!*

At the time of the hearing, I was recovering from total knee replacement back in March, my dog Sandy was sick and later diagnosed with cancer, and I was trying to clear my name from this situation that I never created. Once the hearing officer showed up, my wife stayed in the lobby, and the IA, my attorney, and I proceeded to the hearing room. When I walked into the room, the hearing officer greeted everyone, and we went through the introductions. She informed us that this hearing was going to be recorded. To my right was the IA, to my left was our attorney, in front of me was the DCF investigator, and next to her was her supervisor. The hearing officer was to my left, at the head of the table.

The process of the hearing allowed the DCF investigator to go first. Before she started, her supervisor said, "I reviewed her investigation, and she did a great job. She was very thorough, and you will see that her investigation will prove that Mr. Pepi and the IA are guilty of neglect." *Wow, that was interesting,* I thought. *Right to the end they stick together.* In

Massachusetts, this department ranks forty-fifth out of fifty states in terms of credibility. Just in the last six months, two children died in their care, and here we are fighting for our name. This was not right, we shouldn't even be here. Talk about a broken system.

The investigator continued with her findings, and while I was listening to this fabrication, I kept on feeling a kick from under the table. Who was kicking me? I rolled back in my chair and looked under the table. It was the investigator. I think she was nervous. I then observed her body language. It was obvious she was a wreck, but from what? I wondered, *Does she know she lied? Does she know that the whole investigation is a sham? What does she know that I don't?* She could also have been nervous because this was her first case and she was already in the hot seat.

When she finished, it was my attorney's turn, and man, now I knew why she was worth the $2,000 I paid to have her represent me. She took the investigative report and poked holes in it like it was Swiss cheese. I was then under oath, and the questions my attorney asked me cleared up a lot of information that should have been cleared by the union attorney and the DCF investigator. No one listened to me, and right from the beginning I was the problem even though I was the one who was the mandated reporter and filled out the proper paperwork. Something was very wrong here, and this whole case didn't pass the smell test. It was the IA's answer to a particular question from my attorney that explained how I was railroaded and that their clear goal was to ruin me.

My attorney asked, "How many times were the students in question pulled from the classroom to be interviewed by the principal?" The IA responded that some of the children had three interviews with the principal and they received white wallies. She then explained it was a reward system for students, who could purchase something at the school store for good behavior. In other words, A BRIBE. Then it was exposed that the DCF investigator never fully interviewed the children, only the principal. My eyes popped out of my head, and I was angry about the information I just received.

The hearing lasted about two hours, and the last question came from the hearing officer. "How long, Mr. Pepi, have you been teaching?"

"Thirty-four years," I replied.

"How many of those years did you teach kindergarten?" she asked.

"Fifteen," I said.

She stopped the recorder and said thank you and before long, the DCF employees were gone. The only ones left in the room were the IA, the hearing officer, my attorney, and myself.

The hearing officer looked at me and said, "I am so sorry for this. This should not have happened, especially to a teacher with the experience you have." I thanked her, and as we walked out, the ladies went first, and the hearing officer went to the lobby and saw my wife. She stopped and said, "Your family must have gone through so much. I am so sorry this has happened to your family." My wife thanked her, and the hearing officer turned to me. She then stated she was going to get the report completed immediately, but it had to go to the higher ups at DCF before I could know the results. *Of course,* I thought. *They all have to justify their jobs. Only in Urbanville, only in Massachusetts.*

Still on paid administrative leave, I knew that the city was going to harass me until the results came in. Their ultimate goal was to terminate me instead of waiting for the results. Between the union and human resources, it was all a scam. I knew they wanted me out, especially when I announced I was running for union president three months before this incident. I received plenty of support because the teachers respected how I had gone the distance with the city previously. It was too obvious that they felt this would be their chance to finally get rid of me. I needed to hold strong and fight back. They were not going to manipulate the situation. I was on to them.

The focus changed from this situation to our dog, Sandy. Ironically, we had adopted her in 2004, two months after I started as the director of physical education and athletics. She was a labrador and golden retriever mix, but she looked more like a yellow lab. She was definitely part of the family and was a lot of fun. She would sleep at the foot of our bed, but during colder winters, she would hop right under the covers. When the situation with the city was at its worst, I felt secure that she was keeping watch over the house. The day that the police came to the door to try to take Sandy, the city knew that was going to hurt us. THEY WERE JUST PURE EVIL. I didn't realize that our days with Sandy were going to end sooner than I thought.

The Saturday after the hearing, we took Sandy to the vet because she couldn't bark and wasn't eating. My sister-in-law, my wife, and I took the trip. As we sat waiting for the vet, I could tell she was a very sick dog. We wanted to pay for X-rays, and when the results came in, our worst nightmare came true. She was loaded with cancer. The vet asked if we wanted to "put her down," but we declined until all four of our children could say their final goodbyes. I would never forget Sandy looking at me wagging her tail, like she was telling us everything would be okay. The drive home was rough, and all three of us filled up with tears.

To make it clear, Sandy was the unofficial support dog for our stress and comfort. She would swim in our pool, play outside, and comfort us when we were depressed after being targeted by the mob. As I thought back, I wondered, *Where did the time go? Sandy's time on earth will soon be over, but what about my children?* Gina was in the sixth grade when everything started. My son John was married, and Mark was now in the working field. How about Anthony? He moved to California, but time for me was flying by. I was fighting a never-ending battle, and there didn't seem any end in sight.

The rest of Saturday, we made Sandy as comfortable as possible. Her heavy breathing kept me up all night, but I couldn't sleep anyway. My best friend was dying, and I felt helpless. When the next day arrived, my daughter Gina went off to work, and we had some company over the house. I could care less who was over because I stayed on the floor with Sandy and petted her over and over again. I would tell her everything was going to be okay. I was praying that she would die that day, so I didn't have to make that terrible, painful decision to put her to sleep. Everybody left except for my sister-in-law. She told me she would help me take Sandy outside to go to the bathroom.

We picked her up and brought her outside. She was shaking and weak, but she managed to walk a short distance, stopped, and sat down. She then collapsed onto the grass. We ran to her, "Sandy! Sandy! Oh my God!" No sooner we got to her side, she already took her last breath. My wife and I were devastated, and tears started to flow. Our baby, our friend, had passed on. We quickly brought her blanket, placed her in it, and brought her inside. My wife fell to the floor bawling her eyes out as I sat there numb.

Our children came to the house, and they all sat there saying their goodbyes. Anthony was on FaceTime and witnessed the whole thing. After what my family had gone through, and Sandy was a part of it, it was like getting punched in the stomach. After our goodbyes, we had to find a place open on Sunday to take Sandy. We found an emergency hospital for pets in Natick, which was about thirty minutes from home. We brought her there, and the staff was great. They placed her on a table in a private room, and we were able to say our goodbyes before they took her away. We were in the room for about an hour. After leaving, my daughter Gina and my son Mark made arrangements for Sandy's cremation. As I write this book, Sandy's urn is on the case behind my desk as a reminder of what our family endured through the evil torment of the corrupt school system.

It was heartbreaking to lose a dog, and if you've had one, you understand what I mean. It was difficult to move forward, especially waiting for the results from DCF. I was told that I won my case from my attorney, but that did not mean anything because the DCF administration had to review the findings to officially clear me. In the meantime, the city continued to send me emails and letters about going to an investigatory meeting. In a nice way, they were moving to terminate me. I kept pushing the meeting off, so the city decided to use their operative, the teachers' union. I would battle Wendy, the executive secretary, and Steve, the new union president, on the same issue. The union even told me that it was a Weingarten Rights meeting, but it was another smoke screen. The principal did violate my rights, but the meeting was not about that. I read the letter from human resources and Weingarten Rights were not mentioned, which only means they would do anything to get me to this meeting.

The new superintendent, Sara, who I knew from her days as the assistant principal at Eastly High School when I was the director, I assumed would be on my side during this investigation and would see this was a fabricated case. Besides, when she was principal at Eastly, and she seemed to be the type who wanted to find out the truth. I also knew her husband because I played football for him at St. William CCHS, but when I received this letter on June 16, 2017, I had a different opinion of her. To me, it looked as if she believed the human resources department and the union. which I am sure that Jan, the new director of human resources, whom I never met or knew, was filled in by her assistant Walter because he had been the disciple of Aisha, who had left for Urbanville State University. Another political move.

When I received the letter, I could not have the union walk into this meeting with me because I knew (like in years past) that they did not have my best interest at heart. I had to hire an attorney, and I went back to the same attorney who ran my case back in 2013. The letter was very disturbing, and it read as follows:

*Re: Intent to Dismiss*

*Dear Mr. Pepi:*

*Pursuant to M.G.L. c. 42, I am notifying you of the district's intent to dismiss you from your position as a Teacher with the Urbanville Public Schools for reasons of incompetency, inefficiency, failure to satisfy teacher performance standards, failing to properly supervise students for whom you were responsible or to ensure their supervision by others, and other just cause. Specifically, on December 7, 2015* **(they finally got the date right)** *you failed to maintain a safe learning environment for a class of early childhood students at the* _________ *Road School and, as a result, some of the students were alleged to* *have been victims of inappropriate touching of their peers. The Department of Children and Families initially screened in the report of neglect filed by the District and subsequently supported the allegations of neglect charges against you in a report dated January 2016.*

**Now isn't that interesting. They were going to dismiss me without due process and not wait for the state to investigate further after I appealed the decision by DCF. Incompetency? Where? Inefficiency? Where? I did my job by reporting an incident that a child brought to my attention, and I followed state and local protocols to report a situation. How about teacher performance standards? Where did that come from? The only time I received a poor evaluation was in 2007 when the system painted me as a terrible administrator to justify replacing me. Even my last evaluation was perfect. Ahh, that's right, back to supervision of the students, where Judy fabricated the whole situation and went around saying that there was inappropriate touching. You remember, Judy had to interview children three times to get the answer she wanted. The kicker was the "other just cause" part. In other words, let's throw mud on the wall and see what sticks. The letter continued:**

*Since that time, the district has tried repeatedly to hold an investigatory meeting with you so that you would have an opportunity to answer questions pertaining to our investigation. You have either canceled each meeting or not attended. Through your union, the Educational Association of Urbanville, and in direct correspondence with me, you had requested postponements of the meeting due to your contention that the DCF report was "not complete;" however, you have failed to provide us with any evidence indicating that the case was incomplete or that you remain in an appeals period with the DCF. The information that has been provided to us seems to indicate that the investigation was, in fact, complete; however, in a good faith effort to allow you to exercise your rights through the DCF investigation we have on multiple occasions deferred the meeting while you have remained out on paid administrative leave. To be clear, the findings of DCF are certainly germane to this matter, although they alone do not form the basis of the District's intent to dismiss you from your employment. Your conduct, as alleged, constitutes grounds to support your termination independent of any finding by DCF.*

**They don't get it; or do they? Their whole investigation had nothing to do with good intent, and it didn't matter what the "fair hearing" indicated. The last sentence said it all, "Your conduct, as alleged, constitutes grounds to support your termination independent of any finding by DCF." Forget the rest of the letter, forget the "fair hearing." This said a mouth full. Jan had lied, the union had lied, and the principal had lied. Obviously, they were not looking for the truth. This was revenge, and they wanted me gone. But the letter didn't stop there. The third paragraph read:**

*On July 20, 2016, I sent to you the final letter notifying you that the meeting had been rescheduled to August 8, 2016. On the morning of August 8, 2016, at 7:42 I received an email from you notifying me that you would not be attending the meeting which was scheduled for 9:00 a.m. I responded to you that the meeting was not being canceled and that we expected you to attend. You did not attend. I notified you that the district would be moving forward after multiple attempts to provide you with the opportunity to provide information and/or answer questions. Despite the passage of time, you have not provided any update to the District regarding the status of your appeal of the DCF findings. Given that you have repeatedly declined opportunities offered by the District to participate in an investigatory meeting, the District must now proceed without your input at the investigatory stage. However, in accordance with the provisions of Mass. G.L. c. 71, Section 42, a meeting with the Superintendent on this matter has been scheduled for June 23, 2017, at 10:00 a.m. in the office of the Superintendent of Schools at 20 Irving Street. At this meeting, you may be represented by counsel or other representative, and you may present information pertaining to the basis for the decision and your status. Documents supporting these allegations are included herewith.*

*Sincerely,*
*Jan*

I'm reprinting the contents of the letter to show the intent of the school district. This is the kind of manipulation, conspiracy, bullying, abuse, and corruption that has been done to me over the last eleven years. As the years go by, I realized that I wasn't the only person who endured this behavior. My choice was to fight back. After reading this letter, I contacted my former attorney and set up a time to meet with him. We then prepared for the meeting on June 23, 2017, which I referred to as a witch hunt. I was ready, but again, I had to spend more money on attorneys. It was going to cost me $4,400 to prevent me from getting terminated.

The day of the meeting, I met my attorney in front of the central office building, and we both entered the front door. After signing in we went upstairs to the first floor, and around the corner was the superintendent's office. We went inside and were greeted by two secretaries. One of them picked their head up, and we announced ourselves. We were told to sit down and that the superintendent will be ready shortly. It was an awkward feeling sitting in the superintendent's office. The last time I had been there was for the last grievance hearing back in 2008.

While waiting, I couldn't believe who showed up: the two union representatives, the executive secretary, Wendy, and the union president, Steve. They came in like nothing happened and they were my best friends. I introduced them to my attorney, and they started with small talk. It was a very uncomfortable situation as we waited for the superintendent. Five minutes later, the secretary announced that the superintendent would see us now.

As we walked into the superintendent's office, I looked around the room and I decided to play politician by walking around the long table to greet everyone. I knew by their reactions that I made them nervous. I shook hands with Walter, who I called "the delivery boy" since he kept coming to my house with toxic letters. He didn't know how to handle me and was very uncomfortable in my presence. I then approached a lady standing next to Walter, and I didn't recognize her at all. I asked her name, and she answered that she was Jan, the director of human resources. I acknowledged her and stated that it was nice finally meeting her. I thought, *I've never met the lady, how does she have any knowledge of me as well as my teaching ability?* Yet she wanted to terminate me. When I said, "It's nice to finally meet you," she felt small and knew that I knew she had no clue about me. There was a better way of getting to know someone by not sending them fabricated letters of unprofessional behavior and so on, especially wanting to terminate me. I think that is a little over the top.

Finally, I shook hands with the school department attorney, Brendon, who knew me really well from other lawsuits, and finally, Sara, the superintendent. After our greetings, it was time for me to sit down and prove my case was fabricated. At this point, I was thinking, This meeting will be very interesting.

My attorney started with the same information that my DCF attorney used during my "fair hearing." We used the Goggle Earth view of the school and my testimony, which explained the situation very well. We used the custodian's affidavit and explained how this couldn't have happened during my physical education class. Sara stopped my attorney and said, "We don't have any of these documents," as she stared at Walter sitting across the room. I looked over at Walter, who had his head down as his face was as red as a strawberry. Brendon and the superintendent asked my attorney for copies of these documents, which my attorney agreed to.

After the secretary came back with the copies, Brendon asked for the union representatives, my attorney, and myself to wait outside while they talked in private. As we stepped out into the hallway, all I could hear was yelling from inside the superintendent's office. We were only supposed to step outside for a few minutes, but it ended up being twenty minutes. While we were out in the hall, I kept bumping into principals and teachers I knew, and it was getting embarrassing waiting in front of the superintendent's office. They knew that I hadn't been in school for almost two years. Then, all of a sudden, the noise stopped. Brendon came to the door and told us we could come in.

As I walked into the room, there was a strange feeling in the air. I looked over and saw Walter with his head down, like he had been scolded for taking the last cookie out of the cookie jar. The school attorney spoke first as soon as we sat down. "The district will keep you on paid administrative leave until we get the results of the 'fair hearing' by DCF," he said. We all stood up, I thanked everyone, and we walked out of the office. As I was talking to my attorney, he felt it went well. I wasn't too sure because of the recent past. I was skeptical, but I had a right to be. As we parted ways, I thanked my attorney and went to my car.

Before I left, I called my wife to let her know everything was fine for now. But the last thing that bothered me was when my attorney told me that he would be getting me back to work. I thought to myself, *I don't want to go back to work.* I knew at the time the school system would find something else that would make things worse. My thoughts were all over the place after that meeting: *I am always going to be a target. If they don't get me now, they will get me later. These people are capable of fabricating any story. What's it going to be next, "I saw Mr. Pepi touch a student inappropriately," or a teacher claiming that I touched her? Then what, jail time? I couldn't take that chance. I* had *to get out of the school system, but how?*

I had to be patient and wait for the results of the "fair hearing" before I started to make any decisions. At least they didn't bother me, except once in a while the union would ask if I had heard anything. On November 27, 2017, I received an email from my DCF attorney that she received a decision dated November 22, 2017, the day before Thanksgiving. It was what I had been waiting for. When I printed out the decision, it cleared me from all charges as well as the IA. I was excited and wanted to let the union know. When I called, they told me that they also received a copy and they would get back to me about my position. I figured I wouldn't be reinstated until after the first of the year, so as not to disrupt the schools. That would give me time to figure out how I would leave the school system.

Christmas came and went. New Year's came and went. There was no response until I received an email from human resources notifying me that they had extended my paid administrative leave until January 31, 2018. What's that all about? Now I started thinking that they were up to something. I had felt this before, and they know how to play dirty. I contacted my new attorney who I had hired after the June meeting and expressed what my concerns were. He told me to get a final settlement from them and retire on June 30, 2018. I thought it was a good idea. My attorney sent the superintendent's office a letter of my intension and let them know I did not want to come back after January 31, 2018. He expressed in the letter that the school department, my attorney, and I set up a final settlement to move toward retirement.

Two weeks later, I received a letter in the mail from Jen stating that "The superintendent accepted your resignation." *What?* I thought, *I never resigned!* Then it continued by saying, "You can collect unemployment and your health insurance will be cancelled in March." *Now what do I do?* I wondered. *I still had two of my children on my health insurance. I had medication to fill and physicals coming up in September.* Since they placed me in a hole again by taking away my salary and my health insurance, I had to go back to fighting mode again.

Fortunately, my daughter and my son had full time jobs, so they switched over to their employer's health insurance. I collected unemployment and completed the paperwork to report I had worked in a hostile work environment. I met with representatives from the unemployment office and told them that the school department was corrupt, and that I was happy to leave but not this way. Furthermore, the school department did not give me a letter indicating my health insurance was cancelled until August, even though the first letter stated that my coverage would end in March. They backdated it, so I did not have a proper letter to give to my wife's employer, so we could go on her health insurance.

As you can see, I am a battler, and I will never give up fighting for what is right. We ended up on my wife's health insurance in January 2019 (a year later), where she is an employee at a hospital, and I was able to retire on June 6, 2018. My wife and I still have not had health insurance for nine months. We could not go on Mass Health because my wife worked, so I had to pay out of pocket for my medication and postpone our physicals until after the first of the year. Fortunately, nothing happened that we needed to use health insurance. Again, the city's toxic bullying tactics were affecting my family.

I received five months' pay when I finally collected my retirement at the end of October. I only retired on 38 percent of my pay, while others in the central office were receiving 80 percent of $150,000 or better. I know it hurts, but I can at least place my head on a pillow and sleep knowing that I was always there for the children of the Urbanville Public School. My story doesn't end here, because I continue helping others who have been victims of bullying and those who were wrongfully terminated. The pain is still there, especially going from an $84,000 a year salary to $31,000, but we will continue our journey to expose the truth about this corrupt school system.

I have founded a business called Pepi & Associates, LLC, and my goal is to assist others go from a victim to a victor. My ambition is not only to assist people, but to expose the corruption and abuse that go on in educational systems today. Each school system is a cash cow. Taxpayers assume that their tax dollars are going to provide quality education for the children in their care. Each urban school system is run by politics, and no one seems to hold the school systems accountable for the money they spend. The US spends more money on education than any other country in the world, and at the time of the writing of this book, this country is ranked twenty-fifth in the world. Why? The politicians use excuses for why education is failing, except they don't want to expose the truth, which I will be discussing in the next chapter.

Believe me, there is a war on teachers, with teachers becoming the scapegoat for failing schools. Why do politicians always blame the teachers? How about the administration? Why do we have multiple directors and staff working at the central office making six figures? Why do teachers have to buy their own supplies? The blame for failing schools should fall not only on bad teachers but also on bad principals or bad superintendents? How about school committee members who worry about the small stuff instead of the big stuff such as safety in our schools? These are all valid questions that require answers. It is tough enough for teachers dealing with social issues that keep children from learning. Students go to school wondering where their next meal is coming from and not if their homework is submitted on time. Politicians and administration give parents excuses instead of holding them accountable. Students cannot learn in unsafe environments and teachers cannot teach if violence continues within the school system. For starters, we need to hold our public schools accountable, which includes the politicians who make up the policies, administrators who enforces the policies, and the teachers who implement the policies within their classroom. Most of all, let's hold parents and students accountable for their actions. Enough of the name calling. Let's be part of the real answer. We need to look at the abuse, bullying, and corruption that continues within our school systems and implement real solutions to enhance education.

I would have to thank the Urbanville Public Schools for giving me the tools to expose the truth about public education. Since the abuse, bullying, and corruption that my family and I endured, I graduated with my doctoral degree in educational leadership. My research for my dissertation was on workplace bullying in education. I became very knowledgeable about this hot topic and have found hundreds of references that support my venture within this phenomenon. My story was supported by boxes upon boxes of evidence that were covered up by the system that eventually pushed me out of education. On the plus side, my story doesn't end here.

# 14

# THE ABCs OF PUBLIC EDUCATION: ABUSE, BULLYING, AND CORRUPTION

My story is only the beginning to an ongoing story of abuse in our educational system. If we want children to stop bullying other children, adults should stop bullying other adults. We are supposed to be the role models for our children. Bullied teachers create problems in our school systems, which begins with abuse and then becomes bullying. Exposing bullies will expose corruption, which will expose school district's cover-ups. This is what happened to me. Through my experiences and what I have researched, this will show that there is a severe problem in public education. This will not only affect the teachers, but the whole learning community. Part of me is still angry, but the decision I made was to harness that anger and steer it toward the positive. My dissertation and this book are not only my therapy, they also gave me the opportunity to share what I learned in the hopes of helping others realize that they are not alone. In this chapter, I will use my story to explain the truth of the epidemic that is filling our nation. This epidemic poses not only a threat to our children, but a threat to our democracy that allows our school system to be hijacked by self-absorbed narcissists. It all begins with abuse.

## A = ABUSE

*Abuse:*

1. *To use or treat so as to injure or damage, MALTREAT;*
2. *To attack in words, REVILE;*
3. *Obsolete, DECEIVE.*

(*Merriam-Webster*, Dictionary, 2019)

The reason I wrote this book was I wanted to help teachers understand that their lives can become sidetracked by power-hungry narcissists. If you are not prepared, you can fall victim to these narcissists as well. It wasn't like this in the past. Education was excellent back in the '80s, and teachers were more respected. I loved it. What the taxpayers don't see today is what goes on in the schools: safety issues, teacher abuse, and incompetent educators who are placed into the school system because of political ties. Taxpayers don't see the negatives because the newspapers don't cover important stories that occur. These are important times we face because the future of our country is at stake. That is why I am adamant about continuing my research even after this book is published.

After my first encounter with a bully, the event became psychologically embedded in me, and I carried it with me the rest of my career. I didn't even know I was being abused, but as the years went by, I realized what it was. The points I share below outline some warning signs that should be recognized when dealing with potential bullying situations. If the abuse continues, it then becomes bullying. Remember the difference between a bad boss and a bully. A bully continually attacks the target and commits other acts that will be covered later in this chapter. These abuses are:

1. Verbal aggression: Words can hurt, and the abuser is fully aware of the damage they cause
2. Dominant behaviors: The abuser tries to show they are superior to the abused

3. Jealous behaviors: Jealousy is the root of all evil
4. Abuse-of-power behavior: When administrators use their power for evil and control
    - Through these abuses, the abuser looks to break down the abused and make them feel as if they are worth nothing. The abuser: Destroys the abused's self-esteem or self-worth
    - Places all the blame on the abused when something happens at work (Anastasia, 2017)

When the abuse begins, it starts a change in the abuser's demeanor. They might give the silent treatment or consider the target a trouble-maker for making any comments to benefit the school or work environment. This person is now a threat to the abuser. The abuser also gives work to the target which they may feel is not constructive, but the target does the work anyway because they are following the boss's orders or are trying to get the abused to quit.

The abuse started early in my administrative role. I didn't recognize the abuse right away because it trickled in slowly. It started with principals complaining every day and not respecting me as an administrator. As the abuse progressed, the excessive workload, with tasks that often did not have anything to do with my job, increased. Sarcasm from the grounds crew and abuse from the secretary and other officials in the central office became more evident over the three years in my position. Even when the programs I developed produced positive outcomes, I would never get any praise, just complaints that I shouldn't have been running those programs. It was at the end of my tenure when they were dismissing me from my position that the bullying started. They knew that I was catching on to their antics and their plans. They used the abuse against me, and the only way to back me off was to bully me until I couldn't fight back. Fortunately for me, they underestimated my resilience.

## B = BULLYING

*Bullying:*

1. *Is unwanted, aggressive behavior that involves a real or perceived power imbalance. The behavior is repeated over time.*

(*Merriam-Webster*, Dictionary, 2019)

It is tough to do your job when you're targeted by a bully. Every move I made, I would meet resistance. The city officials were more concerned with their agenda instead of someone else coming up with an idea, even if it benefited the children. If you didn't comply with their agenda, you were the enemy. I encountered bullying on a daily basis through their intimidation and attempts to set me up to fail. Once I showed the administration that I was for safety of the fields and gyms instead of their political agenda, the bullying escalated.

This is what bullies do so they can claim control over the target. Their goal was to intimidate me so that I would live in fear. Fear of losing my job or the fear of doing something illegal that could put me in prison. When you live in fear, it becomes debilitating and leads to psychological trauma. This started when I found out that the former athletic director who left on sick leave was not coming back. I was not aware that the central office wanted me to become permanent. They fixed the interview process so that I would receive the permanent position, and after that happened, the gloves were off. The bullies wanted to control me by intimidation.

My supervisor couldn't do the bullying alone and needed to include others to carry out her hidden agenda by the political hacks that ran the City of Urbanville. The bullying turned to mobbing, which means a group of bullies who are loyal to one another would make sure that I could not recover from the abuse (Anastasia, 2017). No matter what direction I went in, I could not get any justice or relief from the torment of the wrath of these bullies. Everywhere I turned—the school committee, the city counsel, the city officials, the superintendent, and the union—proved to be a dead end. They would tell me, "I will get back to you," but I would never hear from them again. A true team effort to destroy me and my reputation.

The problem with bullying is that the bully has no remorse about what they are doing to their target. Through my study of this phenomenon, I have learned not only how it occurs, but also why. I have also concluded through years of research that there is also another level that the bully escalates to, and it's to hurt the target's family and their finances. The bully is obsessed with power, they will stop at nothing to bring you down. It is even worse if they are jealous of you; that means you are a threat to them. I have become friends with so many who have seen their lives and careers destroyed, and from which recovery is difficult because of the loss of trust, tarnished reputation, ruined finances, and diagnoses of life-altering illnesses.

Bullying in the school districts also place a toll on the educator's health. Performing research for my dissertation has also revealed that the health issues I experienced are real. Even though attorneys that represented school districts played down my stress-related illnesses, it was real. The attorney for the city basically scoffed at the idea of stress-related illness when they were presented in the courtroom during my lawsuit. What I have researched for my dissertation proved that the attorney for the city used junk science and told the courtroom that there were no illnesses and I had made them up. The information I have researched tells a different story.

As I dived into the research of workplace bullying, I have also found that these effects last long periods of time, which can also lead to the loss of a career. Bullying in the workplace does not have any upsides. It affects one's physical, emotional, and mental health, but it doesn't only limit the effect on the individual. It also devastates families, finances, and social activities. If the targets don't have a strong spouse supporting them through their torment, this can also lead to divorce. Other family members, such as siblings or parents of the target, may not believe that they are victims of bullying and could place the blame on them, which could lead to depression. The target will feel alone both at work and at home.

With this information, you may say, "Why isn't workplace bullying illegal?" I would love to give you an easy answer, but it's complicated by politics, and people are uneducated about this phenomenon. It is even worse when due-process laws are violated, and the victim loses their rights while at work. Your rights don't end when you walk into the front door of your place of employment. You are an American, and the US Constitution protects your rights. Under the Constitution, you have a right to life, liberty, and property, which your boss or place of employment should not violate.

What does this mean? Why has the Workplace Bullying Bill not been passed into law? This could lead to what I have experienced in Urbanville that can be the same problem throughout other urban school systems around the country. It's called corruption.

## C = CORRUPTION

*Corruption:*

1. *is the abuse of entrusted power for private gain*
2. *Political corruption is a manipulation of policies, institutions, and rules of procedure in the allocation of resources and financing by political decision makers, who abuse their position to sustain their power, status, and wealth.*

(*Merriam-Webster*, Dictionary, 2019)

The problem with public education is that the school systems become so large that they become "cash cows" for those who are entrusted with power. Like the Catholic Church, the elite titles held by administrators within both organizations happen to use their power in an abusive way and turn around to hide behind these organizations to look for protection when they are being sued for various reasons. Not all public school systems are corrupt, but if you have corrupt politicians who run the municipalities, you have the trickledown effect with other government offices including the school system.

All I was looking for was to be an assistant principal and retire from that position, but it didn't work out that way. In hindsight, I believed that the central office was looking for a stooge to take over the director of physical education, health, and athletics until their political person was ready to leave the Healthy Student Grant. They misread me as a person because I was a nice guy and they believed I was weak. They definitely picked on the wrong person.

I knew the first day I was in the position of acting director, I witnessed the corruption almost immediately. First of all, the director I took over from was at the end of his career, and he was going to retire after three years. It just so happened that the Healthy Student Grant only had three years left. That meant the politically connected replacement was looking to take over my position from the start. It was in their plan. That wasn't the only political person who exposed themselves to me. Let's talk about my secretary first.

My secretary was eligible for retirement at least five years prior to my start date as director. But why leave? She had the gravy train. She was too incompetent to do the job, and for years (well before I took over the director job), she was the brunt of jokes from former athletic directors and other staff members. The mistakes she made and her inability to carry out any instructions to help ease the burden of the director, who had jurisdiction over many schools, was mind blowing. I knew from the start that she knew enough to be dangerous. All her mistakes were blamed on me, and even after I complained downtown multiple times, nothing was done. I tried to evaluate her, but she had already evaluated herself and want me to sign it. I refused.

The worst antic that she pulled was using my signature stamp. I would use the stamp to sign bills and purchase orders, so I didn't have to sit there to sign all of them, especially bus bills of which there were hundreds. My secretary was not allowed to use the signature stamp, and I kept the stamp in my top drawer of my desk. She did use the stamp for items I never purchased and who knows what else. This action was eventually used against me in the September 17 letter from the superintendent, which falsely accused me of insubordination and misappropriation. Was my secretary instructed to do this?

This brings me to the fabricated embezzlement, larceny, and fraud charges, which started in my office under my nose. The secretary and the grounds crew started making a list of the purchased items in my office as well as the items I never purchased. Even though Aisha admitted she never investigated by going to my office, the scene of the so-called crime, human resources took that list and later on claimed that I stole the items. It was also mentioned that I misappropriated funds by purchasing items that I never purchased. What I learned was that my secretary was in the swamp and was part of the deep corruption within the school department with her partners in crime, the two grounds crew members. I also didn't realize at the time that my secretary and the two grounds crew members were also very close to Marsha, and they would exchange gifts with one another. I happen to walk into the conference room unannounced to witness their quaint relationship. These minions made sure that I would sink, but who gave them the orders?

Then there was Aisha, the human resources director, an African-American woman with whom I was close before she was put in this position. I was thrilled for her promotion, but what I didn't realize was how political she was. I guess she put politics ahead of her moral compass. Her true agenda appeared after I became an administrator. She had her marching orders, and she forgot where she came from. She started to hire questionable people, especially when she hired a former union president to become the assistant director. You remember him, Walter. He was the errand boy who dropped off letters to my house. Her second questionable hire was another former union president who placed a dagger in my back, Claire. This union president happens to be very close to my bullying cousin, Antonio, and she was in charge during my lost arbitration case in which the grievances were never filed on time. It was because of her and my cousin that I received NO help from the union. It was obvious that there was collusion between the school department and the union.

Aisha and her assistant's lies and deceptions during my eleven-year battle were nothing but pure evil. She lied about me stealing. Even when I proved her wrong, she took another angle of lying about misappropriation of funds. Even when my attorney presented the hard evidence that I didn't steal or misappropriate, she stuck to her lies. Her lies were part of a colluded effort to destroy me and protect the person who took my place. Aisha was on the Department of Education's board that was responsible for licenses, which concluded how Marsha was licensed in one day, two years after she took over my position. How ethical was the Department of Education to allow this to happen, or did they even know?

Aisha bullied me, which made her the main part of the problem because she used her minions to carry out these lies. It's amazing that Aisha is an attorney because she has no trouble breaking labor laws or contracts. One of her quotes to me would be, "We do things differently here in Urbanville." When she was called out, she would act dumb and try to get away with it. It is almost like when the superintendent retired, his secretary was making $70,000 and must have been promised another position. Sure enough, Aisha decided to place her in a school as a special education teacher at $70,000. Problem was, she had never taught a day in her life. This made big headlines and news coverage over this terrible ordeal. Especially when the students needed a strong teacher since the school was in a low-income neighborhood. When I lost my court case, a year later Aisha left her position and took a job at Urbanville State University. She was being protected, but by who?

Walter became the acting human resources director, and not only did he play a hand in my court case against the city, he was also fully involved in the DCF actions against me that were fabricated. His investigation was just that, "his investigation." There wasn't any evidence, nor did anything happen in my class. The principal, Judy, ran with this false narrative and she brought in the human resources department. Not only did Walter deliver the letter to place me on paid administrative leave, he tried to have people lie for him, so he could support his false narrative with witnesses. His goal was to fire me. What saved me was the honest custodian at this school who would not go along with the fabricated story. The list of custodians, cafeteria workers, nurses, teachers, and other staff members who had severe problems with Walter would often share their stories with me, but again, politics protected him.

They all were trying to protect Marsha, who was a politically connected person and took a position with no qualifications. My research on her not only brought out that she was not licensed but who she was related to. It showed corruption firsthand. For starters, her father-in-law was the former mayor of Urbanville, and even though he passed away in the early sixties, his influence was carried out by his children. My replacement claimed in court she never met her father-in-law because he passed away before they got married, but he did have children and his children had influence. The oldest was a big attorney involved in the courthouse and was good friends of the disgraced Lt. Governor Jim McMurray and was also in public office serving on the Governor's Council back in the early 2000s, but he was forced to resign because of unethical behavior. This was the same courthouse where I lost my case and also happens to be the office of the District Attorney Bob Lately, who was the brother-in-law of one of the city councilors Stan Rush. Pieces of my court case started to make sense. Were they involved?

Marsha's sister-in-law was the former principal of one of the middle schools, and speaking of Jim McMurray, her other sister-in-law was married to city councilor John Andy for whom McMurray campaigned. It just so happened that McMurray became city councilor right after Andy stepped down, and in a short few years he became the Mayor of Urbanville.

It was the quote from my supervisor that stuck in my head when I knew I did not have a chance in this political position: "I have to take care of a friend before I retire." Mary harassed me and was a part of destroying my reputation. It all started to make sense to me. This is why they were all part of the plan to destroy me because I questioned their motive. They couldn't do it alone. They needed someone else on their side, and that was the union.

My cousin Antonio was a union executive secretary for the Education Association of Urbanville (EAU), which was the local chapter of the Massachusetts Teachers' Association (MTA). This was the union that was to negotiate contracts for teachers and IAs, but also protects the teachers of wrongdoing by the administration. Antonio had worked for the EAU since the early '90s. He was the only person outside of my family who knew about the situation in the Catholic Schools, and it was evident when the former principal from that Catholic School came to testify in my court case.

Once I started in the Urbanville Public school system, Antonio tried to bully me any chance he could. He would come into the schools I was assigned to as a Physical Education teacher to threaten me and intimidate me. He harassed me about the family house I was living in when my parents passed. Once I became director of physical education and athletics he would support anyone who wanted to file a grievance against me even when the situation was not anything you can grieve by contract. He would come and bang his fist on my desk and try any bullying tactics he had. Worse than that, any time he had the chance, he would bad mouth me to others. When it would get back to me, I could feel the stress build. I decided to ignore him because I had the job, but ignoring him and my critics got worse, which affected my position later on. When he switched places with someone from the MTA office in the summer of 2006, that raised a red flag for me. Antonio's reasoning was he wanted to spend more time with his family and relax more before retiring, but I knew better. This looks more like collusion.

I do not believe in coincidence. Antonio left the district before they let me go. The union president would not talk to me but referred me to Pete, the person who replaced my cousin. The union lawyer would not defend me on the false narrative about the embezzlement, larceny, and fraud allegations but instead wanted me to resign. The union would not file grievances on my behalf and during arbitration, they told me it was my fault. Finally, Pete lied to the union reps (teachers in the system) that it was a slam dunk on winning arbitration even though he knew without the grievances filed, I didn't have a shot. Was this a conspiracy with the city?

The corruption I witnessed and researched came from the puppet masters of the school department. Why was the city council and the school committee not responsive in helping me? I knew them, and they seemed to like me, but all of a sudden, they turned on me. After working as a director for three years, I saw a gross picture of what was going on in the school department. I would hear two names no matter what decision was made. It was the common dominator which was higher on the food chain that protected the superintendent that was using grant money for salaries and got caught. Who protected the human resource director when she hired that secretary as a special education teacher. Not only protected in her position but was promoted to Urbanville State University when it started to get hot in the kitchen. Why all of a sudden did they decide to pay the head financial officer, Bobby, a lot more money to stay in the system when he was looking to leave? He was in charge of the books. Interesting. The common dominator has a name in the city of Urbanville called the McMurray/Jones connection. Who are they? Let's dig deeper.

After starting teaching in the Urbanville Public Schools, I had a desire to run for political office, but I didn't know how cutthroat it was. There is no discussing issues anymore. If someone disagrees with you, they try to destroy your reputation instead. Anyway, I was running for city council in my district against the incumbent. I pulled the papers to run for public office which I needed 300 signatures to get on the ballot. What I didn't realize was that news of my candidacy had been published in the local newspaper. Three weeks later, I got a phone call from another candidate also running for the same office. He told me he had a lot of money invested already in his campaign and wondered if I would help him instead of running. I decided to drop out of the race because deep down, I wanted to continue with my master's degree in educational leadership.

As I started to campaign for him, it included attending Congressman Tim Jones' fundraiser, and all of the local politicians appeared to show their support for the congressman. I had already dropped out of the race for city council by the time of this fundraiser, but the notice of my suspended candidacy was never published. I bumped into Jim McMurray, who was mayor at the time, and he knew who I was from mutual friends. Instead of saying hi, he started in on me by asking, "Pep, what are you doing?"

I was confused and said, "What?"

"I want you to drop out of the race, I already have MY BOYS in place," he said. MY BOYS? What does that mean?

I responded with a wisecrack. "You can't tell me to run or not to run. What do you think we live in, a communist country?" I never told him that I dropped out of the race because I was so upset by that comment. I believe he held a grudge against me because of it, but I didn't care. I believe we are in a free country. If I wanted to run, he couldn't stop me.

It does make sense because other politicians who ran for office told me that they were dragged into Congressman Jones' office and were told it was not their time to run. What happens in Urbanville is that the elections are controlled by the congressman. If you got his blessing, you would be protected. If you were an adversary, your reputation would be destroyed. They would use racism as their biggest defense, and they didn't care what they did to destroy the person's integrity and/or character. Sound familiar? Just like how they fabricated a story about me. I was falsely accused of embezzlement, larceny, and fraud with a dose of neglect. I too was called racist, and they would have no problem destroying my reputation in and around the city. This is why exposing these narcissists will help in my healing process and also help others in theirs.

If you are still skeptical on the McMurray-Jones connection, I have two other pieces of evidence that shows this was a cover-up. The first was a young woman I knew who worked in the election committee at city hall. She was bringing out some unethical and illegal activities within the department. Election fraud? Nepotism? I don't know, but when she started to ask questions, they started to bully her and then fired her. She ended up filing a lawsuit, and she was given a settlement by the city. So, what did she know? I guess we will never find out that information, or will we?

The second story was about our disgraced Lt. Governor Jim McMurray, who was mysteriously out on a winter morning after a storm to "inspect storm damage." It was 4 a.m., and he crashed his state-issued automobile doing 110 MPH on the interstate. Why was he speeding, and who was he running from? He was also in trouble with campaign money involving another politician who was from the Boston area. Again, everything was covered up. The next thing we knew, he resigned from the lieutenant governor position. All he was given was a fine from the attorney general for $80,000, which he can use his campaign funds to pay. He came back to Urbanville and became the president of the chamber of commerce for a whopping $200,000 with a company car. How did this happen? Especially when the former president never made more than $100,000 a year. Who helped him out?

This is what I was fighting against, the minions who were controlled by the puppet masters Congressman Tim Jones and disgraced Lt. Governor Jim McMurray. There is no doubt that the courthouse, school district, school committee, union and the city council all were under their spell. Call it what you want, group think, following their plan or just plain corruption. This is how I connected the dots but for what I endured over an eleven-year span gave me the opportunity to put everything together to write this book. It was the Abuse + Bullying = Corruption which my family and I experienced. The McMurray/Jones connection didn't care about my finances, or my family, or my health because I was a threat to them, they decided to attack me through their minions, so I could not fight back. They wanted to crush me, but I am the one that kept on going by helping others, receiving a doctorate degree, and watching my family flourish through the adversity. "What the enemy intended for evil, God meant it for good" (Genesis 50:20).

Where do we go from here? My passion is to push for accountability and look for justice for anyone who endured abuse. The reduction of violence, suicide, and health issues depends upon the help the target receives in holding bullies accountable. This is important so that our children will have the best education that public school can offer, and the money spent on court cases, mediations, workers' comp, and other legal avenues can be redirected to our classrooms where it belongs. After my experiences and the research, I have done through the writing of my dissertation, I have learned how to create avenues to assist others who have been inflicted with this phenomenon. Please follow me on my Facebook page at *Workplace Bullying: Stop the Abuse*, and remember, there is STRENGTH IN NUMBERS.

# REFERENCE

Anastasia, A. (2017). Signs of Emotional abuse at work (and how to react). *Journal of abused workers, 3*(4), 23–33. Retrieved from http://www.cleverism.com

# ABOUT THE AUTHOR

Dr. John J. Pepi Sr. grew up in Worcester, Massachusetts, in the Grafton Hill area of the second largest city in New England. He was the last of five children, and he credits his parents with instilling in him integrity, character, and a strong work ethic. Even though his parents only had an eighth-grade education, they believed in advancing oneself through education. All four of his siblings were successful in their careers in and around Massachusetts. Two of his sisters were teachers, one sister was a nurse, and his brother was a carpenter. John himself worked in education and has a doctorate in educational leadership.

He has taught school for thirty-four years at all levels between grades K–12. His career started in the Diocese of Worcester and finished in the Worcester Public Schools. During his lengthy career, he worked at Worcester Academy Sports Camp and coached at Tahanto, St. John's, Quabbin Regional, and Nashoba Regional high schools. He was also a football official and baseball umpire; through sports, he spent many years helping young people develop lifelong skills. His most senior position was as the director of physical education, health, and athletics in Worcester Public Schools, where he created many programs that are still in use today.

John has been happily married for the past thirty-five years and has three sons and a daughter. Having support from his family was essential to his pursuit of a career of which he was proud. Today he works to help children, parents, and educators to seek justice in the areas of bullying and abuse. He is the founder and president of Pepi & Associates LLC, which looks to educate and assist people in due-process violations, injustice, and other abuses. John's goal is to bring awareness to the problem of not only bullying but also to failing public schools throughout the country.

# ABOUT THE AUTHOR